CINEMA OF THE OTHER EUROPE

CINEMA OF THE OTHER EUROPE

THE INDUSTRY AND ARTISTRY
OF EAST CENTRAL EUROPEAN FILM

Dina Iordanova

WALLFLOWER PRESS
LONDON & NEW YORK

First published in Great Britain in 2003 by
Wallflower Press
4th Floor, 26 Shacklewell Lane, London E8 2EZ
www.wallflowerpress.co.uk

A catalogue for this book is available from the British Library

ISBN 1-903364-61-2 (paperback)
ISBN 1-903364-64-7 (hardback)

Printed in Great Britain by Antony Rowe, Chippenham, Wiltshire

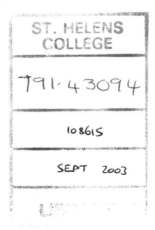

CONTENTS

LIST OF ILLUSTRATIONS

ACKNOWLEDGMENTS

First and foremost, I would like to thank those from whom I have been learning about East Central European cinema over many years; my gratitude in particular is offered to Barton Byg, Ian Christie, Paul Coates, Nancy Condee, Herbert Eagle, Janina Falkowska, Wiesław Godzic, Dan Goulding, Marek Haltof, Peter Hames, Ron Holloway, Vida Johnson, Ewa Mazierska, Maya Nadkarni, Bohdan Nebesio, Volodia Padunov, Graham Petrie, Cathy Portuges and Yuri Stulov.

Then there are the many colleagues working in related areas who taught me a great deal – Slavists, and scholars of both film and media; thank you to Dudley Andrew, Fiona Björling, Julianne Burton-Carvajal, John Downing, Geoff Eley, Thomas Elsaesser, Lóránd Hegyi, Piotr Kuhiwczak, Peter Lev, Yosefa Loshitzky, John Orr, Anna Reading, Robert Rosenstone, Colin Sparks, Janet Staiger, Richard Taylor, Katie Trumpener, Ginette Vincendeau and Nancy Wood.

I am also grateful to those who eased my access to the films discussed here – not all of which are, alas, easily available: Bill van Wert, Andrzej Pitrus, Angela Nanasy-Irwin and Hiltrud Schulz; special thanks to festival programmers Ludmila Cvikova (Rotterdam), Peter Fischer (Cottbus), Hans-Joachim Schlegel (Berlin), and to Milos Stehlik, the driving force behind Facets Multimedia.

Very special thanks to those colleagues at Leicester whose support allowed me to successfully complete this project – Prof Robert Burgess and Phillip Lindley.

Thank you too Natasa Ďurovičová, Anikó Imre, Boris Jocić and Daniela Berghahn for providing much needed conceptual feedback, and Zahira Ahmed for helping out with numerous technical details.

Last but not least, my deepest gratitude to those who helped my peace of mind in different ways – Yoram Allon, Andrew James Horton, Jim McKenna and Milos Lazin.

This book grew out of material I have been gathering over the past ten years and which I have used in my teaching and in various talks and shorter pieces. Two earlier sources of this text are the Course File in East European Cinema published with *The Journal of Film and Video* in 1999, and a text which I wrote in 2000 for a major comparative literature project co-ordinated by Prof John Neubauer from the University of Amsterdam Parts of chapters four, six and seven draw on papers and talks given at a variety of locations – at the American Association of Teachers of Slavic and Eastern European Languages

(AATSEEL) and American Association for the Advancement of Slavic Studies (AAASS) conferences, at the University of Illinois at Urbana-Champaign (1996, 2000), the University of Western Ontario (1998), the University of California at Berkeley (1999), the University of Tübingen (2000) and at the Imperial War Museum in London (2001). Earlier versions of some parts of the text have appeared in publications such as *Media, Culture and Society*, *Media Development* and *Javnost/The Public*. Research related to the film industries was made possible due to the generous support of the Arts and Humanities Research Board (1999) and the Leverhulme Trust (2001–2).

This book is dedicated to George.

INTRODUCTION

This book is intended to contribute to two fields of study: first, to European film studies and second to studies of East Central European culture.

More than a decade after the abolition of the 'iron curtain' that divided Europe into 'proper' and 'other' parts, the cinema of the regions in the Eastern part of Europe remains largely excluded from the concept of European cinema. While all European nations are believed to be part of a relatively homogeneous cultural and intellectual community, the culture of East Central Europe from the second part of the twentieth century has not yet been fully integrated into what is seen to be European. The concept of European cinema is still more or less synonymous with West European film-making, and the teaching of European cinema barely covers East Central European traditions. This study will not attempt to present East Central European cinema as an organic part of a West European one: there are numerous differences in preoccupation, theme and style, and the overall 'feel' of Polish or Hungarian cinema can differ substantially from the 'feel' of French or British cinema.

What this book does aim to do, however, is encourage a more inclusive and comprehensive understanding of European cinema, one that is necessary for a new and unified Europe which has extended towards its eastern periphery. The integration of East Central European cinematic tradition can be meaningful only if appropriate attention is paid to its idiosyncratic characteristics. This study will thus attempt to foster an inclusive understanding by mapping out the interactions, key concerns, thematic spheres and stylistic particularities that make the cinema of East Central Europe part of the European film tradition.

This book is divided into three parts, all of which aim towards the same objective: to provide an overview of the cinema of the region that is both comprehensive and general. Comprehensive, because it puts the material in a regional context: it places the 'trees' within this particular 'forest'. Generalised, because the goal is to discuss the forest not the trees and to stay focused on the whole.

As the intention is to present a survey of East Central European cinema, the approaches in separate sections vary and the result is occasionally eclectic. In every case, an investigation into the cultural policies and industry set-up of the institutions of cinema is included as important background knowledge. A second range of issues is related to the main themes of the discourse on history, ethics and social order, and it is here where issues of style and narrative specifics are considered. A third range of issues pertains to the major schools of film-making and specific groups of film-makers.

Part I, 'Film and Context', largely sets the scene for the investigation. The first chapter attempts to position the study of East Central European film within the wider context of contemporary film studies. It argues in favour of taking a fresh look at this remarkably rich part of the world's cinematic heritage and considers its place within the 're-mapping' of global cinema in accordance with regionalist discourses. The second chapter investigates the specific industry structure of film production, distribution and exhibition under state socialism, considers the fine traditions of animation and documentary film-making, and elaborates on issues of censorship and Socialist Realism. It also looks at the international moves and migration patterns of film-makers from the region that are of interest in the study of contemporary transnational film-making.

Part II, 'Film and History, Ethics and Society', investigates the large body of work that explores the moral decisions of an individual faced with uncontrollable and often adverse historical circumstances. While, as it is argued on several occasions here, many other themes and aspects of the region's cinema deserve attention, it is certain that the films dealing with issues of history, memory and morality make up the core of East Central European film. The investigation of these films is divided into three parts: chapter three surveys the range of those historical films that focus on the specific relationship between an individual agent of history and historical processes at large, as conceptualised within the region's discourse; chapter four explores the specific intersection of moral and historical issues as found in cinematic representations of the Holocaust, a remarkable corpus of work that remains insufficiently known; chapter five discusses a further dimension of the explorations of individual ethics, focusing on films that looked at urban life under socialism, as well as those works ultimately concerned with issues of modernity (as revealed in films dealing with the crisis of village patriarchal lifestyles).

Part III, 'Films and Film-makers', covers issues of an interdisciplinary nature at the intersection of creativity and social conditions. The investigation in chapter six, 'Women's Cinema, Women's Concerns', is twofold. On the one hand, it surveys women's film-making and tries to explain the specific 'reluctant feminism' characteristic for many of the area's female directors. On the other hand, it offers an investigation into some of the key patterns in female representation in the cinema of the region, by looking into gendered images of communal confinement, intimacy, sexuality and social realisation. Chapter seven surveys the post-1989 period and maps the new industry landscape, marked by turbulent changes in production patterns and sometimes by generational incongruities. As far as themes and styles are concerned, however, continuation prevails over rupture, even when rupture rather than continuity appears to be the more likely course of events.

This study comes with the inevitable shortcomings of a survey. By choosing to outline trends and general stylistic and thematic areas, important details are inevitably omitted. Some films deserve to be written about at length, yet here they may appear only in a listing of relevant works. Some directors deserve dedicated monographs but the coverage they receive here is a mention in passing. It is not possible to be fully politically correct in a study like this, nor to pay equal attention to all deserving films and directors, and occasionally decisions to highlight some films or individuals without mentioning others may appear arbitrary. Sometimes balance was forfeited in order to outline tendencies and make important points. This was done knowing that the attempt to focus on the general picture at the expense of details would be compensated and complemented by the growing body of writings on the cinemas of Poland, the Czech and Slovak republics, and Hungary.

The appendix at the end of this book points to other research and further reading and outlines the resources available to those who may be interested in teaching and studying the cinema of East Central Europe in more detail. The filmography and bibliography that follow provide further information regarding the cinema of the region.

PART I

FILM AND CONTEXT

OVERVIEW

The end of the Cold War encouraged a renewed interest in the cultures of Europe's eastern part, the 'other' Europe as it was sometimes called. The focus here is on the cinema of what, after the rapid disintegration of the cultural entity of the so-called Eastern Bloc, came to be known as 'East Central Europe'. We will mostly explore the cinematic traditions of Poland, Hungary and Czechoslovakia during the period of state socialism (1945–89) as well as the post-1989 changes in the field of culture, when the idea of East Central Europe as a unique cultural space was revived and re-constituted. Rather than looking at national cinemas and directors, we will consider the shared topics that, from the 1950s to the times of post-Communism, defined the major concerns of the people in the region as addressed in their cinema.

As far as area studies are concerned, film is still treated as a medium of secondary importance to literature within the discipline of East Central European cultural studies (which only recently started emancipating itself from Sovietology). Yet it is often the moving image rather than the printed word that carries more persuasive weight in today's world of electronic media, and students are frequently more familiar with the cinema of a given area than they are with its literary heritage.[1] Looking at cinematic texts thus helps bring to light the underlying dynamics of cross-cultural image-making as it occurs within the wider context of communicated concepts and interpretations. It seems, therefore, that it is time for area studies to recognise the crucial role that film plays in discourse formation, and ideally this book will contribute to a better understanding of the importance of the cinematic medium in revealing essential features of the region's culture.

CHAPTER ONE

East Central European Film Studies

Periodisation

Cinema established itself as an art form early in the twentieth century, and its development often depended on technological and industrial innovation, such as the use of sound or the advent of television and video technologies. Yet it is historical events that determine the changing modes of production and remain the main criterion for periodisation. In the case of East Central Europe it seems most appropriate to speak of three major periods – cinema before the Second World War, cinema during state socialism and post-Communist cinema.[1]

As in all other European countries, film was introduced across the region shortly after its advent in 1895. Soon thereafter, during the early decades of the twentieth century, most nations in the region launched their own film industries (a process that developed even before some of them would gain political sovereignty). Ever since, maintaining a cinematic tradition has been seen as an intrinsic part of modern nation-building. While the attention in this book is mostly directed to films made in the period after the end of the Second World War, it is important to mention that there was a thriving film industry (producing silent films initially, and switching to talkies in the early 1930s) in each of the countries covered in this book.[2] At that time, film production in the region was more or less of the same quality and quantity as the film production in other similarly-sized European countries, and the links with the cinemas of Western Europe were particularly intense, including exchanges of actors, directors and other creative personnel. And if Polish, Hungarian or Czechoslovak cinema from the 1920s and the 1930s remain lesser-known today, it is mostly due to the imposed isolation that these countries had to live through after the Second World War rather than to a less significant cinematic output.[3]

The period after the Second World War saw the film industries across the region re-established: they were nationalised and from the 1950s started receiving substantial financial injections, with the Communist state taking serious interest in the propaganda potential of this mass medium. The artistic output of the period was marked by a common stable of themes, aesthetics and genres, all of which were in part pre-determined by the shared post-war political constraints. However differently applied by the respective national regimes, the subordination of cinema to the authority of state institutions was a common denominator across the region.

Shared experiences and trends established shared traits in the diverse range of nationally specific forms of cinematic expression under state socialism. What was happening in the politics and culture of the region closely mirrored the situation in the Soviet Union. In the late 1940s and early 1950s, a number of Socialist Realist dramas were produced. Soon thereafter, in the late 1950s, a number of socially-conscious films reflecting the spirit of the 'Thaw' in politics were made. In the 1960s, the region experienced a 'new wave' of film-making, encouraged by reform-orienteded domestic political developments, and in-fluenced by Western experimentation with narrative and style. Realist drama, historical epic and comedy took leading positions among the genres produced and films concerned with the Holocaust, the destruction of traditional village lifestyles and urbanisation occupied a specific place in East Central European cinema.

In some cases film historians, focusing more on style than socio-cultural and industrial criteria, have opted to discuss developments in film art around 'decades'. It is interesting to note that even if the periodisation is determined by socio-political criteria, the 'decades' approach works well for these cinemas. Most important political events in the region (the 1968 Prague Spring, the 1981 imposition of martial law in Poland, the 1989 'velvet revolutions') have taken place close to the turn of a decade. In such a schema, the 1950s would roughly be classified as the period of totalitarian, Stalinist-Zhdanovist Socialist Realist cinema. The 1960s would be characterised by the establishment of a new generation of more liberally minded film-makers who increasingly received wide international recognition. The seemingly unremarkable 1970s are also a period of consolidation leading towards to the advent of the cinema of moral concern and committed political film-making at the end of the decade. The 1980s can be seen as the autumn years of socialism, ultimately marked by turmoil and growing political discontent, as well as political film-making inspired by the Soviet policies of *glasnost* (openness) and *perestroika* (restructuring). The 1990s can briefly be described as the period of post-Communist transition and transformation.

Here, however, we will opt to use a post-Second World War periodisation that evolves around five distinct periods. Here is a schema (adapted from Hegyi 2001) that compares the developments in fine arts and cinema (see table overleaf). The first period, characterised by totalitarianism and isolation, begins in 1949, the time when the power of the Communists in the region is consolidated, coming to control all aspects of economic, social, political and cultural life. The period ends in 1956, a year which is important in two respects – the official end of Stalinism (Stalin had died in 1953, but Stalinism was officially denounced only three years later) and a failed anti-Communist uprising in Hungary. The second period, 1956–68, 'between two revolutions' (the Hungarian one and the Prague Spring), begins with the collapse of the Stalinist regimes and coincides roughly with Nikita Khrushchev's 'Thaw' in Russia: a slow and contradictory process of liberalisation and transition that ultimately led to the emergence of the Prague Spring in Czechoslovakia. This popular movement, however, soon became too radical to be acceptable to the Soviet Union, and it was promptly suppressed via the invasion of Warsaw Pact forces leading to a bleak period of political oppression across the region, ironically called 'Normalisation' in Czechoslovakia and which constitutes a third period of film-making in the region. The time between 1980 and 1989 saw a growing dissident resistance (also fuelled by the imposition of martial law in Poland in 1981) and some of the best works of politically committed cinema. This 'fourth period' was an era of the gradual weakening of state socialist regimes, enhanced by the important impact of the policies of *glasnost*, *perestroika* and the various reform movements targeting the undemocratic political structures and the inefficient economies of the Eastern Bloc.

The post-Communist era brought state interference in film-making to an end. However, it also meant massive cuts and the withdrawal of centralised government funding. The shift to a market economy affected every level of the film industry from its basic infrastructure to its mode of financing and administration. It is this change in basic operational premises, and not so much the specifics of the artistic output, that make it necessary to distinguish the time of post-Communism as a new and separate period.

Regionalism

The concept of East Central Europe has proved particularly influential in cultural discourse and literature since the time it was first established. The countries of the region had historically been parts of Russia, Germany and

	Art History	Film History
1949–56 Totalitarianism	• Suppression of modern, alternative, avant-garde periods in Art History and Film since the Second World War. • 'Official' art endorsed aggressively.	• Development of state socialist film production and distribution system. • Template of Socialist Realism imposed on cinema.
1956–68 'The Thaw'	• Borderline phenomena between 'official' and 'unofficial' art. • Aesthetic rehabilitation of historical avant-garde. • Penetration of some Western influences.	• Liberalisation in respect to theme and style. • New generation of film-makers, born in the 1930s. • Czechoslovak New Wave. • 'Polish school'. • Films from the region internationally acclaimed.
1968–80 Convergence and divergence	• Co-existence of various ideological and aesthetic strategies in the art scene. • Intense artistic developments in major cities after 1968. • New models of artistic interaction between East and West. • Perspectives for new positions in the international art context and awareness of an avant-garde.	• Articulate interest in contemporary topics, particularly in moral explorations often implying political connotations ('cinema of moral concern'). • Occasional situations of subversive dissident film-making. • Continuous interest in historical topics, often as allegories. • Mass production of mediocre and politically correct socialist dramas and comedies.
1980–89 Preparations for upheavals	• Intensification of artistic contacts with the West. • Artists gained more solid financial backing, they were also able to put their aesthetic intentions into practice.	• Film-makers often politically committed, engaged in subtler or more open dissident confrontations. • Yet some express disillusionment with politics and interest in more existential themes (Kieślowski). • Intense interest in re-visiting awkward historical topics and continuation of the moral concern type film-making triggered by glasnost. • Growing recognition for popular cinema.
1989-present: Euphoria, disillusionment, normalisation	• Contemporary art in the new post-Communist democracies in Central Europe. • Opening up for intense interactions with artists in the context of 'new Europe'.	• Profound restructuring of the film industry, initial crisis and turmoil, gradual adjustment and establishment of new (more commercial) production patterns. • Generation gap. • New cinematic works within traditional thematic spheres.

the Austro-Hungarian Empire, and had continuously struggled to achieve independence. At the same time, their geographical place and political function in Europe had often led to questions about their belonging to the 'properly European'. In the context of the imposed Communist regimes after the Second World War, the idea of 'Central Europe' gradually grew in importance. As expressed by H.M. Hughes:

> There now developed among the small, neighbouring states of central Europe a new conception of *Mitteleuropa* to rival (or supplant) the unpalatable Pan-German version, which had been at the origin of two World Wars and the subsequent division of Europe. This new version was based, in part, on a nostalgically tinged recollection of the multi-ethnic, multi-cultural and multi-lingual Habsburg Empire, pre-1918, and, in part, on Tomas Masaryk's democratic vision of a 'close friendship with our neighbours to the East and Southeast' and an 'amicable group of small nations, extending from the Baltic to the Adriatic'. (1999: 43)

In the 1970s, and particularly in the 1980s, the idea of 'Central Europe' gained wide currency among critical intellectuals in the region. Besides strengthening the regionalist vision, the concept of 'Central Europe' established by intellectuals from the region stressed the distinction of these cultural traditions from the imposed Soviet domination and cultural Russification.[4] In addition, this categorisation allowed a demarcation line to be drawn between the Central European and the Balkan countries, which were also part of the Soviet sphere of influence at the time (see Todorova 1997; Iordanova 2001). Ultimately, it was a concept that asserted the region's cultural belonging to the West European tradition.

Thus, the concept of 'Central Europe' was a key instrument in the struggle for establishing a desirable cross-cultural image of the area. The self-conceptualisation of the region was of a buffer zone doomed to an imposed cultural subservience and to bear the repercussions of the eternal clashes between the two big powers in the region (Russia and Germany). The fact that at the end of the Second World War countries like Poland, Hungary and Czechoslovakia were sacrificed and betrayed by the Western Allies, effectively excluded from the community of Western democracies to which they believed to naturally belong, was often seen as a tragic fate that had befallen the region. Throughout the 1970s and 1980s, East Central Europe was to be conceptualised as a region that fitted culturally within the West but was still colonised by barbarian Eastern powers, as a region that longed for democracy yet had to endure tyrannical Communism. The intense rhetoric of cultural claustrophobic grievances gradually built up to the idea of a 'return to Europe', which soon became a leading trope in the region's public discourse and played a key ideological function in the aftermath of 1989 (see Gal 1991; Wolff 1994; Iordanova 2001). In the post-1989 period, the regionalist essence of the 'Central Europe' concept played an important role not only for these countries' favourable cultural re-positioning but also in the fields of economics and politics.

Today, the concept of 'Central Europe' is still influential and important. It grew in the context of a regionalist discourse, with contributions from intellectuals in Czechoslovakia, Poland and Hungary, giving us one more reason to reassert the regionalist approach favoured by this investigation: the focus is more on developments and issues as they are revealed across the region rather than national specifics.

Most of the scholarship on East Central European film still adheres to the 'national cinemas' framework and pays attention to the cultural and cinematic process only within a given national cultural context. Indeed, if cinema is studied as part of the national cultural tradition, the national approach is justified and necessary. But there are also transnational developments that can easily remain overlooked as a result of choosing the country-by-country approach: what is observed in Polish cinema is often similar in Czech, Slovak and Hungarian film. The regional framework allows us to reveal leading stylistic or narrative trends and other general aspects, thus supplementing the scholarship on individual countries. While it has a number of advantages for the study of film, the national framework also has limitations; by looking regionally we see trends that otherwise remain neglected.

As with Scandinavian cinema, which is often approached regionally, the cinema of East Central Europe can be studied successfully in regional terms. This is, to a great extent, presupposed by the proximity of the national cultures that the region is comprised of, a proximity that can be described as diversity in unity. The countries in the region have an extensive shared history and the parallels in their social, political, economic and cultural background prevail over the differences (in language, ethnicity and religion). Another important factor is that throughout the second half of the twentieth century these cultures were confined to the Eastern Bloc, which predetermined similar socio-economic development and positioned them seemingly within Europe; their struggle to overcome the isolation from the West and the pattern to which they have developed since 1989 is also rather similar. The countries in the region have continuously shared common values and traditions in literature and the fine and performing arts, as well as in the wider tradition of the role of critical and diasporic intelligentsia within public discourse. For the long years of Communist rule, intellectuals from the region were interested in each other's spiritual quests, reading each other's novels, watching eachother's plays and films. Hence the symbiotic and synergetic phenomenon of East Central European intelligentsia and their struggle to establish the idea of Central Europe as a shared cultural sphere, albeit one under constant revision and marked by occasional divisions.

As far as cinema is concerned, in the context of regional cycles and regionalism (versus national consolidation), we can trace shared features in several important areas:

- Industrially – The industry structures have been very similar across the region throughout all periods of technological and political development.

- Thematically – The leading concerns and stories that figure the artistic imagination are ultimately the same across the region. As pointed to in the following discussion, this cinema is mostly preoccupied with investigations of morality, of the relationship between the individual and social and historical processes.

- Stylistically – Contrary to the wide-spread belief of the leading importance of Socialist Realism, it is elaborate camera movements, complexly staged long takes, meticulously choreographed scenes, mastery of black-and-white photography and extensive use of documentary techniques that characterise all national cinematic traditions of the region.

- Geopolitically – The forced 'togetherness' of these countries within the context of the Eastern Bloc led to numerous artistic interactions and mutual influences that are inevitably left out if these cinemas are explored within the national framework, and can only be made explicit if studied in the regional context proposed here.[5]

Re-mapping

In the 1990s, the line that split Europe into two was abolished; but did the new era lead to an abolition of the mental division of Europe between 'the West and the Rest' (Hall & Gieben 1992)? Was there public consensus on the avenues towards mutual understanding and harmony in a pan-European shared home? The end of the Cold War seemed to suggest that 'Eastern Europe' had ceased to exist. Larry Wolff has indicated, however, that this did not mean an automatic deletion of the entrenched ideas of European fault lines; either new associations were to be found to mark the differences, or older division lines from before the Cold War were to be re-established (1994: 14). Other historians and anthropologists observed the longevity of the wish to 'join Europe' and the crucial role of the construct of 'Europeanness' (in this case played out as consciousness of backwardness and peripheral positioning) for the assertion of East Central Europeans' modern identities (Gal 1991).

Russia, the constantly overbearing force, was finally ousted into the shadows by an ideologically desirable image of Europe as a revered site of inherent affinity, the bond with which had been continuously disturbed throughout history. The rush for emancipation from the coercive satellitism of the Soviet sphere and the turn westwards was often supplemented by the assumption of a sycophant role in the 'new Europe' that easily translated into the culturist terms of 'kinship' and 'civilisation' (Huntington 1993), which, in our particular case was closely linked to the re-constitution of the Habsburg and the Ottoman spheres. The discourse on 'Europe' that had evolved around the vision of the vulnerable 'in-betweenness' of Central Europe now stressed the rhetoric of 'return' in which the term 'Europe' was ambiguously used both as a geographical location and a symbolic destination.

One of the most important reasons for emphasising this 'Central' European standing, as distinguishable from the Soviet Union and 'Southern' Europe, was due to the increased importance of studying cultural continuities with added weight granted to the various pre-World War Two cultural legacies. The concept of East Central Europe would be void without considering this diachrony which, when taken into consideration, would include the heritage of nationalist romanticism in the post-1948 states, or the modernism of the 1930s.[6]

When it comes to politics of place, cultural topographies fluctuate and ideas about belonging change in time. The recent major social and political changes in the former Eastern Bloc led to a situation in which cultural historians also had to make geopolitically motivated choices. As far as film history is concerned, it meant that film history specialists were to engage in an often unspoken re-mapping that implied a significant degree of potential distortion in the historical record on cinema. Some of the main lines of the post-Cold War geopolitical re-positioning were directly reflected in the re-mapping of film history.

A change that does not appear to be of immediate concern here and yet needs to be mentioned is the post-Soviet period re-mapping taking place within the concepts on Soviet cinema itself. At the time of writing, the study of Soviet cinema has been more or less reduced to the study of Russian cinema, which scholars almost exclusively treat as synonymous with Soviet cinema. It is extremely rare to see writing on the cinemas of Ukraine, Belarus, the republics in the Caucasus (Armenia, Georgia, Azerbaijan) or the Baltics (Latvia, Lithuania, Estonia).[7] Where do these cinemas belong today, one wonders? They are left in a sort of vacuum – the Russian specialists are no longer interested in them, and scholars of 'Eastern Europe', that other periphery of Russian influence, think they are in the 'realm' of the Soviet specialists. It is a paradoxical situation that has yet to be addressed and resolved.

In the post-Communist era, the dynamics of 'North' and 'South', previously deemed inapplicable as the emphasis was on East and West, seem to have begun to translate onto the region, with all the characteristics of the orderly and affluent 'North' juxtaposed to the chaotic and poor 'South'. The old Eastern Bloc underwent a process of dissolution into two general areas, East Central Europe and the Balkans. It was now possible to rediscover consistent stylistic and thematic features shared by the cinemas of the Balkan countries, including the former Yugoslavia,[8] Bulgaria, Romania and Albania, as well as Greece and sometimes Turkey, a combination unthinkable until recently for political reasons. This newly consolidated concept of Balkan cinema was juxtaposed to the concept of East Central European cinema, which now includes the film histories of Hungary, Poland, the Czech Republic and Slovakia (but, paradoxically, not that of East Germany).

During the Cold War, the culture of East Germany (or more formally, the German Democratic Republic, GDR) was an intricate part of the culture of the Eastern Bloc, and its cinema had correspondingly shared similarities in terms of ideology, style and thematic interests with the film traditions of other Bloc countries. Yet as soon as the GDR 'returned' to Europe (via the reunification with its Western twin) the culture of this country vanished from all East European conceptual contexts. Less than a decade after the reunification of Germany, East German film no longer features as part of the film studies concerned with East Central Europe, and the cinema of the ex-East Germany is now studied exclusively within the context of German film.[9] Even though an investigation of East Central European film history can barely be complete without including East German cinema, this book will comply with the general trend and only occasionally refer to film examples from the former East Germany.

When state entities in the region dissolved, as in the Czech-Slovak split, the new nations claimed their respective territories. Dividing the artistic heritage along the new fault lines, however, appeared to be even more complicated than drawing new state borders. 'Exclusive' cinematic traditions could be granted only by separating coherent national film histories into units that would fit into the new political entities: a fairly problematic and somewhat arbitrary act, easily susceptible to disputes and disagreements. In the case of Czechoslovakia, two cinematic cultures (a Czech and a Slovak one) co-existed in a symbiotic cultural interaction, a relationship that has been compared to the one between British and Irish cinemas. Given that these are two different countries today, from now on we are compelled to think of Czech and Slovak cinemas as two different entities. That Slovakia's main co-production partner remains the Czech Republic, or that leading Slovak directors such as Juraj Jakubisko or Martin Šulík live and work as much in the Czech Republic as in Slovakia does not change the fact that from this point on Czech and Slovak cinemas would exist as distinct entities.

It is difficult to determine if these reconfigurations, taking place both in literary scholarship and general cultural studies of the region, simply echo processes in politics and economics or represent an unbiased and lasting corrective to confining paradigms. The undertaking of hurried creation of distinct film traditions appears particularly problematic. This relabelling is being carried out at a moment when, in the world at large, national cinematic borders are collapsing and increasingly giving way to transnational film-making. Creating new theories of national cinemas at such time is a lost cause – *causa perduta*.

In addition, we are left with a range of situations where the politics of place has made no provisions for those sites of shared imagination or remembrance, as seen in the cinematic usage of places like Transylvania or the Terezín (Theresienstadt) concentration camp. On the other hand, within the East Central European film tradition, we encounter situations whereby certain cinemas are devoid of a clear-cut culture of belonging. Such is, for example, the case with the Yiddish-language film-making that thrived in the 1920s and 1930s in Poland under Joseph Green, a Polish-born American – a cinema that belongs not only to Poland, where it was produced, but is rightfully claimed as part of the Hebrew cinematic heritage.[10]

Beyond the Post-Cold War Era

The Cold War between the East and West expanded beyond economy and warfare and well into a cultural realm. East and West functioned as two independent spheres, competing in all fields and co-existing in permanent negation of each other.

Not much Western culture crossed the Iron Curtain to reach the East. Still less of the culture of the Eastern Bloc was known in the West, and a high proportion of the features that were known had been highlighted selectively for ideological considerations (for example the well-publicised lack of creative freedom and the suppression of the individual under state socialism). The one-sided Western coverage of artistic life in the Eastern Bloc resulted in a relatively incomplete Western picture of the way state socialist culture was organised and functioned.

For a situation that was so highly ideologically charged, such bias is not extraordinary. What is more worrying, however, is that after the West won the propaganda battle over the hearts and minds of people of the Eastern Bloc, the culture of the East remains as little known in the West as before. The resulting situation is that more than a decade into the post-1989 'transition', many of the Cold War-era clichés about East Central European culture and cinema remain unchallenged in the wider context of post-Soviet area studies.

This is why it seems important to try to overcome the remnants of the approach that is still 'dominated by a Manichean, and sometimes apocalyptic, view of the ideological struggle between East and West' (Hughes 1999: 4). Today it no longer makes sense to keep pointing out the wrongs of state socialism; it is something that has already been accomplished successfully. It would be more meaningful to engage in a project that would be less ideologically loaded and simply try to explain the specific logic of the state socialist system of cultural production as a system that had its own justification, advantages and disadvantages.

While no longer a dominant paradigm, the conceptual framework of the Cold War often continues to be uncritically reproduced and unimaginatively perpetuated in popular journalism that reveals a lack of sensitivity to new social and theoretical developments, and has not been effectively countered by the more serious studies into East European culture that, unfortunately, remain isolated within academia. It is necessary to scrutinise some basic premises of the Cold War framework, as recent explorations of the culture of the post-Soviet sphere have yet to connect with the mainstream of disciplines such as cultural and film studies.[11]

While it is unlikely that all such difficulties may be resolved here, we can at least identify some of these previously obscured and neglected issues. To begin, it is worth pointing out some of the important areas where more work needs to be undertaken in a reassessment of the region's cultural legacy as manifested in cinema. By mapping out some of the central ways that film scholarship of the region can be brought up to date, we may come closer to outlining a more adequate (and desirable) picture of East Central European film.

Firstly, we need to reassess industry configurations and considerations. During the Cold War, the system of state-owned and state-controlled film production and distribution under socialism was vilified as cumbersome, inefficient and plagued by the intervention of censors. The time has come to give a new, less ideologically biased, assessment of the rational aspects in the organisation of the film industries under state socialism. Once the ideological critique (which can also be called propaganda) is bracketed out and the industry structure is explored in the context of straightforward concepts of political economy such as ownership and control, a new view of censorship is also needed. Chapter two of this book will propose a different way of looking at these issues, an approach that also allows for a critical assessment of the commercialisation of post-1989 film-making offered in chapter seven.

It is also particularly important to reintroduce the study of style. Once the focus on political film-making is overcome, we can pay greater attention to dimensions previously ignored simply because they did not fit. We can explore in more detail those cinematic trends that pertain mostly to the film form, such as Surrealism, Constructivism, Dadaism, experimentation with non-linear narrative and so on. We can also study these cinemas from the point of view of their contribution to cinematic language. Such study has long been part of courses in cinematic language and theory, where films by Miklós Jancsó, Jan Němec and other masters from the region are regularly screened and studied solely from the point of view of film form. We should also foreground the specific absence of glamour, the sobriety, the moderation and the somewhat antiquated and out-of-fashion feel that East Central European cinema carries in its specific, more existential idiom.[12] Such exploration of style, however, is not regularly a feature of the study of film as part of area or national culture studies. Bridging the gap between the study of the thematic range and narrative strategies of East Central European film and the studies of style is an essential task for forthcoming studies.

In addition, one of the most needed steps is to rehabilitate popular cinema. In the polarised international context of the Cold War, films that bore, or seemed to bear, a political message were given more attention at festivals by distributors and journalists. This effectively led to neglecting a whole range of cinematic works that were not political, and resulted in the absence of studies into the popular genres of East Central European film. The commonly held opinion today is that popular genres did not exist under state socialism, which is a serious distortion of the facts. The neglected genres of comedy, melodrama, mystery, true crime and even horror still remain invisible.

It is also time to begin a critical discussion of cinema's role in forging nationalism. Because of the overwhelming interest in politics, those aspects of East Central European film where the effort was clearly geared towards forging the nation (historical epics and other explorations of historical nature) remain ignored. We need to acknowledge that film was not only used for Communist propaganda, but also for promoting a nationalist agenda. Some of these issues are addressed in chapter three.

Further insights in these cultures and cinemas can be gained if we examine cinema's exploration of moral issues independently of politics. A wide range of the region's films are informed by moral or existential concern that, even when played out in the context of a politically confining environment, is not limited to the political. East Central European cinema has offered classic explorations of the existential aspects of guilt, isolation, betrayal, responsibility and patriarchy, to name just a few moral conditions that have been approached. In addition, cinema in the region has a tradition of exploring the relationship between the individual and the course of history in a uniquely innovative way. These issues are addressed in chapters three, four and five.

Encouraging new studies in the sociology of culture of the Cold War and post-Cold War periods would have a significant impact on the understanding of film from East Central Europe. Very little has been done so far, for example, to study cultural production and consumption patterns (audience structure, cinema-going habits, spectatorship), and other related categories under state socialism.

A further important task is to reassess existing views of cultural dependency versus transculturation and globalisation. So far, cultural studies dealing with the former Eastern Bloc have done little to investigate the cultural relationship between the Soviet Union and the countries in its sphere from a new perspective. Nor have the cultural exchanges and co-operation between the countries of the region themselves been re-examined. Such investigation would lay a much-needed foundation for further studies into the more recent processes of globalisation and new cultural dependencies, as well as establishing viable links with important strands of contemporary cultural theory such as post-colonialism and globalisation. This book considers the cinemas of East Central Europe primarily in relation to European cinemas, but some of the recurring questions raised – nationalism and cinema, politics and morality, auteurism, issues of gender, history, allegorical form, realism – beg comparison with other non-European cinemas, most of all the cinema of the Third World and American independent film-making. It would also be important to encourage the examination of Western film and the cultural influence, both populist and arthouse.

A fresh look needs to be taken at the motives and commitments of émigré film-makers. In the polarised and politicised context of the Cold War, most of their migratory moves have been presented as driven by political disagreement and dissent. The picture is more complex, however, as will be discussed in chapter two.

Last but not least, it is important to encourage studies in documentary film-making, the least explored cinematic form. Another misleading assumption is that documentary film of the region was strictly politically controlled and mostly used for propaganda purposes. This view is incorrect: while it may be true that newsreels and documentary films were often made with propaganda in mind, it was within the documentary realm that some of the most important socially critical works materialised. Serious work in this area is necessary in order to correct prevailing misconceptions.

While it is not possible to cover all these areas in depth here, they are kept in close view throughout the study. Re-evaluating industrial context, liberating the study of style from dissident political content and rethinking political content as nationalist or politicised in multiple ways, rehabilitating popular cinema, intitiating studies of spectatorship and consumption, resituating East Central European cinema within the context of globalisation and focusing on documentary are all key areas that need to be developed further with renewed energy and vigour.

CHAPTER TWO

The Industry

Prior to 1945, the economic and cultural circumstances of the countries of the Eastern Bloc varied and uniform development was not characteristic of the region as a whole. Between 1945 and 1989, however, the development of these countries was levelled to a significant extent and dictated by Soviet policies in the spheres of economics and culture. It is thus necessary to choose a wider survey approach to the region, one that cuts across nations and identifies general trends in cultural administration and definitive advantages to the traditional one-country investigation.

Many important aspects of pre-1989 cultural production in the Eastern Bloc remain insufficiently studied today. While disproportionate attention has been paid to the propaganda contest, issues of censorship and state leverage on artists to conform, areas such as the geopolitics of culture (exchanges with Third World countries and within the Eastern Bloc itself), state socialist popular culture, and the rationale of socialist cultural administration remain overlooked. It is time to redress these shortages, to cast a new look at the activities of cultural policy agencies, and to reassess the relations between cultural activities and political agendas in the Cold War era.

This chapter will discuss the main features of the film industry from before 1989 and cover the specific Cold War realities in the cultural policies of the region; the structure of film production and studio arrangements; practices in film distribution and exhibition; and additional aspects of film-making such as animation and documentary. Issues regarding state socialist censorship practices, the concept of Socialist Realism and the migratory patterns of East Central European film-makers are also discussed here.

Cultural Dimensions of 'the Bloc'

At the end of World War Two, Poland, Hungary and Czechoslovakia were assigned to the sphere of influence of the Soviet Union. They rapidly became satellite states in political, economic, military and cultural affairs. Whatever happened in the Soviet Union directly influenced the cultural climate in the countries of the Eastern Bloc, and often events in the USSR were replicated in the Eastern Bloc (such as the 'Thaw' that followed the demystification of the cult of Stalin's personality in the late 1950s or the stagnation of the Brezhnev period).

The Soviet Union and the 'satellite' countries from its sphere thus existed in a closed system that was relatively self-sufficient and isolated from the rest of the world. Economic or cultural exchange beyond the Eastern Bloc, and particularly with Western countries, was discouraged and systematically interfered with. Within the Bloc, however, political, economic, defense and cultural co-operation was strongly endorsed and facilitated by the respective international organisations. There was a well-functioning system of cultural exchanges within the Bloc, with the 'brotherly' countries of the Third World and with select Western representatives (usually moderately left-wing writers or film-makers). The only thing off limits was mainstream Western mass culture, particularly those products that were believed to promote uninhibited violence or pornography.

Under state socialism, film production and distribution worked within a specific framework of cultural administration. Each country had a government body in charge of film-making (that is, a ministry of culture, a film commission); film financing was centralised and came exclusively from the state. Thus, many film-makers did not need to be familiar (and were not familiar) with the fundraising aspects of film production. The key film-making enterprises were the state-owned studios, and in most cases their work was organised within the so-called 'units' – relatively permanent teams consisting of directors, screenwriters, cameramen, and set and costume designers often sharing similar interests, views and tastes.

Once completed, films were distributed by a nationally owned monopoly, shown within the system of state-owned theatres and eventually screened on national television. A system of exchange of feature films between the Eastern Bloc countries was in place, thus the films were getting guaranteed exposure in a range of 'friendly' countries.

While we cannot underestimate the paternalistic omnipresence of the state within the film industry under state socialism, we have to acknowledge that this different industry model also had some positive aspects, such as maintaining consistently high production output and being less dependent on commercialism. The control was often driven by an underlying intent to rationalise, streamline and facilitate the production/distribution/exhibition mechanism. However, good policy intentions were often carried out by means of heavy-handed enforcement practices.

As was the case with arts and literature, political leaders took a personal interest in film-making and occasionally interfered with it. The unions of film-makers were controlled by the state and represented a strong trade organisation, membership of which was by election and was considered quite prestigious (while non-membership effectively meant isolation, making working impossible). Each country maintained a respective national film institute engaged in education and research, and a cinematheque with an archive. There were at least two leading film periodicals, one academic and one targeting wider audiences. Film scholarship was not seen as a separate discipline but was considered part of art history, and film scholars would often act as film critics.

Specialised film schools included, but were not limited to, FAMU (the Film and Television Faculty of the Academy of Performing Arts) in Prague and the Łódź Film School (along with VGIK in Moscow), where many of the film-makers from the region learned the nuts and bolts of the trade. International education has always been a mechanism for reinforcing desirable geopolitical influences, and – as in the case of the Eastern Bloc – a tool for forging cultural and economic links with the former colonial countries through the period of decolonisation. The international educational arrangements – acceptance policies, quotas, grants and alumni relations – were part of the system of film schools across the Eastern Bloc, all of which had a permanent contingent of international students from the 'brotherly' countries.[1]

The system was created with the view to persist. According to the official Eastern Bloc ideology socialist revolutions were to gradually occur in every single country and it was simply a matter of time to see state socialism being established all over the world. Thus, cultural policies were directly determined by the belief that communism was soon to triumph, and were meant to further cultural interactions within the Bloc and with those other countries that were designated 'brotherly' or 'friendly'. To what extent ordinary people believed the official ideology was a different matter.

Production and Studios

The film industries in the Eastern Bloc had the capacity and the size of their West European counterparts. This allowed the East Central European countries to have film output numbers comparable (and sometimes surpassing) those of similarly sized countries in Western Europe. The table below, extracted from data quoted in the *Encyclopedia of European Cinema* (Vincendeau 1995), illustrates the size of feature film production in the three countries of our focus. The average annual output of the region ranged between 100 and 130 feature films (this does not include the annual average of around 20 feature films made in East Germany). If we add the 150 films on average produced in the Soviet Union (Menashe 2001: 10) and another 100 made in Romania, Yugoslavia, Bulgaria and Albania, we arrive at an annual cinematic output of the Eastern Bloc of 350 to 400 features a year. The cinematic legacy of each single country for the period spanning 1948 to 1989 thus averages around 1,000 feature film titles. (The East German feature film library contains over 750 features.) Thus, we are talking of a film library of over 4,000 feature films (including the East German ones).

It is important to take into consideration, however, that the data given in this table only goes back to 1945, the year when the war ended. Before 1945 all three countries in question enjoyed thriving film production, despite flucuations. In each country, there was a general pattern: the beginning was strong with good production output throughout the silent period; they then suffered set-backs in the 1920s, and particularly with the advent of sound technologies. This was followed by a recovery in the second half of the 1930s, but the rise in output numbers was sooner or later (depending on the political alignment of the country) brought to an end by the effects of World War Two. According to Bryan Burns, for example, Hungary had produced 28 feature films in 1939 and 53 in 1943 (1996: 14). In Czechoslovakia, Peter Hames observed a rise of only eight features in 1930 to an average of over forty in the late 1930s (Hames in Taylor *et al.* 2000: 54). The record number of 27 feature films in Poland was established in the year 1937, two years before the German occupation of the country (Witkowska in Taylor *et al.* 2000: 185).

Regarding the specific organisation of film production under state socialism, most state production companies were structured after the Polish model of film units (*zespol filmove*), introduced in the early 1960s. Under this system, the film units within the studios of the Eastern Bloc functioned as the basic film production entity and had relative creative autonomy. Usually led by a well-established director (for example X was run by Andrzej Wajda and TOR was headed by Krzysztof Zanussi), the units comprised of several other directors sharing an artistic vision, as well as screenwriters and other specialised dramatists, cameramen, set and costume designers, and sometimes even actors, all salaried employees who only received bonuses upon the completion and release of a new film. The national television companies were also involved in production and often ran their own studios. The average cost of film production varied significantly over the Cold War period, which spans several decades, but has generally been set in the range of $200,000 per film.

Year	Hungary	Poland	Czechoslovakia
1945	3	0	3
1946	no data	1	12
1947	no data	2	22
1948	6	4	20
1949	no data	4	no data
1950	4	4	20
1951	8	4	8
1952	5	1	17
1953	8	9	18
1954	7	6	15
1955	11	9	17
1956	9	13	22
1957	16	10	27
1958	13	23	29
1959	18	15	35
1960	15	21	36
1961	19	24	45
1962	16	23	39
1963	19	27	39
1964	20	23	41
1965	23	20	45
1966	21	25	40
1967	22	no data	49
1968	37	no data	45
1969	23	no data	50
1970	23	24	54
1971	19	27	59
1972	21	19	49
1973	21	19	68
1974	20	27	66
1975	19	21	62
1976	19	no data	68
1977	25	27	64
1978	28	31	48
1979	26	32	47
1980	26	39	52
1981	25	19	48
1982	no data	26	no data
1983	25	36	66
1984	17	35	no data
1985	21	37	50
1986	26	34	63
1987	26	35	55
1988	20	34	58
1989	37	22	70
1990	23	27	62

Table 1: Number of films produced annually in East Central Europe 1945–1990. Source: Vincendeau (ed.) *Encyclopedia of European Cinema*, 1995: 464–5.

With a joint annual output of around (and sometimes over) 400 films, the Soviet Union, East Central Europe and Balkan countries established a well-developed system of film studios.[2] Primarily meant to serve the ambitious undertaking of national film industries, most studios were built in the 1950s, but the largest ones had been in existence since the early 1930s. Besides feature film production, they were home to smaller administrative film production units, such as studios for documentaries and shorts, television films and animation.

Studio executives of the Communist era maintained good contacts with the international film community, and while the studios were mostly meant to serve domestic film production, some began hosting international co-productions. With time, the studios started attracting foreign film crews, and a number of Western productions were made here, even during the Cold War. These studios were especially sought after for period dramas and historical super-productions as large numbers of extras and cavalry were easy to secure.

The Polish state cinematography committee, Film Polski, ran four main studio spaces: WDFiF in Warsaw, Leg Studios in Kraków, Łódź in Central Poland, and Wrocław in Silesia, where production was realised via the administrative entities of the film units. Hungary operated three state-owned studios under the umbrella film agency Mafilm. The facilities belonged to a state monopoly until the 1980s, when production was somewhat decentralised to give autonomy to established directors, who started playing a more prominent role in management.[3] Besides the facilities for mainstream film production, Hungary also had a dedicated experimental film studio – the Béla Balázs Stúdió. Founded in 1959, it evolved as a burgeoning centre for independent short and documentary films, and throughout several decades it functioned as a leading centre of avant-garde cinema.[4] One of the largest studios was DEFA near Berlin in East Germany.[5] In existence since the 1930s, DEFA had the most advanced production facilities for its time and was at the centre of the thriving East German film production. Secondary production facilities for Czechoslovakia were the film studios in Gottwaldov (now Zlín) and Koliba in Bratislava, which was the centre for Slovak film production.

The main production centre in the region, however, was Prague's Barrandov studios, comparable in size to the Italian Cinecitta near Rome. Alongside the former East German DEFA studio in Berlin (now again called Babelsberg), Barrandov today claims to be the largest studio on the European continent. It has 11 sound stages with a total capacity of 7,000 square metres. Barrandov also has post-production facilities and an enormous collection of costumes and props.

Barrandov was built at a small plateau near Prague in the late 1920s and was named after Joachim Barrande, a geologist who had worked in the area. The studio, which opened officially in the year marked by the advent of the 'talkies' (1931), came into existence due to the entrepreneurial efforts of the

Havel brothers, direct ancestors of the former Czech president Václav Havel. The facilities had been further improved during the occupation of the country by the Nazis, whose ambition had been to make Barrandov a third German film-making centre alongside the studios in Babelsberg and Munich. After the Second World War, Barrandov was nationalised and continuous state investments made it possible to build a special effects stage, a projection tunnel, and a water tank allowing for underwater photography. Barrandov was where most of the celebrated films of the Czechoslovak New Wave were shot; it also attracted international co-productions, such as Miloš Forman's *Amadeus* (USA, 1984) and Barbra Streisand's *Yentl* (USA, 1984).

In the post-Communist era, cinema industries soon witnessed the loss of guaranteed state funding. Profound changes in production financing included the substitution of film units with independent producers, the introduction of new strategies in state subsidies (which are now awarded on a per project basis and only cover a percentage of the production costs), the growing role of television as co-producer in feature film-making, the increased dependency on international co-productions, and the emergence of private investment in film-making. A number of smaller production companies are now working on a contractual basis with the studios. Under the new conditions, production levels stabilised relatively fast and the balance in output numbers, disturbed originally by the drastic cuts in centralised financing, was restored in many of the East European countries.

Initially, the studios' budgets were reduced to a bare minimum. Equipment was becoming out-of-date and scores of employees lay idle. However, production costs were still much lower compared to the West, and studios throughout the former Eastern Bloc came into fierce competition with each other in the struggle to attract Western co-productions that would keep the skilled local personnel, also known as 'below the line' staff, busy. Gradually, various degrees of privatisation were carried out at all the studios. The story of the initial privatisation of Barrandov and several subsequent changes in its ownership reflected the dramatic and volatile essence of the post-Communist transition.[6] For the time being Barrandov is thriving, mostly due to a great demand for its facilities from Western 'runaway' productions (that is, ones that are financed entirely by the producing country and only use locations and services in the host country, without co-production participation or significant creative input from them). Studios in Slovakia and Hungary also heavily rely on runaway productions to maintain their operation.[7] The business of runaway productions, however, is considered a 'portable industry', suggesting that all this film commerce currently going to the region may simply 'run' elsewhere as soon as the current cost-advantages disappear, especially with the accession of the countries in the region to the European Union in 2004 (and the likely rise in prices to West European standards).

Distribution and Exhibition

The cycle of production, distribution and exhibition throughout the region in the postwar period was run in a centralised manner, with all components co-ordinated by the state. It was an arrangement comparable to the classic American studio system where the big Hollywood studios exhibited their films in a system of theatres they owned. This 'vertically integrated' system had been in operation before 1948, when the studios were forced by anti-trust legislation to break up the well-consolidated production/exhibition mechanism, a split which in effect enhanced the role of distribution as a key intermediary operation within the film industry cycle.[8] As the socialist system was concerned neither with fighting monopoly and securing freedom for competition nor with stimulating private enterprise, here vertical integration was encouraged rather than confronted. Box-office revenues did matter but were never of crucial importance, and distribution was a well-orchestrated activity, which allowed for rigorous non-commercial and sometimes highly ideologised promotion. While frequently muddled up with dull politically correct films, this system was effectively safeguarded from the drawbacks of commercial competition. Works of higher artistic quality, particularly from across the region, were exhibited in a system of art-house theatres. A well-developed system of cinematic barters between the Eastern Bloc countries included not only theatrical distribution, but also a range of special events. The export of films was part of a wider promotional effort, including national film weeks abroad run by dedicated organisations.

Due to the sporadic and limited character of film exports beyond the Bloc, Western audiences were mostly familiar with products of a 'high-brow' nature. They were often left with the impression that the cinematic output of the region consisted either of cerebral or of highly politicised (and usually censored) works. Such a view was corroborated by scholars from the region, who, on the rare occasions when they were invited to contribute to Western scholarship, claimed that the popular genres were non-existent.[9]

In fact, there was a thriving popular culture, which remains little known and understudied. Naturally, not being commercially dependent on audience attendance, these cinemas may not have produced as many works of mass appeal as the cinemas of the West European countries. However, there was a range of films in popular genres such as comedy and adventure. Some were extremely successful and rivalled Hollywood blockbusters in popularity, including the two Polish television series *Czterej pancerni i pies/Four Tank Soldiers and the Dog* (1966) and *Stawka większa niż życie/More Than Life at Stake* (1969), Juliusz Machulski's Polish box office hits of the 1980s (*Vabank/Va Banque*, 1981; *Seksmisja/Sex Mission*, 1984), the Czech spoof western *Limonádový Joe aneb ko/Lemonade Joe* (Oldřich Lipský, 1964), the Czech television adventure series *30 případů majora Zemana/Thirty Cases of Major Zeman* (1975), and the DEFA native Indian adventures, for example *Osceola* (Konrad Petzold, 1971) and *Die*

Söhne der großen Bärin/The Sons of the Big Bear (Josef Mach 1966), which were both Karl May adaptations starring the dashing Gojko Mitić, a Serbian-born actor. Today many of these films enjoy cult status in their respective countries.

Another common (and equally erroneous) belief is that during the Cold War people in the Eastern Bloc lived on a 'diet of Soviet war films'. While this is partially true (some countries had quotas for Soviet film imports, in turn reciprocated by quotas guaranteeing their cinematic exports to the Soviet Union), it is a view that obscures the real picture. In fact, film exhibition was much more diverse. Imports from the West were not as limited as widely believed, but were made selectively, effectively resulting in distribution of quality Western films. A versatile system of barter exchanges was in place with the 'friendly' countries from the Third World as well. Thus, films produced in the region were granted wide distribution within the Bloc (while today many are not even released in their home country). The active distribution networks also consisted of non-Western countries like India, the newly independent countries of the Third World and of other 'brotherly' nations such as Cuba or Vietnam. In this way, Polish, Hungarian and Czechoslovak productions enjoyed a type of exposure that was truly international, reaching far beyond the usual distribution channels traditionally limited to Western Europe and North America. This international film distribution was part of a crucial political

Figure 1: The Polish television series *Four Tank Soldiers and the Dog* (1966) was extremely popular with mass audiences.

Figure 2: Gojko Mitić in the Karl May adaptation, *Osceola* (1971).

effort to rebalance the configuration of the world's (cultural) powers and was thus a politically sensitive activity, replicating the logic of geopolitical priorities in the area of cultural exchanges.

Another, traditionally neglected, form of film distribution included the system of film festivals, which worked as a complementary distribution network. National festivals had been in existence in all countries of the former Eastern Bloc since the 1950s. Usually showcasing the entire annual production, the awards at these festivals directly reflected the dominant political line and were considered a litmus test for the political climate within a given country.[10] In some cases, however, festivals were major sites of dissent, for example in Poland in the late 1970s and early 1980s when awards went to politically subversive films, and where the Gdynia festival effectively provided a venue for the important political activities of the independent trade union Solidarność (Solidarity) and its predecessor KOR (Workers' Defence Committee), thus signalling the first cracks in the system.

During the Cold War, film festivals in the East and in the West alike were important instruments of cultural diplomacy. They were often seen as undisguised flag-waving exercises, where award distribution reflected the geopolitical configurations of the day. Individual film-makers were usually not permitted to promote their work themselves, and which film would be entered at which international festival was decided centrally. The most important international venues within the Eastern Bloc were the festivals in Karlovy Vary (Czechoslovakia) and Moscow, both in existence since the 1950s. Generally speaking, politically correct output was traditionally sent to Moscow, while artistically significant films would compete at Karlovy Vary. These high profile events were supplemented by an extensive network of smaller festivals (all subjected to supervision by the cultural ministries in the respective countries) that were very popular with audiences. Films from Hungary, Poland and Czechoslovakia regularly competed and won awards at the prestigious international festivals in Cannes, Berlin, Venice and elsewhere.

Since 1989, the festival scene has undergone a substantial transformation. Some older festivals became defunct while new ones proliferated. There was even a short-lived attempt (1995 to 1996) to shut down the venerable Karlovy Vary festival and replace it with a new one in Prague, which was perceived to be a more commercially viable location.

The proliferation of film festivals in the 1990s is a world-wide trend, and East Central Europe is no exception.[11] In a world where theatrical screens are increasingly dominated by commercial Hollywood productions, the festival circuit is clearly emerging as an alternative distribution network for independent, international and art-house cinema. In this new context, venues specifically dedicated to East European cinema include the Cottbus Festival of East European cinema which takes place in eastern Germany and the Alpe-Adria film festival in Trieste, Italy.[12]

Animation and Documentary

While this book is primarily intended to survey feature film, it is necessary to at least outline the scope of animation and documentary film-making in the region as two other equally important areas of creative cinematic output. Eastern Europe's contribution to animation art is particularly significant, marked by the co-existence of many original artistic visions and by highly innovative approaches in a range of techniques, such as puppet animation and cut-outs, as well as aspects of cel animation.

Centrally subsidised, animation was one of the costlier film arts to flourish here. However, it had begun much earlier, in the first decades of the twentieth century. Some of the East European pioneers of animated art – such as Polish-born Władysław Starewicz (also known as Ladislav Starewicz) or the Hungarian-born János Halász (better known as John Halas) – are also considered to be patriarchs of West European animated art.

Until 1989, animation in East Central Europe was almost exclusively financed, produced and distributed within the state-run studio system – Krátký Film and Trick Brothers in the Czech Republic (in existence since the 1940s), Pannónia Film Studios in Hungary, the Experimental Cartoon Film Studio and

Figure 3: The contribution to animation art was particularly significant in puppet animation: Jirí Trnka's *Old Czech Legends* (1953).

SeMaFor in Poland (as well as busy animation studios in Romania, Bulgaria and Yugoslavia). These studios put out works that earned scores of international awards and turned the region into a world leader in the art of animated film.[13]

Best known for their unique style were Czech animators Jiří Trnka, Karel Zeman, Hermína Týrlová, Jiří Barta, Břetislav Pojar, Stanislav Látal and surrealist Jan Švankmajer, as well as the Slovak animator Viktor Kubal. The Czechoslovak animation tradition in particular has a strong emphasis on puppetry. The great Polish school includes the work of popular animators such as Witold Giersz, Walerian Borowczyk, Jan Lenica, Daniel Szczechura, Jerzy Kucia, Piotr Dumala and émigré Zbigniew Rybczyński. The best-known animators from Hungary include Gyula Macskássy and Edit Fekete, Ferenc Rofusz, Ferenc Cakó, Csaba Varga, Mária Horváth, Csaba Szerda and the Los Angeles-based Gabor Csupo, co-founder of the animation production company Klasky-Csupo, which came into prominence in the 1990s with the cartoon series *The Rugrats*.

Animation is an expensive art, and in the post-Communist period the countries in the region could no longer afford the level of generous subsidies they had previously maintained. After 1989, state funding was reduced to a minimum and the studios underwent various forms of privatisation; the new box office-oriented approaches in production and distribution led to a drop in the output of animation. There was a massive emigration of animation professionals, many of whom are now employed by companies across Western Europe, Canada and the US. Many of those who stayed are involved in working on international orders, in an industry context that Toby Miller *et al.* call 'off-shore cartooning' (2001: 44). The Zagreb Animation Festival in Croatia is still one of the two most important animation venues in the world, alternating every other year with the Annecy Film Festival.

Documentary film-making was an important part of the cinemas of all East Central European countries during the years of communism, regularly awarded prizes at the specialised festivals in Oberhausen, Mannheim, Amsterdam, Leipzig and Kraków.[14] Documentaries were produced either by dedicated studios or by units attached to the respective national television companies. There was also a well-developed network of amateur film clubs where grass-roots documentaries were produced and then showcased at special national meetings.[15] Many of the leading feature film directors from the region – such as Andrzej Munk and Krzysztof Kieślowski in Poland, Miloš Forman in Czechoslovakia, or Márta Mészáros in Hungary – started as documentary film-makers. Others – such as the Slovak director Dušan Hanák – have actually preferred the documentary format for their most important films. Crucially, documentaries brought a range of innovative approaches to cinema, some of which include the inventive use of re-enactment or the mock documentary (a technique used by Andrzej Wajda within his 1976 feature *Człowiek z marmuru/Man of Marble*). In a conscious effort to give features the feel of authenticity, documentary methods were widely used in features, often expressed in approaching feature film as a sociological snapshot (as in early films of Miloš Forman like *Černý Petr/Black Peter*, a.k.a. *Peter and Pavla*, 1963) or as a socio-psychological investigation (as seen in Andrzej Munk's *Człowiek na torze/Man on the Tracks*, 1957).

Even though many documentaries glorified socialist construction (particularly those commissioned by the authorities), documentary film-makers did not hesitate to explore the sores of society wherever possible and offered rather subversive commentaries on the affairs of the Eastern Bloc countries. Documentary film-making in Poland even played an important role in undermining the Communist regime.

In the 1990s, many documentary film-makers took the chance to revisit moments of the past and to critically re-evaluate the official history. There was a temporary decline in output, but nonetheless remarkable documentaries have been made in the region carrying out investigations of historical topics that were previously taboo. Several subjects were favoured by documentary film-makers, such as the difficult process of political transformation, relations with the Soviet Union, and the complex interaction between different ethnic groups. After 1989, in the context of a general financial crisis, documentary proved to be one of the most popular genres and managed more than any other film form to yield serious and meaningful works chronicling various aspects of transition. The success of documentary forms in the post-Communist period may also be due to the fact that such works were often financed by television networks and thus had more chance than features to be shown on television and watched by wider audiences.

Censorship

While there are a number of well-known embarrassing examples of censorship from all the countries in the Eastern Bloc, within the ideologically tense atmosphere of the Cold War censorship in the region was often given disproportionate attention by commentators in the West. Art was part of the ideological battles between the two camps, and it was mostly in this context that censored art from the Eastern Bloc was celebrated in the West. Film festivals were thought of as Cold War instruments, and in the West there was a tendency to judge the artistry of cinematic works coming out of the Eastern Bloc according to the level of dissent displayed. There was an unstated assumption that all good films were shelved and only the mediocre ones released.[16]

Even today, more than a decade after the official end of the Cold War, this presumption persists. Censored art from East Central Europe is still given privileged attention. It is still assumed that censored films had a higher artistic value than those that were not censored. The continuation of this thinking, however, is not productive, and some corrective discussion on censorship is necessary here; it is important that we replace the politicised and distorted Cold War-era picture of cinema in the region with a more comprehensive and ultimately more truthful one.[17]

When discussing censorship, it is imperative to avoid simplistic explanations, which regrettably are widespread, and try to understand the logic of Communist censorship. The elaborate censorship mechanisms of Communism are notorious; but then, thinking of the number of daring and serious works of art that were completed here, we also need to explain how was it possible to make and release films of superb artistry and aesthetic quality under such a repressive system. In the West many of these films would not be censored – they simply would not have been made. In each case, there is a measure of control, be it commercial or political. While in the West market considerations were predominant but rarely acknowledged or identified as freedom infringements, in East Central Europe political considerations were the guiding force.

It is most useful to explore censorship contextually, within a framework that takes ownership into consideration. Whoever considers themselves to be the owner of a product – be it the state within the system of state socialism or the corporation within the system of capitalist production – also exercises control over the marketing of the product. Such an approach to censorship was proposed by Hungarian Miklós Haraszty in his excellent 1983 treatise *The Velvet Prison*. Here, he extensively compares the limitations of the artist working under state socialism with those faced by corporate employees (for example film-makers working within the Hollywood system) and the interference that both categories of film-makers experience. The main difference between the two, Haraszty points out, is that under state socialism there was nothing beyond the state. Thus, if the artist rejected the socialist state, he would not have access to any other creative possibilities. The situation of the corporate artist in consumer society is only a little better – if he was to reject corporate control, he could at least choose to remain free in obscure independence.

The control of cinema under state socialism should be seen as a logical consequence of the state ownership of the film industry. Yet the owners did not exercise this control particularly effectively. Their censorship was plagued by irony: rather than preventing films from being made, the Communist state would often commit production funds that could have easily been withheld, but then shelve a completed film. Under the economic logic of capitalism such waste of funds would not be allowed and the shelved films would never be made in the first place, let alone censored.[18] This paradoxical situation was largely due to the semi-autonomous standing of the film units where most production decisions were made, and where mechanisms to evade direct surveillance and interference were developed. Within the units, ideological supervision was fairly relaxed and sometimes intentionally overlooked.

Looking at censorship practices at large, Haraszty noted that state socialism even practiced relative permissiveness – direct glorification of the state was not expected, even criticism was permitted, and the only thing really off limits was to express doubts of the pure and genuinely humane intentions of the socialist enterprise. What the socialist state actually wanted (and failed) to achieve was to retain the public consensus over the commonly accepted purpose of social and historical development. While variations were permissible, each and every work of art was supposed to corroborate (or at least not dispute) that everything was moving forward according to the general plan to build a perfect classless society of affluence and equality. While censors often looked into petty details, their ultimate responsibility was to ensure that art preoccupied with 'small truths' (that is, socially critical films focusing on economic and moral problems) did not distract audiences from the 'big truth' (the generally accepted vision of glorious ascendance to communism).

The organisations committed to carrying out censorship control in the Eastern Bloc differed from country to country. While Hungary did not have a dedicated censorship body, it was still believed to have had the most sophisticated and elusive censorship mechanisms in place. Poland, on the other hand, had a special body in charge of media censorship, The Main Office for Control of the Press, Publications and Public Performances. In other countries, the studios had artistic commissions working under the close supervision of the Communist

Party's ideological department in approving completed films. In Czechoslovakia, a two-tiered censorship mechanism was in place: first, scripts needed to be pre-approved by internal censors, a level where the rules were set out clearly and thus possible to circumvent; then the completed films were to be approved by a Party commission, a stage at which most problems occured. In the aftermath of the infamous East German Eleventh Plenum, almost everything put out by DEFA in 1965 was shelved. As Daniela Berghahn notes, however, while the total number of banned DEFA films stayed within the range of a couple of dozen, 'the extent of editorial interventions at the stages of script development and pre-production [was] much harder to gauge' (2002: 1). The mechanisms of censorship differed, and while a film like Jan Němec's absurdist *O slavnosti a hostech/The Party and the Guests* (1966) was 'banned forever' in Czechoslovakia, many other films were never officially condemned but were only given a limited release, thus effectively ensuring they were seen merely by a handful of spectators.

The paternalist omnipresence of the state found expression in censorship mechanisms that covered both form and content. 'Formalism' (everything suspected of paying more attention to form than to realist content, usually associated with avant-garde and experimental film-making) was out of favour. Censors often failed to combat formalism so a variety of cinematic styles that were not strictly realist were in existence. The censors, however, were particularly vigilant to not let films play a subversive role within the political context and operated through a mechanism of forbidden and permitted subject matters, although these often changed with the political circumstances of the period. Whole periods of history were off limits to film-makers: the volatile period between 1945 and 1948, for example, when Communist governments were imposed throughout the region (history books claimed that Communist governments came into power as a result of the spontaneous choice of the people). It was also not possible to speak directly of the repression and show trials against free-thinking Communists, the gloomy Stalinist period, the Communist-run prison camps, the biased judicial system, the Hungarian uprising of 1956 and the rising 'new class' of *apparatchik*s and nomenclatura members. In Hungary, for example, films like Péter Bacsó's *A tanú/The Witness* (1969) and *Te rongyos élet/Oh, Bloody Life!* (1983) were withheld from distribution due to their critical take on the Communist regime. In Czechoslovakia, many directors suffered from censorship and were not given the chance to work for years, particularly in the period of 'Normalisation' that followed the Prague Spring of 1968. Jiří Menzel's *Skřivánci na niti/Skylarks on a String* (aka *Larks on a String*, 1969), for example, which was started during the period of the Prague Spring and completed after the Soviet invasion, was only released in 1990. In Poland, censors halted the release of Ryszard Bugajski's *Przesłuchanie/The Interrogation* (1982, only shown after 1989) and Janusz Zaorski's *Matka królów/Mother of Kings* (1983, shown after 1986), both films dealing with the Stalinist period. In East Germany, most of the banned films were only released at the time of 'die Wende' (associated with the fall of the Berlin Wall and Germany's reunification).

Film-makers who had to work in such a context were particularly inventive in their efforts to avoid interference and to work on their desired projects. In such a context, an important aspect to censorship was the subtle artistic conformity, sometimes defined as 'self-censorship', which was a direct consequence of the state's treatment of the intelligentsia as a highly prestigious social group.[19] It is important to note that not all film-makers whose films were censored were automatically prevented from making more – such were the experiences, for example, of Jiří Menzel in Czechoslovakia or Kurt Maetzig and Konrad Wolf in East Germany (who were even important establishment figures). The banning of Péter Bacsó's *The Witness* was not an impediment to either of his parallel careers, as a director and a film unit head. In Poland, film-makers like Aleksander Ford and Andrzej Wajda suffered from censorship and yet enjoyed a wide public recognition and high office.[20]

Putting up with the censors clearly bothered film-makers, and they subtly tackled the issues of censorship in many films, from Jiří Trnka's classic animation *Ruka/The Hand* (1965) through Wajda's *Man of Marble*, Kieślowski's *Przypadek/Blind Chance* (1981), and Károly Makk's *Egymásra nézve/Another Way* (1982), to Wojciech Marczewski's *Ucieczka z kina Wolność/Escape from Liberty Cinema* (1990), and many more.

Many of the censored films were released around 1989 – some before, some soon after the change. Film scholars have noted, however, that only rarely did the shelved films receive the public appreciation they were denied at the time of their making. As Daniela Berghahn notes, by the time of 'die Wende', audiences seemed to be too caught up in the massive social changes 'to take much notice of something that had already become history'; moreover many of these films 'had lost their explosiveness and topicality' (2001: 1, 4). Furthermore, for the time, it appeared that with the very end of state socialism, most of the social problems identified in these films would soon be made obsolete during the course of impending social changes.

Realism

The claim is frequently made that cinematic art under state socialism was confined to the straightjacket of Socialist Realism. Yet it is difficult to think of films made after 1956 that could exemplify Socialist Realism in its purest form. Thus in the case of East Central European cinema we have a situation where the Socialist Realism directive was formally in place but no longer enforced in practice or complied with after the end of the Stalinist period. As H. M. Hughes writes:

Socialist Realism was only pressed into service in the satellite states of Czechoslovakia, Hungary and Poland, in the period from 1949 until the death of Stalin, in 1953 or, at the latest, 1955. It barely survived, as a style, though the link between socially committed art and some form of realism lasted a great deal longer. At the very least, Socialist Realism provided independently inclined artists with a negative model, against which they felt an urge, and even a moral compunction, to react, often by retreating into a private world of denial or by explicitly renouncing the possibility of social engagement. (1999: 6)

The Socialist Realist doctrine was a set of guidelines on style and content mostly concerned with the narrative arts. Elements had been launched as early as 1934, and its main proponent, Stalin's cultural policy advisor Andrei Zhdanov, had been particularly strict in applying the rules to the Soviet intelligentsia over the following two decades. At the time of the creation of the Eastern Bloc after the Second World War, the stipulations of the Socialist Realist doctrine were transferred to the East European region and were used as guidelines for cultural policies.

Socialist Realism was supposed to be the art best-suited to cater for the revolutionary masses in their endeavour to build a bright socialist future. There was a pre-determined direction that was to be followed by every work of narrative art; after a period of socialist construction one would then arrive at the threshold of a just social state called communism where all people will be equally respected as important members of society, and where every individual will contribute according to their abilities and will receive according to their needs. Works of art that fell in line with this way of representing social and historical development were encouraged; those that doubted it were discouraged.

Socialist Realism made several demands: the suppression of 'formalism' and all experimentation with the art form and commitment to 'realist' content; an outspoken commitment to the cause of building socialism and communism; the presence of a strong hero, a member of the working class, who promotes the party line; and a plot developing in the cannon of 'historical optimism' (occasionally expressed with the concept of 'revolutionary romanticism'), namely one that keeps in view the ultimate triumph of the socialist idea – no matter what tremendous difficulties the hero may encounter in the course of his struggle to build the bright socialist future, this future should never disappear from sight, thus determining all outcomes in a historically optimist framework.

It is important to keep in focus the distinction between Socialist Realism and critical social realism (as seen in the Italian neorealism, for example). In the Socialist Realist framework the realistic reflection of reality was not sufficient; with the strategic goal of social development (building Communism), the narrative needed to be underpinned by historical optimism. Far-reaching critical examinations of the current state of society were discouraged and Socialist Realist narratives had to evolve to assert the imminent triumph of clearly identifiable forces of history (for example the proletariat) working towards class equality and social justice. Even if it did not result in an immediate triumph of Communist ideals, these forces were to be shown winning over the minds and hearts of protagonists (hence pessimistic endings were not acceptable). The protagonist was supposed to be shown first enduring social (preferably capitalist) oppression and then rebelling against it. Having become socially conscious, the individual was to commit to a struggle for change where he would join forces with others, and become involved in a mass resistance movement for the ideals of equality and ultimate social justice. The protagonist could perish along the way if that destruction was taking place in the context of the forward-looking optimism for it was assumed that in order to build the bright future one should first radically confront all obstacles.

This official stylistic paradigm was not rigidly imposed for cinema, and the framework was mostly used as a critical measure in the assessment of films upon completion, but was not strictly complied with at the planning stage, when new ideas were developed. While seemingly in compliance with the Socialist Realist recipe, most films would be more works of *social* realism rather than Socialist Realism; they would focus more on the subtler exploration of the concrete historical and social confines and less on the declared framework of the pre-determined advent of the perfect state of Communism. Such films were usually honest accounts that, even in a fragmented and elusive manner, commented on the contradictions and limitations of socialist reality. The works of directors like Károly Makk, Péter Bascó, Péter Gothár, Jaromil Jireš, Krzysztof Zanussi, Antoni Krauze and others, formed the backbone of the strong tradition in socially critical film-making.

Distinct film styles that were at odds with the generally prescriptive context of officially endorsed art developed their 'formalisms' and thrived nonetheless. Such were the various avant-garde tendencies or experimental aestheticism as discovered in the work of the Czechs Věra Chytilová, Jan Němec and Jan Švankmajer, Juraj Jakubisko in Slovakia and Wojciech Has in Poland.

The 1980s experienced an increased acceptance of various artistic developments in narrative and style that did not fit within the straitjacket of Socialist Realism (non-linear narrative experimentation since the 1960s, dream sequences, fantasy flashbacks, and so on). The state's cultural policies gradually became more accommodating and flexible (alongside the growing tolerance in issues of faith). Albeit reluctantly, a wider variety of artistic forms of expression, until recently largely excluded from the official public life, came to be integrated within the sphere of permissible cultural practices. As Lóránd Hegyi notes, in the context of this 'soft dictatorship', the concept of 'official art' was no longer a clear-cut term but rather a 'constantly changeable multi-layered system dominated by tactical considerations', and as a result some 'hybrid' forms emerged between the poles of Socialist Realist and avant-garde art (1992: 37). Moreover, state cultural policies and the 'soft dictatorship' were applied differently in the three countries. In this context, the strict distinction between what was perceived as 'officially' endorsed and 'unofficial', or 'dissident' culture was not so important any more. Realism was no longer an imperative, and film-makers could abandon socially committed 'realist' film-making altogether and declare their interest in existential themes.

Movements and Migrations

Like in literature, migrations of talent, exilic and diasporic creativity, and participation in transnational artistic projects have played a defining role in cinema.[21] Unlike literary studies, however, film historiography is yet to acknowledge and chronicle the various dimensions of such movements of people and visions that effectively transcend the confines of national borders, geographic regions, time periods, linguistic systems, diasporas and idiosyncratic traditions. It is increasingly important, therefore, to centralise the discussion of movements, loyalties and detachment here.

The topic of migration in film has claimed a constant presence in East Central European film-making, even though at times it was suppressed by censorship as a subject matter better left untouched. The decision whether to migrate or not has been a theme in numerous films, such as István Szabó's *Szerelmesfilm/ Love Film* (1970), whose protagonists must choose to stay or go, and Wanda Jakubowska's *Zaproszenie/The Invitation* (1986) and Krzysztof Zanussi's *Rok spokojnego słońca/Year of the Quiet Sun* (1984) which both feature heroines in love with American-based men.

More important, however, were the actual migrations of film-makers from the region. Film historiography has paid some attention to the European and transatlantic migrations of the first part of the century, when East Central Europeans such as Michael Curtiz contributed to the establishment of Hollywood's prosperity.[22] These earlier moves of cinematic talent – between America and various European locations – do not differ essentially from the moves of West Europeans, and largely replicate patterns that have been explored in a variety of existing studies (Lev 1993; Elsaesser 1999).[23]

The migrations of East Central Europeans, however, came to differ substantially during the Cold War, when, with the advent of the Soviet sphere, severe limitations were imposed on film-makers' movements beyond the Eastern Bloc and on their international creative contacts. The situation was complicated by the added dimension of the mutual exclusion and isolation of the two political camps. Those film-makers who left the countries of East Central Europe during the Cold War knew that by leaving their respective countries they were crossing critical fault lines and forefeiting the chance to return. To migrate meant to take sides and effectively renounce the conditions of work in the Eastern Bloc.

That these artistic migrations had to be interpreted as 'taking sides' had myriad implications. For example, the work of East Europeans who opted to work in the West was scrutinised for political messages even when it was not meant to be political; each and every one of their artistic utterings was routinely evaluated as if it were a political pronouncement on the regime they had left behind.[24] Yet, many of the directors who left the Eastern Bloc to cross over to the other side of the Iron Curtain were not as preoccupied with politics as is commonly believed; the dissident East European émigré film-maker was a Cold War stereotype more or less constructed in the West. Given the deep political divisions of the period, it appeared that every film-maker that migrated was doing so through a disapproval of the Communist regime, even though politics was not necessarily the main factor in each and every case.[25] For the sake of truthfulness in this investigation, it is necessary to 'complicate' this simplified picture 'by doubling the political dimension with another one: that of trade and competition, of contacts and markets' (Elsaesser 1999: 98) and looking into a more diverse range of migratory moves.

First, not all migrations were taking place along the East/West axis, and while film-makers' crossings of the Iron Curtain were well documented by journalists and film historians, the sanctioned (but equally important) creative moves of cineastes within the Eastern Bloc remain largely neglected and unexplored. The systematic study of these movements would reveal an array of creative collaborations fostered by interactions within the Easern Bloc.[26] It is essential to consider that besides the regular co-productions with the Soviet Union, there were intense co-productions between most of the countries in the region, alongside the respective industry agreements. While exchanges with the West were controlled and largely suppressed, many film-makers took advantage of the freedom of movement they could enjoy within the Eastern Bloc; there was an intense and lively international artistic scene, albeit self-contained and isolated from the West.[27]

Second, a number of East Central European directors did have the chance to work in the West without emigrating. Admittedly available to a select few before the fall of the Berlin Wall, such opportunities proved of crucial importance for the careers of some directors – such as István Szabó – who remained based in their native countries and nonetheless rose to international fame. Andrzej Wajda kept himself occupied with various European-financed productions at times when conditions at home prevented him from working, but would always return to Poland (during the period of martial law, for example, he made *Danton* in France in 1982 and *Eine Liebe in Deutschland/A Love in Germany* in Germany in 1983). Likewise, some of the émigrés would return occasionally to make films in their home countries: during a sejour in Poland, Paris-based

Walerian Borowczyk worked on *Dzieje grzechu/Story of a Sin* (1975, based on Stefan Żeromski), a psychological drama of sexuality and class taking place in a period setting, and New York-based Miloš Forman filmed his acclaimed *Amadeus* in Prague in 1984.

Third, the equation between the 'outside world' and 'the West', which is often presumed in texts dealing with the Cold War period, obscures another important dimension of cultural interactions – those with 'the rest' of the world (to use Stuart Hall's dichotomy of 'the West and the rest'). East Central Europeans' contacts with the West were indeed obstructed but they were able to have active interactions with film-makers from other parts of the 'outside world' such as Africa, Latin America and Asia. In the area of film, there were extensive creative and industry contacts with countries such as India and other post-colonial states.

In view of this assortment of international interactions, it is important to revise the inflexible template that reduces all migrations of East Central European cinematic talent to a straightforward reaction to oppressive political regimes at home. Taking a closer look at the career paths of some well-known East Central European directors who migrated to the West is proof that they did not necessarily follow the simple 'dissident' scenario. Moreover, if many émigré film-makers were viewed as political dissidents then their behaviour was extrememly inconsistent.

While film-makers were certainly attracted by the promised freedom of Western societies, once there only a few remained principally committed to the fight against Communism and were not particularly keen to use their artistry in exposing its faults. Only a few did, remaining explicitly engaged with social causes related to the political situation in the Eastern Bloc.[28] Also, most of those who left in the 1960s and 1970s did not have much sympathy for leftist causes, given that they had mostly been exposed to the totalitarian version of socialist ideology. So it is not surprising that many émigrés articulated aversion to the Western Left. Some even showed a preference for conservative or even right-wing causes, simply because they appeared to be logical adversaries of the Communists. Only a handful of intellectuals committed to the Left, automatically accepting to be branded as dissidents within their newfound context as well. Many directors who emigrated did participate, at one time or another, in political initiatives, such as signing manifestos and petitions, and had their names listed alongside those of other leading dissident exiles. However, their true commitment was to making films of a more existential nature rather than to resisting oppressive politics back home.[29]

Once in the West, most émigré directors from the region did not behave as exilic intellectuals, did not engage in political battles to subvert and destroy totalitarianism, did not form groups and did not commit to making political cinema preoccupied with the system they were escaping. Nor did they form film-making collectives to make political films about Communism.[30] Unlike the 'exilic' cinema of film-makers from the post-colonial countries, the pain of displacement, the strain of exile and the concern of oppressive politics did not seem to be a defining influence here. The East Central European émigrés did not work in intense dialogue with each other, and most often took up individual paths that allowed them to merge into the mainstream fairly easily. They rapidly integrated with their host community and started to make a contribution. Unlike Third World film-makers, most of whom were profoundly leftist in political beliefs and often remained marginalised in the West, East Central Europeans, by virtue of their act of defection from the Communist system, were welcomed and granted access to the mainstream of the cinematic establishment.

The career paths of the major film-makers who emigrated during the Cold War period took various directions, not all of them equally successful. With a few exceptions, the traumas inflicted by communism did not remain as central themes in their work. They either developed high profile commercial careers or created specific cult following, and only occasionally did directors stay committed to political causes. The spectacular success of émigrés like Roman Polanski and Miloš Forman, however, undoubtedly increased the profile of their respective national cinemas.

PART II

FILM AND HISTORY, ETHICS AND SOCIETY

OVERVIEW

The defining contributions of East Central European film to world cinema are films concerned with the discourse on morality and history, with the relationship between the private and the public. These are also the films in which stylistic innovations in developing narrative and cinematic language are most clearly visible.

As a result of the ideology of their region, the people of Central Europe look at history from a specific angle: they come from small countries which are usually powerless to make developmental decisions, yet need to react to whatever political shifts and advances occur (usually at the instigation of a neighbouring great European power). So the stories told here are not so much those of people heroically influencing the course of history but of those who cannot do much more but stand by and witness events; they are stories of the vulnerable and the powerless, the small and the weak, the pawns and the underdogs. The actions of these protagonists are marked by the overpowering consciousness of their own limitations. There are no uplifting imperial conquests, no triumphing over new lands or ruling over new peoples. The protagonists belong to nations that are more likely to be conquered and ruled, who know painfully well that in their historical experience it is the foreign will that has been victorious, and that their role in history is usually a supporting one.

It is in this sense that Lóránd Hegyi refers to a prevalent 'peculiar political emotionality' (2001: 5), where the artistic exploration of history is used as a way to address existential concerns or as an opportunity for idiosyncratic appropriation and examination of the subjectivity of an individual protagonist. Hegyi writes:

> Personal memory by necessity has to be addressed in the context of collective experience because the distinction between individual and collective experience has become almost impossible given the absence of common ground and the emotionally charged nature of history. Historical references such as they appear in the contemporary art of Central and Eastern Europe should, of course, not be misinterpreted as a form of historicism but are evidence of an ongoing critical appropriation of events and of an idiosyncratic examination of certain processes that have retained their power to provoke, that demand some sort of response as they have become an integral part of individual history. (2001: 35)

The key concern of East Central European cinema is the interplay between historical and social process and the personal experience of these processes. It is within this relationship, tilted towards the individual, where most identity issues and existential insecurities are played out. The never ending identity quest is often accompanied by an underlying frustration; there is an ongoing friction between objective historical events and their critical appropriation that limits the range of choices available to the individual. This is part of an eternally unresolved process of identification where all subjective moves are ultimately determined by the dialectical interplay with history.

In the course of this discussion, we will examine films that portray individuals who, even with very limited means, make attempts to act creatively, be it by opportunistically adjusting or by tragically challenging their historical and social limitations. The behaviour of these protagonists is defined to a great extent by an overall satellite attitude; to them history often comes across as a burden, as something adverse that one needs to outsmart.

However, before looking at these issues in detail, it is necessary to point out three key ideological premises of East Central European film which would seem to defeat the commonly shared view that this is a cinema preoccupied with class struggles and politics, and argue that this is in fact concerned with the individual and questions of personal ethics and behaviour.

First, as no other interpretations of Marxism were made public in these countries besides the official state socialist one, for many film-makers the concept of Marxism was practically synonymous with the repressive practices of state socialism (which in turn led to a certain degree of aversion to all things 'Marxist'). Yet, consciously or not, most of them subscribed to the materialist, and ultimately Marxist, view that it is the social context which defines people's subjectivity and behaviour. This is a perspective that sees the individual as a malleable entity mirroring social context rather than as an independent bearer of inborn moral values. Their protagonists are not led by providence or by the will of a superior being, as the idealist view of history would have it, but react to immediate triggers found within their concrete social surroundings. Thus, while most film-makers disliked the officially propagated version of Marxism, they still accepted its inherent premise of the individual as a socially conditioned being.

Second, it is a cinema that displays a paradoxical aversion to representations of mass history. While the assumption may be that governments would encourage film-making that reflects the historical experiences of the masses, in East Central European cinema it is extremely rare to see films that tackle collective history (with the exception of heritage cinema, which is considered in chapter three). Although public ideology stressed the importance of mass movements and events, the cinematic output has not been, as one might expect, dominated by films featuring the history of class struggle. This may be the reason why one of the greatest Polish directors, Kazimierz Kutz, whose most important films deal with Polish themes, in particular with workers' struggles, is inevitably spoken about as an idiosyncratic maverick (*Sól ziemi czarnej/Salt of the Black Earth*, 1970; *Perła w koronie/Pearl in the Crown;* 1972; *Śmierć jak kromka chleba/ Death as a Slice of Bread*, 1994). The focus of the most important films made in this region has regularly been on exploring the individual's experience of history. The concrete rights and wrongs of history, while important, have mostly served as backdrop for moral investigations, and the concern over personal ethics is definitely a trademark.

Third, East Central European film displays an aversion to a straightforward social realist approach in its exploration of contemporary themes. As we will see in chapter five, the films that address contemporary topics are better understood as examinations of existential concerns rather than works of critical realism that characterise socially conscious film-making in the West. Thus, where state socialist public ideology put the emphasis on social consciousness and would not let individuals enjoy privacy outside of politics, the cinematic output vigorously asserted the right of the individual to be apolitical. It is also noteworthy that the concrete rights and wrongs of modern society, while important, mostly served as backdrop for existential investigations, and it is concern with intimately personal experiences that has dominated the best work from the region.

CHAPTER THREE

Historical Film I: Narratives of Identity

Preoccupation with History

Historical topics have long been the centre of interest for film-makers across East Central Europe, and particularly prominently in the period of state socialism. As in other regions, films with such themes visualised the historical narratives governing the respective nation's (or government's) imagination and thus helped consolidate the 'imagined community' (Anderson 1983). However, historical films have played one more important function here – to provide a forum for a discourse on universal moral concerns.

Given that the general political line was to see the individual as a function of the socio-economic process, the focus on the individual's existential and moral concerns could only develop in the context of film-making that formally explored the socio-economic (historical) process. In this specific case, it is thus important to stress that many of the films which can be classified as historical can equally successfully be described as existential. As analysis here will show, some of the most important historical films were structured around the inherent tensions found at the intersection of historical master narratives and smaller, individual accounts and personal views of history, and often evolved around personal memory and remembrance. The following claims will be developed during the course of this discussion:

- Contrary to the commonly shared view of East Central European historical film as synonymous with straightforward realism, they have an astonishing stylistic diversity. Historical cinema has produced films in a variety of genres and styles, from lavish period blockbusters through surrealist fantasies of bygone eras to superb satires about opportunistic individuals overpowered by the irony of history.

- Films dealing with the relationship of individual and historical process are the most important works that the region's cinematic tradition has contributed to cinema at large. This is illustrated most clearly in the range of films discussed in the section on 'burden of history', below.

- Although there are notable exceptions, the most important films of the 'auteurs' in East Central European cinema have all dealt with historical material.

- In many cases historical film-making has closely depended on literary sources and has brought the art of adaptation to new heights.

Film and history theorist Robert Rosenstone distinguished two main approaches that he claimed characterised historical film as a corrective to 'real history' (1995: 6). The first was the 'explicit' approach, led by concrete political and social concerns of the time a film is made (many of the 'socialist realist' films would fall under this category). The second was the 'implicit' approach, where an existing cinematic text was judged by historical criteria at a later point.

In the context of this dichotomy, it should be stressed that many of the 'historical' films discussed here have not been made with 'real history' in mind. Quite often the historical episode of the plot has served as a backdrop for the examination of universal ideas from the realm of ethics and aesthetics, as seen in the work of Miklós Jancsó, for example. Thus, historiography is often subsumed under the investigation of the individual's moral reconciliation in the face of what has usually been experienced as an adverse and hostile flow of history.

Manipulated remembrance and biased reconstruction of the past have often served passing political needs, and the recycling of historical myths has frequently been a feature of state-sanctioned historical film-making. In such context, fictional explorations of history have often been particularly influential in shaping the intellectual discourse and attitudes of a given time. Personal cinematic accounts, which do not claim accuracy but choose to appeal to the shared historical imagination, have ultimately influenced public perceptions of history as much as officially endorsed versions. The study of mainstream historical film is an important tool for the identification of the doctrines that shape the prevalent national discourse on history. However, considering cinematic works that represent non-conventional cinematic approaches to historical material, found in a range of satirical, fantasy, science fiction or animated features, is of equal importance.

Heritage Epics

Before we come to discuss examples of the specific interplay of individual moral choices and the objective flow of history, let us look at another, more straightforward aspect of historical film-making: literary adaptations and historical super-productions.

Lavish heritage epics make up an extensive part of the East Central European cinematic output but remain largely unknown in the West, where 'heritage cinema' is now frequently considered as a 'new genre' (Vincendeau 2001: xvii). Such large-scale historical blockbusters, usually based on epic novels from the nineteenth century, chronicled episodes of the glorious past of the country in question and fulfilled the needs of romanticised representations of national history. The case of Poland, in particular, deserves special attention.

As historian Norman Davies has appropriately remarked, 'Polish literature could always supply the nation's needs whenever Polish politics was found wanting' (1981: 22). And, indeed, most of the important works of authors such as Henryk Sienkiewicz, Stefan Żeromski, Władysław Reymont, Adam Mickiewicz and Bolesław Prus have been adapted for the cinema by directors such as Andrzej Wajda, Jerzy Kawalerowicz, Aleksander Ford, Jerzy Hoffman, Filip Bajon and others.[1]

More than any other country in the region, Poland has pursued a systematic programme of adaptations of literary classics as part of a concerted heritage management effort. While the interest in heritage and period cinema in other European countries has developed in spurts, since the 1960s Polish cinema has consistently produced at least several major historical super-productions or literary adaptations per decade. Some memorable films have come out of the government-sponsored efforts to film officially endorsed epics focusing on important episodes in the nation's formation (and particularly those showing resistance to a variety of invading powers), thus fostering an articulate consolidation of sovereign Polish national identity.[2]

If one looks at the wider European context, Poland's record in producing heritage cinema may yield only to France and Britain. The trend of expanding Poland's assortment of filmed epics of national heritage not only continued but even accelerated in the 1990s; some of the most expensive heritage productions, commanding budgets in the range of $20 million were released towards the end of the decade and the early 2000s.[3] The release of nearly each one of these blockbusters has been accompanied by a promotional crusade, involving critics, festivals, diasporic organisations and, since the 1990s, the Vatican.

Poland's continuous commitment to heritage epics has occasionally appeared overwhelming and has made some critics question the politics of sustaining such a programme of adaptations. Long before the lavish historical epics of the 1990s were even planned, film scholar Anita Skwara admitted she was fed up with films glorifying the Polish nation and longed for cinema that would no longer be 'based on dates of national upheavals, meditations of freedom fighters, and a sense of the inviolability of national archetypes' (1992: 231). Writing a decade later, in 2001, Ewa Mazierska classified the heritage blockbusters from the 1990s as 'nostalgia business', which, by continuously reiterating the idealised romantic image of the 'land of noble knights and mute princesses', ultimately asserted nationalist xenophobia and misogyny (2001a: 167).

Many of the Polish heritage films indeed feature a dashing blue-eyed blonde-moustached romantic hero, proudly riding a stallion, wearing a red military jacket and a fur hat concealing wavy hair. He is devotedly committed to the cause of Polish national liberation, driving back hordes of invading enemies with his sword. Between battles, he fights for the heart of a fragile beauty with long braids. Like other heritage films from across Europe, where 'the class hierarchies of the period remain unchallenged' (Medhurst 2001: 13), the status of nobility is rarely made a subject of critical exploration, which is particularly noteworthy given that East Central European films were made in a supposedly class-conscious socio-cultural context.

Discussing British heritage films, Cairns Craig notes that, 'The same cast in the same period costumes gives the feel almost of a repertory production, with actors who know well each other's strengths and limitations, and directors who know perhaps too well their audience's expectations' (2001: 3). This observation could as easily be made about Polish cinema, where actors segued from one heritage into another (for example Beata Tyszkiewicz and Daniel Olbrychski), and directors certainly knew what to deliver to satisfy audience expectations. The heritage genre has undergone very little stylistic change over time, and watching films made in the late 1990s is not that different from watching those made about thirty years earlier. They are all ambitious projects, over two hours in duration. They are all spectacularly shot, with stunningly-set battlefield scenes that involve elaborate props and costumes, and make extensive use of cavalry and artillery, and thousands of extras divided into groups of fleeing peasants, brave Polish soldiers and rude foreigners. As a Canadian journalist remarked, to a Western audience these films appear 'all the more fresh for [their] reliance on low-tech horsepower and old-time storytelling in an age of digital-FX blockbuster madness' (Matt Radz, *Montreal Gazette*).[4] The most important difference is that with time these films have become more expensive. Within the system of the state socialist film industry, the historical blockbusters usually had the army at their disposal, an arrangement which kept staggering production costs within reasonable limits.

Figure 4: In 'the land of noble knights and mute princesses': *Pan Tadeusz* (1999)

The sustained interest in massive scale historical blockbusters in Poland through the 1990s and the early 2000s suggests a continuous need for romanticised representation of national history. Mickiewicz's 1834 classic poem *Pan Tadeusz* seems still to be 'filled with a lyrical serenity of truly universal appeal' (Davies 1981: 22), thus its adaptation by Andrzej Wajda was perceived as the ultimate patriotic act in the year preceding the director's Academy Award for lifetime achievement.[5] The making of Jerzy Hoffman's blockbuster *Ogniem i mieczem/With Fire and Sword* (1999) was yet another patriotic act. It had taken the director twenty-five years to bring the project to fruition, and it had been a matter of pride for Hoffman to finance and complete the trilogy, which was put on hold by unfavourable political circumstances.[6]

It is not only Poland that invests in this type of heritage film-making, though. The genre of the historical blockbuster is alive and well in other parts of the region, an important feature of the identity consolidation of domestic and diasporic populations. In recent years, for example, Hungary has released a number of big budget heritage super-productions. Some were made by director Gábor Koltay, best known for his 1984 cult historical rock opera *István, a király/King Istvan*, who has more recently committed his name to historical blockbusters such as *Honfoglalás/The Conquest* (1996) and *Sacra Corona/Sacred Crown* (2001). In 2002, Hungary saw the release of another epic *A Hídember/ The Bridgeman*, directed by Géza Bereményi. This was the most expensive film in Hungarian history, and controversy raged over the millions of dollars spent

Figure 5: Heritage film-making is flourishing in Poland: Andrzej Wajda's adaptation of Mickiewicz's 1834 classic poem *Pan Tadeusz*.

on production and the allegations that it was right-wing 'patriotic' propaganda, particularly since the film was released in the middle of an election season (see Becker 2002).

Surrealist Proliferation of History

Some of the most interesting contributions to historical film are found in the works of directors such as Wojciech Has and Juraj Jakubisko, whose specific surrealism is intrinsically linked with the discourse on history.

Discussing Hans-Jürgen Syberberg's historical biopic *Hitler: ein Film aus Deutschland/Hitler: A Film from Germany* (1977), film scholar Anton Kaes notes the use of 'strategies of proliferation', the addition of superfluous experiential dimensions to the primary account of events, where 'events' are not so much reconstructed in the texture of the film but are more often alluded to through the way they are remembered. The surrealist enhancement found in *Hitler* makes it a particularly suitable example of postmodernist creation of a *post-histoire* (Kaes 1992: 218). It is a view of history that ventures into a meta-level of historical examination by including not only a straightforward account of the concrete historical events (which usually relies on referencing of familiar historical episodes), but also expands into rich symbolic cross-referencing of the impact that these events may have had on various seemingly unrelated dimensions of human experience, be it earlier or later, close or far away. Kaes' framework of investigating the means by which historical discourse is 'proliferated' into the meta-reflective level of *post-histoire* is also well-suited for discussing the East Central European surrealist tradition, a rich field crying out for investigation by postmodern historians. It is precisely such proliferation that is discovered at every step in the work of Has and Jakubisko, be it in their radical doubt of the possibility of any truthful knowledge of past events or in their cyclical replay of intertextual historical references. As in Syberberg's better-known and yet fairly esoteric work, in the surrealist tradition of historical film-making in East Central Europe we have a situation where 'various temporal layers are interlocked through blatant anachronisms, radically undermining the illusion of continuity and linear development in narrated history', and where the directors 'favor a self-reflexive play with images and linguistic signs that refer to history in associations that are not bound by time and place' (Kaes 1992: 210).

The best-loved film by the doyen of Polish surrealist tradition, Wojciech Has, remains his 1965 adaptation of Jan Potocki's romantic epic *Rękopis znaleziony w Saragossie/The Saragossa Manuscript*. Like the novel itself (an early example of Gothic horror), this three-hour film shot in crisp black-and-white is in a category of its own: it is rich and labyrinthine, elliptic and elusive, convoluted and astonishing.[7] *The Saragossa Manuscript*'s cult status is due to the multi-layered sprawling narrative, which would qualify it as a prime example of phantasmagorical romanticism, elegantly combining humour and adventure, mystery and eroticism. Even though critics have made parallels to literary works such as *The Arabian Nights*, *The Decameron* and Jorge Luis Borges, the film's inspirations appear more closely related to Pedro Calderón de la Barca's seventeenth-century play *Life is a Dream* (which is, coincidentally, set in Poland) and E.T.A. Hoffman's fairy tales. Appropriate cinematic parallels would be the work of Alejandro Jodorowsky and Pier Paolo Pasolini's adaptations of literary classics.[8]

Set at the end of the eighteenth century, the film focuses on the experiences of a Belgian officer, Alphonse van Worden (Zbigniew Cybulski), who is travelling through Spain. In a non-linear narrative which comes together only in the interlocking jigsaw pieces of Alphonse's subjectivity, his experiences, ranging from erotic through mischievous to nightmarish, are recounted in a maze-like manner that mixes dream and reality and often makes it impossible to distinguish between the two. There are multiple references to the Spanish Inquisition, the Arab Khalifate and the Hassidic Kaballah, as well as to Moors and Gypsies. It is a world of imagination, inhabited by ghost-like creatures, constantly challenging the protagonist and the viewers to doubt and question the reality of what is presented. This is achieved by combining bizarre dream sequences, Fata Morgana, déjà vu flashbacks and spoken accounts of added vignette plots, enhanced by the haunting score of Krzysztof Penderecki, one of the founding fathers of modern music. Ultimately, in an endless escapade of playful romantic zigzags, the film presents an extended meditation on the problematic relationship between reality and illusion. What is true and what is imaginary? It is not possible to tell dream and reality apart. And even if it were possible, one would still wonder if in our moves we were not influenced more by dreams than by 'real' experiences.

Equally bewildering and fascinating is Has' *Sanatorium pod klepsydra/ Sanatorium under the Sign of the Hourglass* (1973), an adaptation of the work of Polish surrealist Bruno Schulz that deals with issues of guilt, illness, isolation and Jewishness, narrated through a doomsday mentality. Once again dream and reality overlap in a storyline where the imaginary is indistinguishable from the real, and once again nightmarish demonic hallucinations affect the moves of the protagonist more than concrete causes.

Another Polish director who would not exactly qualify as surrealist and yet should be listed in the ranks of those who approached history from a more imaginative angle, is Jerzy Kawalerowicz. The aesthetically exquisite period films made by the director in the 1960s are works of superb philosophical quality that explore the ironies in history's twists and turns as experienced by ordinary mortals who have to confront historical treachery and the vicissitudes of power and fortune. The austere and beautifully crafted black-and-white *Matka Joanna od Aniołów/Mother Joan of the Angels* (1961), based on Jarosław

Iwaszkiewicz, dealt with Catholic restraints and should be regarded as an artistic precursor to better-known later films on religious soul-searching such as Andrei Tarkovsky's *Andrei Rublev* (1969) and Ken Russell's *The Devils* (1971). Set in a remote part of Poland in the seventeenth century, the film follows the moves of a cleric who is sent on an exorcist mission to a convent where a group of nuns are possessed by demons. Struggling with physical temptation and exposed to extreme experiences, the priest gradually comes to question the fragile boundary between the 'normal' and the 'possessed'. Self-flagellation does not help him resist or avoid blasphemy, and the priest gradually yields to 'demons' and grows 'possessed' as well. In his search for insights into human nature he even undertakes the controversial step of visiting with a representative of an antagonistic religion, the local Rabbi, soon realising that the Rabbi is his own reincarnation. *Mother Joan of the Angels* is a film about profound identity quest leading to the realisation that the crisis of faith is not so much caused by aggressive demons but rather by 'lack of angels'.

Kawalerowicz's spectacular and stylish *Faraon/Pharaoh* (1966), adapted for the screen by Tadeusz Konwicki from the novel by Bolesław Prus and shot amidst the desert sands of the Soviet republic of Kazakhstan, may look at moments like the better-known lavish Hollywood blockbuster *Cleopatra* (Joseph L. Mankiewicz, 1963), yet is an artistically exquisite achievement bearing the clear marks of Sergei Eisenstein's aesthetics.[9] In this philosophical

Figure 6: Kawalerowicz's *Mother Joan of the Angels* (1961): austere and beautifully crafted.

exploration of the manipulation of a historical personality, the young pharaoh Ramsès faces the decline of his empire and the challenging traps of democracy; he has to cope with betrayal and make difficult decisions. Condemned to live in a reality marked by endless intrigue and surrounded by a range of personages who pursue their specific agendas, from slaves and mercenaries to duplicitous priests and seductive priestesses, the pharaoh's experience is one of disoriented wandering in the labyrinthine corridors of power. Like the priest from *Mother Joan of the Angels* (and also like Eisenstein's *Ivan Grozny*), he gradually grows alienated and ends up confronting his personal 'demons' in a magic realist encounter with his own double.

Slovak Juraj Jakubisko is one of the most important representatives of the surrealist tradition in Czechoslovakia (one that boasts an extensive roster of Czech and Slovak literary names), particularly with his two internationally co-produced avant-garde historical fantasies of the late 1960s: *Zbehovia a pútnici/The Deserter and the Nomads* (Czechoslovakia/Italy, 1968) and *Vtáčkovia, siroty a blázni/Birds, Orphans and Fools* (Czechoslovakia/France, 1969).[10] Rich in symbolic referencing (including protagonists such as Death and Yorick), both films address the difficulties in coping with a destructive and adverse historical fate that ultimately limits individual freedom. The director bends the objective chronology for the purposes of an extremely subjectified narrative that changes the sequence of events and subverts

Figure 7: Jakubisko's *The Deserter and the Nomads* (1968): barbarity and vengeance carried out by perpetually tense and unpredictably troubled people.

Figure 8: Jakubisko's *Birds, Orphans and Fools* (1969): avant-garde surrealist film-making.

traditional ideas of linearity. Like Syberberg's historic chronicle, where at moments 'the present is itself no more than an assemblage of quotations from the past' (Kaes 1992: 218), in Jakubisko's films associations often take over from the straightforward action. However, it does not come down to faithful referencing of concrete texts or events; the 'quotes' from the past are yet another interpretative layer, burdened with haunting visions of violent orgies staged by invaders and nightmarish projections of impending devastation over a vulnerable countryside. The three parts of *The Deserter and the Nomads* supposedly take place in concretely defined historical periods (First World War, Second World War and a future nuclear conflict), yet the boundaries between these historical episodes are often blurred to allow crossings back and forth in time. The action jumps from one war into another, from one act of barbarity into another episode of vengeance, carried out by perpetually tense and unpredictably troubled people. The storyline is interjected with moments of peaceful oblivion in idyllic village settings juxtaposed with panoramic shots of battlefields covered by anonymous scattered corpses or episodes of excessive drunkenness. The feeling of chaos and disorientation that the film maintains throughout is achieved via a 'proliferation of perspectives', a key element of postmodernist poetics in cinema.

Birds, Orphans and Fools, in the words of the director, is a chronicle of 'madness in the world'. The story, marked by deliberate narrative incongruity, is about three adult orphan friends who live amid cynicism and violence, where the feelings of chaos and disorientation are proliferated to create a disturbing but powerful cacophonous effect. Jakubisko widely uses pastiche technique and grotesque imagery, often triggering visceral reactions that work more on the sensory than the rational level.

Some critics have interpreted these two films, and particularly *Birds, Orphans and Fools*, as the cineaste's reaction to the crushing of the Prague Spring.[11] The director himself admitted that he was particularly worried by the severe limitations on artistic freedom that came at the end of this uplifting period. Yet the films powerfully assert the idea of cycles of violence so that the events of 1968 can only be seen as another point in a nightmarish allegorical chain of horrific historic memories.[12]

This type of surrealist historical film-making radically diverges from the allegedly dominant Socialist Realist view of history that required cinema to show social processes as a struggle for class equality leading to the triumph of social justice. The concern of surrealist film-making is profoundly different: each one of these ventures into history implies an exploration of *post-histoire*. It is a film-making centred on the subjective experiencing of the past that cannot possibly be defined by concrete co-ordinates of time and place and proliferates into repetitive cacophony. It is a *post-histoire* in which the perception of objective continuity is illusory, ultimately locked in the prism of subjectivity.

The Burden of History

Some of the most important films, made by leading directors such as Wajda, Munk and Szabó, explore the interaction of the individual with history. As a precursor to looking at specific examples, there are several points to stress.

First, taking into account the volatility of the region's history, Lóránd Hegyi has spoken of the inherent tension between two visions of the individual, one that casts him in a 'prophetic, missionary, and irrationally overrated role' and one that sees him playing 'the same role in mechanist-determinist, hopelessly subordinate terms' and as being 'helpless in the face of forces outside its control', thus constantly maintaining an inherent tension between the 'unrealistic delusionary over-assessment' and the 'pessimist nihilist minimisation of the individual's power to influence events' (2001: 37). So it is no wonder that this range of films often deals with insignificant, small protagonists rather than the 'hero'. The individual is more likely to be overpowered by history, so the typical protagonist is less heroic in nature and more like an anti-hero.

Second, some of the finest East Central European films belong to the strong tradition of personalised interpretations of history. In such films, the relationship between individual experience and national fate is conceived in an entirely different manner than is officially sanctioned memory. The adverse social events that abound in the history of the region are particularly favoured because they invite investigation into complex moral dilemmas. Personal accounts here often substitute for public ones. Hegyi notes, however, that such an approach ultimately lessens the consciousness of history as process and stresses history as fate, reducing it to a relationship between private biography and paradigmatic records of political events where private memory does 'not claim to recount some grand narrative' (2001: 24) but is of utmost importance nonetheless. Among other effects, he underlines, this frequently also causes a certain demonisation of history as a *fatum* (fate) which in turn is addressed by numerous artists who on the one hand seek to demythologise history and rid it of its fetishist quality, while at the same time trying to personalise it and to render it a metaphor (2001: 37).

Third, in the films of East Central Europe the individual and history are often seen as adversaries, or as rivals in a game. The individual is conscious of his/her weakness and tries to 'outsmart' history, trying to guess the direction in which events will develop in order to take the 'correct' side. Yet, whenever a purely pragmatic choice is made, the protagonist is punished, and lands on the inopportune, 'wrong' side of history. Playing with history is a form of gambling, an extension of the entrenched satellite mentality that stems from the awareness that someone else has already made decisions that affect you, that the best you can do is to opportunistically adjust your reactions.

Having identified these ideological premises, we can now examine some concrete examples to reveal how they are played out in film. For Europe, the Second World War was undoubtedly a key historical event: in terms of the twentieth century, European historical record falls into two distinct periods, before and after the war. Even though one could give many examples of films that explore other historical periods and events,[13] wartime duress is the frequent subject of attention. The principal historical films from the region are those that deal directly with wartime experiences or those set in periods of build-up to war or its aftermath.

Films made in the decade following the end of the Second World War dealt with wartime realities or with the war's immediate aftermath, and largely belong to the genre of the so-called *Trümmerfilme* (films of the ruins). Some of the most important titles in this range include the first post-war (East) German production *Die Mörder sind unter uns/The Murderers are Among Us* (Wolfgang Staudte, 1947), the Hungarian *Valahol Európában/Somewhere in Europe* (Géza von Radványi, 1947) and the Polish *Piątka z ulicy Barskiej/Five Boys from Barska Street* (Aleksander Ford, 1954), directly comparable to better-known West European post-war dramas such as Roberto Rossellini's *Germania anno zero/Germany Year Zero* (1947) or René Clément's *Jeux interdits/Forbidden Games* (1952) . The ruins of bombed cities make up the natural setting of these films; they all reflect the post-war European realities of disorientation and despair, and it is not by chance that many focus on the experiences of children, adolescents and young people, questioning what possible future lies ahead for this lost generation.

Andzej Wajda's early war trilogy (*Pokolenie/A Generation*, 1954, *Kanał/ Canal*, 1957, and *Popiół i diament/Ashes and Diamonds*, 1958) can also be classified within the *Trümmerfilme* range. More importantly, however, the films of the trilogy approach the contradictions of recent history through the controversial fates of individual protagonists. And even though the stories told here all focus on the 'burden of history' and the uneasy fates of protagonists who perish in the uneven struggle with destiny, Wajda manages to sustain a flare of heroism throughout the films.

The first part, *A Generation*, depicts the self-sacrificial resistance struggle of a group of young Poles. *Kanał* chronicles the 1944 Warsaw Uprising by focusing on the doomed escape of a group of rebels through the sewers of the city. Shot amidst a shocking scale of destruction, the film is a grim realistic tale of desperation and futility. The third part, *Ashes and Diamonds*, based on a novel by Jerzy Andrzejewski, is Wajda's recognised masterpiece. Set on the last day of the Second World War, it is another treatise on individual limitations in confronting the mighty flow of history. Maciek, the protagonist (played by Polish screen idol Zbigniew Cybulski), is on assignment to kill a local Communist leader; the action occurs at a time when the Communists are to emerge as winners from the bitter internal wartime splits between Poles loyal to the exiled government in London and those who look to Moscow, a context which renders the planned assassination meaningless. Maciek has chosen the wrong side of history and is doomed to die tragically at the end of the film. Yet Wajda's protagonist, having made a conscious choice, confronts his fate with the heroic readiness that one expects from fully mature characters prepared to take responsibility for their actions.[14]

Wajda's protagonists are tragic characters, consciously taking on the limitations of the individual against history and confronting hostile, often desperate situations: the resistance fighters from *Kanał* endure the horrible journey through the underground sewers only to turn up at the feet of a Nazi waiting for them at the other end; Maciek from *Ashes and Diamonds* is on the wrong side of history from the outset, and he knows he is destined to die.

In the general context of East Central European cinema, however, the heroic view of confronting history is the less typical one. More often, the story is about protagonists who are not as idealistically assertive as Wajda's characters. It is common to come across stories of individuals who are not prepared to make tragic mistakes, and who, in order to avoid taking wrong steps, model their behaviour entirely in a responsive mode. Among the many examples of such an attitude (some of which we will discuss in chapter four), the best are found in the films of Andrzej Munk.

One of the leading auteurs of Polish cinema, Munk is often compared to another cinematic genius, Jean Vigo, who also died prematurely leaving only

Figure 9: Wajda's *Ashes and Diamonds* (1958) featured Polish screen idol Zbigniew Cybulski as Maciek, a tragic loner on the wrong side of history.

several works of great artistry.[15] The films that Munk managed to complete are seen today as key contributions to cinema's narrative style, innovatively telling the same story from several points of view (in *Człowiek na torze/Man on the Track*, 1957), offering fragmentary viewpoints in order to highlight a theme from various angles (*Eroica*, 1958), including leaps forward between the main episodes of a story to cut to its narration (*Zęzowate szczęście/Bad Luck*, 1960) and using extensive subjective reconstructions of highly personalised memories in flashbacks (*Pasażerka/Passenger*, 1961).[16]

Two of Munk's films, *Eroica* and *Bad Luck*, are directly relevant here, focusing as they do on the plight of the individual against the 'burden of history'. Originally intended to contain three novellas, the completed version of *Eroica* only has two parts that show unrelated episodes from the time of the Second World War, both intended to mock widespread wartime attitudes which the director saw as faults in the Polish national character. The second part, 'Ostinato-Lugubre', features a group of high-ranking Polish PoWs who are trapped in a camp near the Alps shortly before the end of the war. Deprived of all heroic glamour, the officers are stagnating; with failing spirits, preoccupied with petty animosities, they are barely able to stand each other. One of them has escaped the camp and is talked about as a hero; yet it soon becomes clear to the viewer that he is still hiding within the compound: the scenes of his fearful existence in a cramped attic radically undermine all the heroic rhetoric that surrounds the myth of his persona.

The most memorable story of *Eroica*, though, is the one from the first part of the film, '*Scherzo alla Pollacca*'. It is the tragi-comic story of Dzidzius (Babyface), an opportunistic small-timer who also happens to be a member of the Resistance. Even though Dzidzius is on the 'correct' side of history and manages to accomplish some good deeds while the 1944 Warsaw Uprising is in full swing, in the course of the story it becomes obvious that he is more concerned with the little pleasures of life – wining, dining and womanising – rather than the outcome of the struggle. In a quintessential moment, he is seen taking a gulp from a vintage bottle of wine which he has just managed to pull away among a hail of enemy bullets; he sits on a bank and drinks with relief not noticing the German tank approaching from behind. Concentrating on the immediate pleasures of the moment, Dzidzius is ultimately unable (or unwilling) to deal with the bigger picture of life and history.

The anti-hero from *Eroica* was developed further in Munk's next film, *Bad Luck*, where the inopportune encounters of the protagonist with the whimsically unpredictable course of history span several decades. Jan Piszczyk (played by Bogumił Kobiela) is a middle-aged man who tells the farcical story of his life in a series of flashback episodes chronicling all 'unfortunate' choices he has made at the crossroads of history.[17] Several decades of volatile Polish history, from the 1930s to 1960, are presented via Piszczyk's account of continuous opportunistic side-switching, an act that he performs so many times in the course of the film that by the end it becomes excessively complicated to juggle the disparate pieces of his past in a coherent account. It is the choices that one has to make when history takes about-turns that the protagonist describes as his 'cock-eyed luck', taking sides in harsh historical moments is again compared to the act of gambling. Typically, Piszczyk reacts not according to principles but according to his (somewhat unintelligent) judgement of the

Figure 10: Busy with his bottle, Dzidius does not even notice the enemy's tank: Andrzej Munk's *Eroica* (1958).

immediate situation. In an episode from the 1930s, for example, within a single month he is beaten up by the police twice, once as a Jew and once as a member of an anti-Semitic organisation – he is neither. In one of the film's finest scenes Piszczyk's encounter with 'history' is so direct that it all comes down to a silent pantomime: caught in the middle of a field when German bombs start falling from all sides, Piszczyk literally has to hop in a zigzag to keep alive each time there is an explosion on his right or left side. Ultimately, though, he is a survivor; opportunistic, he still has his specific practical wisdom. In this, Piszczyk is an anti-hero who can be viewed as a precursor to his younger but better-known and popular counterpart Forrest Gump.

Within Polish cinema, Munk's films are often compared to Wajda's.[18] Both directors have tended to focus on individuals who were conscious of the limitations they faced and who were trying to guess which way the sequence of historical events would unravel. Watching these films with the benefit of hindsight, the viewer can clearly identify the ironies of historical twists and turns that remain unknown to the protagonists. In Wajda's films, not knowing which way the winds of history may blow presupposes that the protagonists will make tragic mistakes and thus become tragic characters. In Munk's films, the protagonists are equally unaware which direction history will next take so they try to seize the moment and react opportunistically, coming up with short-term solutions. Munk's petty souls are caricatures of Wajda's tragic heroes. Both types are disoriented, both have to take decisions in the face of uncertainty and try to outsmart the challenges of history. With their quick-fix tactics, however, Munk's characters never rise to tragedy dwell in the realm of tragi-comedy. Wajda's protagonists are heroic; Munk is at his best creating the anti-hero.

Furthermore, Munk approaches the 'burden of history' with a humour that makes his films particularly watchable today; not simply a biting commentary on the shortcomings of the Polish national character (as his intention seems to have been), they contain fine observations on the human condition in general. One of the most important points that Munk has made with these films is that people's experiences of history differ, and that the encounters with important historical moments may not necessarily trigger heroic reactions from the individual.

The ironies of the uneven match between the individual and history are also a subject of interest within Hungarian cinema. Taking a very different narrative tone, the problems of the protagonist who has to take sides amidst painful self-torment are captured by István Szabó in the three acclaimed historical films he made in the 1980s, all featuring unforgettable performances by the remarkable Austrian actor Klaus-Maria Brandauer. The first in the series was *Mephisto* (1981), winner of numerous international awards (including a best foreign film Academy Award); the second was the Austro-Hungarian period, character study *Oberst Redl/Colonel Redl* (1985); *Hanussen* (1988) was the third. As in so many other films from the region, each work in Szabó's trilogy represented an account of an individual who had to adjust and face difficult political choices; each was about carrying the burden of history.

Figure 11: Bogumił Kobiela in Munk's *Bad Luck* (1960).

Figure 12: Klaus-Maria Brandauer in Szabó's *Mephisto* (1981).

Mephisto, based on Klaus Mann's 1936 novel, was a fictionalised biography of German actor Gustav Gründgens, who in the 1930s chose to side with the Nazis and, having taken on the directorship of the Staatstheater in Berlin at a time when other leading intellectuals opted to emigrate, became one of the pillars of Hitler's conformist intelligentsia. This remarkable film is about the disorientation experienced by intellectuals who compromise consciously, hoping to give a boost to their careers while not realising that success and fame will ultimately be judged within a more general ethical context. It is about the tragedy of people who pick the wrong side of history and about the inherent link between individual commitment and worthy social cause. Similar problems were tackled in *Hanussen*, which was based on the real-life story of a flamboyant clairvoyant whose main credit was 'predicting' the infamous 1933 Reichstag fire (which is widely believed to having been the result of a Nazi conspiracy).[19]

Given that the Nazi period is well known, well-crafted films like *Mephisto* and *Hanussen* are fairly easy for wider audiences to understand. A film like *Colonel Redl*, set during the lesser-known final years of the declining Habsburg dynasty and (based on John Osborne's 1965 play *A Patriot for Me*), is rather more difficult to follow. Yet this is the most subtle film of the three, and certainly the one that best reveals the complex web of prejudice regarding class and ethnicity that defines and confines the protagonist. As in the other two films, *Colonel Redl* closely follows the fate of an individual who is compelled to confront history and take sides, his choices often restricted by the rigid rules of military honour and army hierarchies. An offspring of a lower-class family, from a background that places him in the lower ranks of the Austro-Hungarian ethnic hierarchy, Redl's dubious officer's credentials are further compounded by his suppressed homosexuality. In the course of the film, he is painfully aware of his inferior beginnings and constantly hides his embarrassingly low origins. By doing so, he manages to get himself accepted in aristocratic circles and be promoted to the rank of colonel. His rise, however, can only be limited, and when a scapegoat is needed he is promptly picked by the army and requested to commit suicide. Redl is a truly tragic anti-hero, a protagonist who is overpowered by the course of events to which he is prepared to adjust.

Colonel Redl is an extremely rich exploration of the multiple layers of public prejudice pertaining to class, ethnicity and sexuality that make the individual susceptible to subtle forms of abuse such as isolation and denigration. The film has captured the spirit of East Central Europe, with all the suppressed tensions and fine weaknesses, where the burden of history hangs over the protagonist from cradle to grave. It is an investigation into the moral choices a person must make and a never-ending source of inspiration for film-makers, as we will see in the next chapter.

CHAPTER FOUR

Historical Film II: Discourse on Morality

As already noted, the periods of duress in the history of East Central Europe have attracted much attention from film-makers and been the subject of some of the best films of the region. Of course, these were the periods in which dramatic moral dilemmas were most likely to occur, but film-makers also chose to investigate historicity because it allowed them to venture into a particular existential investigation. In order to empahasise this peculiarity of East Central European cinema, this chapter will consider a further range of examples that reveal how historical film ultimately enhanced the discourse on morality.

First, we will look at some of the films by Miklós Jancsó and Zoltán Fábri, and explore their use of historical material in postulating rationally constructed moral theorems. We will subsequently focus on select examples of Holocaust cinema, in particular films that have developed the issue of moral choice. After investigating how specific humour has been used in stories to reveal the way in which the moral choices of ordinary individuals turned them into accidental heroes, we will discuss the films featuring the moral damage inflicted on ordinary people during the totalitarian period of state socialism.

Moral Theorems

Miklós Jancsó's and Zoltán Fábri's best-known films can be described as historical, dealing as they do with concrete episodes from the past. However, using the substance of history in order to deal with moral concerns, ethical matters are elevated above historical material.

Their films revolve around political conflicts of one kind or another, but quite often the focus is on an almost forgotten and thus nearly fictitious incident. The fact that the event holds little significance is particularly important, as it supplies an opportunity to explore general moral problems such as the relationship of public and private interest, and concepts such as betrayal, honour, power, humiliation, leadership, devotion, individual guilt and responsibility. This idiosyncrasy is excellently articulated by Graham Petrie in his discussion of Jancsó:

> From an overall theme of great national importance [...] he deliberately isolates a peripheral and complex episode (often giving no other explanation or background than a mere date) and works this through to a rigorously logical conclusion. In isolation, the problem, without losing its specific local relevance, becomes more abstract, allowing the inner realities of power, oppression, violence, cruelty, and dehumanisation inherent in any similar historical situation to come to the forefront. (1978: 30)

Let us briefly consider how this approach works in two of Jancsó's films – *Szegénylegények/The Round-Up* (1966) and *Csillagosok, katonák /The Red and the White* (1967) – both co-written by Gyula Hernádi.

The Round-Up is only loosely based on historical events. It takes place in 1868, twenty years after the suppression of the anti-Austrian revolution of 1848 and during a time characterised by overall reconciliation. Only the followers of legendary rebel Sándor Rósza still maintain occasional warfare. A number of peasants suspected of belonging to this underground army of outlaws are arrested and herded into a fort's courtyard. For the duration of the film they are held there by the pro-Habsburg police, and for the duration of the film we observe them continuously bargaining over their lives while the captors constantly change the rules of the game.

The proclaimed objective of the operation is to capture the leader, yet it looks more like an exercise in intimidation: groups of prisoners are taken in different directions in almost geometrical patterns, escorted by officers in black capes and by guards wearing feathered hats. We are not made party to the premise or to the goal of this 'investigation', all we see is its physical mechanics – back and forth, up the steps and down the steps, unlocking cells and then locking them – and repetitive prison routines that are played out numerous times. We cannot possibly tell who is right or wrong; all we know is that the violent captors claim that the unarmed captives are bloody killers.

Jancsó's approach to the story, Brechtian and alienated, enables him to expose ethical dilemmas by staging situations where the viewers observe and judge the moral choices made by the protagonists. The elliptical plot shows the men attempting to negotiate in their forced confinement, sometimes punished with immediate devastating effect. Father and son are led to renounce each other in an attempt to save their own lives. Dialogues are brisk and abrupt; confinement and enclosure are pervasive, and the protagonists are envisioned as types rather than individuals. The promises of the guards are deceptive and only lead to further brutal violence.

The remarkable aesthetics of the film glorify the beauty of the barren Hungarian *puszta* (plain), a landscape bearing a Giorgio de Chirico-like quality where the wide, open spaces come across as confining and claustrophobic. The camerawork juxtaposes extremes of high and low angles in a context of persistent medium close-up. There are multiple visual and semantic layers in each frame and an elaborate interplay of light and shadow, an approach that Jancsó brings to perfection in his next film, *The Red and the White*.

The Red and the White is set in 1919, at the time of the Russian Civil War, and shows Hungarian troops fighting alongside the Communists. Once again, the events are arbitrary and abrupt, the warring parties are interchangeable, and the causes they represent do not seem profoundly different; moreover, they assert them with the same brutal means. The action moves back and forth, through attack and counter attack, the taking over and giving up of positions: an endless series of clashes between the Tsarist 'Whites' and the Bolshevik 'Reds' featuring meaningless violence and clearly indicating that both sides are equally bad.[1] While the film's message is a pacifist one, the absence of individually character-ised protagonists means that *The Red and the White* is perceived as an exercise in formulating and solving moral theorems.

Most of all, *The Red and the White* is a further development of Jancsó's highly stylised approach: the long tracking shots and the rigorously planned episodes where people appear as moving dots on a pointillist canvas. With its contrasting dark and light spots, vertical and horizontal moves, uniforms and vulnerable naked bodies, it looks like a modernised avant-garde version of Leni Riefenstahl's strictly geometrical patterns cross-fertilised with Andrei Tarkovsky's Breughel-influenced compositions. The camera is craned up and down to provide vertical balance to Jancsó's largely horizontal compositions, augmented by carefully choreographed movements of groups of people across, through and round the screen frame.[2] The purpose of focusing on these seemingly meaningless movements is to show that they all take place within a wide open but nonetheless confined space. Though the protagonists appear free to move across the wide spaces, the direction of their movement is more than limited, and thus futile.

Figure 13: The camera craned up to provide vertical balancing of horizontal compositions, augmented by carefully choreographed movements of people across the frame: Jancsó's *The Red and the White* (1967).

Although officially formalism in art (cinema included) was one of the named offences that state socialist censorship was supposed to harness, Jancsó's work is unabashedly formalist. Towards the end of the 1960s, the director's preoccupation with form became so pervasive that critics like Petrie have questioned whether his 'scrupulously worked-out' compositions 'exist largely for their own sake, or whether they contribute to be fused with the political and humanistic concerns' that the director is ultimately known for (1978: 36).[3]

It is difficult to say if the specific emotional detachment from the protagonists in these films is due to an obsession with the form or is an expression of the extreme rationality of the director's approach. At moments, it appears that Jancsó's entire attention is devoted to the choreography of the group and he is unable to handle the individual. Or, perhaps, he is so obsessed with the geometry of his screen compositions that he forgets to inject the emotion. Whatever the answer, there is certainly more reason than emotion in the depiction of his protagonists, and the focus is on group behaviour rather than on individualisation.[4] Giving Jancsó the benefit of the doubt, it is possible to accept that his mode of film-making effectively undermines any emotional approach to historical material and asserts a sceptical view of the past.

Zoltán Fábri's entire oeuvre is also marked by a preoccupation with the ethical foundations of behaviour in everyday life. Like Jancsó, Fábri's main concern is to pursue a moral investigation; the historical material he uses serves as a backdrop to a philosophical inquest. Unlike Jancsó, however, Fábri's films are always structured around clearly defined moral dilemmas and he is particularly interested in capturing the subtle psychological nuances that go hand in hand with difficult moral choices. A versatile director, Fábri has made films focused on urban workers and village life, as well as dramas set in the period of the First World War, the Second World War, Stalinism and state socialism. Most of his best-known films are based on novels by Hungarian authors, including Ferenc Molnár, Ferenc Sánta, József Balázs and István Örkény. An ethical investigation into past experiences from the time of village collectivisation, for example, is at the centre of Fábri's 1964 *Húsz óra/Twenty Hours*, a semi-documentary account of imposed governance structured around the inquiries of a newspaper reporter. Told in a combination of flashback memories, the emerging story tells of several friends who gradually drift apart after being involved in carrying out post-war agrarian reforms that were not particularly welcomed by the peasants. It reveals a complex picture of petty dogmatic prejudices disguised as high moral considerations, and of 'personal vindictiveness disguised as social justice' (Petrie 1978: 177). The struggle for power is also at the centre of attention of Fábri's Academy Award-nominated *A Pál utcai fiúk/The Boys of Paul Street* (1967). The film, which resonates with Peter Brook's *Lord of the Flies* (1963) but focuses more on the social foundations of morality rather than on inherent flows of human nature, depicts the clashes of warring boys' gangs over a contested vacant lot in Budapest in the first part of the century. In fact, the storyline gives the director a chance to make a strong statement about the meaninglessness of war. Moral choices again are the central themes of *Pluszmínusz egy nap/One Day More, One Day Less* (1973), where indignation over the behaviour of others leads the protagonist to commit an act of violence, and of *Magyarok/Hungarians* (1978), in which a group of peasants become reluctant witnesses of historical violence and have to make tough moral choices between overpowering fascists or assisting the oppressed Jews. The plotline of *Fábián Bálint találkozása Istennel/Balint Fabian Meets God* (1979) follows a peasant-protagonist whose personal record of violence, torment and remorse intersects with the historical swings of the short-lived Hungarian Soviet Republic in 1919. In Bryan Burns' view, it is a film that is 'more concerned with the moral meaning of actions than with their social repercussions' (1996: 46). The protagonists of *Requiem* (1981), one of Fábri's last films, are also overwhelmed by moral choices that prove so difficult that they make their relationship impossible. Set in the early 1950s, the film chronicles the encounters of a handsome young man and a beautiful young woman, who come together to talk of the last days of a dead comrade who was the woman's lover and the man's cellmate. They are powerfully attracted to each other; their fairly formal, restrained conversations and self-possessed behaviour are supplemented by added dream-like flashbacks and erotic fantasy flash-forwards. Yet, they are afraid to let themselves get carried away by this mutual arousal as they feel it would be disrespectful to the memory of the dead friend who perished in a Stalinist prison.

Fábri's best-known work, however, remains *Az Ötödik pecsét/The Fifth Seal* (1976), set during the time of World War Two. It is a dark and austere film, in which the director's sparing use of light reaches an astonishing level of mastery: at the culmination of the film he slots in an instant of blinding light, as if to make a strong statement contrasting the monotonous, gloomy lives of the protagonists with the illuminating moment of moral revelation.[5] There is extensive use of medium close-up shots and continuous cross-referencing of familiar images of bodily anguish from Jeronimus Bosch, of watches and of mechanic music, all supplying the theatrical feel of the film. The events are set in two acts, taking place over two consecutive nights on unremarkable ordinary dates that would not show up in any historical annals.

During curfew, four friends gather together around a table in an empty pub; it appears they have been doing this for years. They are all rather bland and harmless, ordinary middle-aged men: a peddler, a joiner, a watchmaker and the pub owner (joined temporarily also by a photographer-war veteran). The companionship goes undisturbed by the reverberating sound of soldiers marching in the night and their occasional forays into the pub. The protagonists become involved in a leisurely but deeply disturbing discussion of the morally acceptable reasons to go to war. They soon come to deliberate over a disquieting example that one of them, the watchmaker Mr. Gyuricza, supplies. It is a fable about two men, a slave and a tyrant, each one of whom has moral justification to be the way he is. (The slave endures endless humiliation and pain yet, as he himself has not perpetrated any crimes, does not suffer and his conscience remains clear. The tyrant engages in horrific despotism and autocracy and yet, as guilt does not exist if one does not feel guilty, he is not troubled and his will to rule remains undisturbed.) Mr. Gyuricza then asks his friends to choose who they would prefer to be: the slave or the tyrant from the fable? Would one prefer the moral superiority of the slave who allows himself to be victimised but remains vindicated, or would one opt for the tyrant's unlimited supremacy?

The friends remain reluctant to make a clear choice: it is too much of a challenge and why, after all, would they need to choose? A little later, however, they will be faced with difficult decisions and will have to choose. Before this moment, there is an intermission, during which each one of them is shown going about their daily lives before reconvening again the next evening, spending time with the respective families. This intermission is particularly important for it is here that each of the protagonists is given an individual moral characterisation. While the peddler rushes toward his lover's bed, the inn-keeper counts money and tries to figure out how to outsmart the volatile economy. In the watchmaker's home we learn that he hides Jewish children who would have otherwise have been deported.

When the men join together at the pub the next evening, they are arbitrarily arrested by Hungarian fascists, taken to police headquarters and brutally

Figure 14: The illuminating moment of moral revelation is stressed by the blinding light behind the Christ-like martyr amidst prevailing darkness and austerity in Fábri's *The Fifth Seal* (1976).

tortured without any clear charges. A superior officer (played by leading Hungarian actor Zoltán Latinovits) wants to use them to test his theory about taking charge over the minds and actions of such ordinary people: there is no need to kill them, he claims, one can fully control them if they are made to disrespect themselves. Near dawn, the protagonists are taken to a spacious room where they are put to an appalling moral test: they will either be killed or they can go free if they twice slap the nearly unconscious tortured resistance fighter who is hung up in middle of the room.

Faced with the moral choice to renounce this Christ-like martyr figure or die, three of the innocuous protagonists perish. But they allow themselves to be destroyed somewhat hastily, without much heroic assertion about the moral superiority of their choice. The only one who slaps the martyr and is subsequently let go is Mr. Gyuricza, the watchmaker who was telling the fable and was teasingly testing his friends' moral readiness. He can now walk back toward his home where the Jewish children are hidden. He is also the only one who had made his moral choice before it was imposed on him by someone else, and who, having established a superior ethical goal, had the moral justification that helped him survive the moment of crisis that proved fatal for the others.

The protagonists of *The Fifth Seal* experience history in the same way as most people: they are bystanders who remain inactive, contemplative and scared. It is only one of them, who is equally ordinary, who finds the modest strength to engage with history more actively, be it in a quiet and inconspicuous way. *The Fifth Seal* is a film entirely dedicated to the difficulty and the importance of making moral choices. Thus it identifies the trepidation of taking moral responsibility as the foundation of the troubled modern experience.

Jancsó and Fabri's leading ideological interest is in the tough moral choices imposed on the individual by socio-political events. The people who inhabit their films ride the tides of history; and the mobility of those who come and win is positioned against the sedentary view of those who stay and endure. Rather than the baroque battle scenes, cavalry and artillery of heritage cinema, these films rely on an impassive presentation and rational reading of moral theorems. History is suspended in favour of existential inquiry. Temporal and spatial movement is claustrophobically encapsulated, stressing the pre-defined limitations of all grandiose historical undertakings.

Ways of Remembering: Victims and Perpetrators

The worst events of the Holocaust took place across the countries of East Central Europe, and it was mostly Jews from these countries that perished. Thus, Holocaust discourse has been and still is one of the major themes of filmmaking in the region. Due to limited distribution, however, many remarkable Czechoslovak, Polish and Hungarian films on the Holocaust and related issues are not nearly as well-known as they should be, despite receiving numerous international film awards.[6]

These Holocaust films range stylistically from gritty and grim realist dramas to poetic and cathartic tragedies. Numerous documentaries and feature films focused on various dimensions of the Jewish experience in the region, sometimes casting a nostalgic look at past examples of harmonious co-existence of diverse ethnicities, sometimes investigating earlier manifestations of anti-Semitism.[7]

A number of perceptive films explore the diverse range of attitudes of Gentile neighbours who, supposedly possessing no hint of anti-Semitism, end up involved in helping the Jews in one way or another. The complex and controversial experiences of those hiding Jewish escapees were sometimes presented in an overtly idealistic light, and sometimes they were radically deglamorised.[8] Then there are the films which examine the Jewish experience itself, telling stories of death and survival during the time of the war.[9] A number of films focus on the life in ghettos. The notorious Nazi 'model city' of Terezín (also known by the German name Theresienstadt), a place where the shadow of death rules over a reality that pretends to follow a normal everyday routine, is the backdrop for some of the finest Holocaust films from Czechoslovakia.[10] There are also the unforgettable films set in the Warsaw Ghetto and other ghettos across Poland.[11] Some of the most memorable films about the concentration camps and the Final Solution were made here.[12] Post-Holocaust traumas are explored in films based on the work of the survivors Arnošt Lustig and Tadeusz Borowski.[13]

To give a more or less comprehensive overview of East Central European Holocaust-themed cinema is not an easy task, given that there are so many important films making it particularly difficult to decide which to highlight and which to mention in passing. Our attention here will focus on films that explore subtle psychological issues and dissect the mechanisms of the post-war readjustment of memory, areas that best reveal East Central European cinema's specific contribution to Holocaust cinema.

First, there are the films that attempt to explore the psychological state of the victims, a category that comprises some of the finest Holocaust-themed works. The dynamic expressionist camera in Jan Němec's masterpiece *Démanty noci/ Diamonds of the Night* (1963), for example, follows two teenage Jewish boys who have escaped from a camp-bound train and who are running through a forest, desperate to stay alive. It is a black-and-white film with little dialogue, featuring superior camerawork by Jaroslav Kučera and his assistant Miroslav Ondříček, who was responsible for the remarkable hand-held photography sequences (both men would become key cinematographers for the Czechoslovak New Wave). The boys are fully dependent on their surroundings and experience hunger, cold and exhaustion. Everybody is an enemy. Yet the urge to live overcomes and lessens their sense of danger. A peasant girl who gives them a bite to eat then reports them, and the men of the local hunting squad soon hunt them down.

The most important feature of this film is not its direct, grim narrative, but the remarkable cinematic portrayal of chilling fear and daydreams of salvation, expressed in the viscerally rough representation of the escapees, whose psychological state is largely defined by the doomed hope that they may succeed to break loose from a bleak fate. The extreme exhaustion impairs their ability to distinguish between the reality of miserable confinement and the vision of glorious redemption. Throughout the film Němec uses scattered surrealist references, juxtaposing contrasting dark shots of the escape (overlaid with a soundtrack of heavy breathing) with shining shots of tableaux-like dreams (on a muted background); of streetcars that take them back to a peaceful neighbourhood, of sunny facades, of calm women at windows overlooking empty afternoon sidewalks.[14]

In another attempt to look into the Holocaust victims' state of mind, Jerzy Skolimowski uses different artistic means. In his *Ręce do góry/Hands Up!* (1966) Skolimowski makes his present-day protagonists, a group of young people, engage in an imaginary re-enactment that replicates the transport experience. It is all staged as a happening in a train car, an experience that does not reference a real event, yet this fairly schematic stage play leaves a nightmarish effect and enhances the possibility of identification with the victims by the painful reaction it triggers. It is a remarkable replay of a traumatic experience, a scene where real time is suspended and taken over by subjectively reconstructed continuity of terror.[15]

At the other end of the spectrum are the films that look into the minds of perpetrators.[16] As a rule, these films engage in reconstructing the twisted rationality of the arguments that perpetrators would conjure to justify their actions. East Central European cinema has contributed at least two superbly crafted psychological films to this range: András Kovács' *Hideg napok/Cold Days* (Hungary, 1966) and Andrzej Munk's *Passenger*.

Cold Days features protagonists who, though well aware and remorseful of the awful suffering they have perpetrated, still live in denial and struggle to accept their guilt. Like Fábri's *The Fifth Seal*, the story focuses on the moral and emotional tribulations of several men, four officers of various ranks, who are confined to a single room and remain engaged in a tense conversation for most of the film. In this instance, the protagonists are captive Hungarian officers, locked up together after the end of World War Two. They have all taken part in the horrible massacre that took place on the frozen Danube in the occupied Yugoslav city of Novi Sad in 1942 and are awaiting trial.[17]

The film is set in 1946 and most of the action takes place in an ascetic chamber, a restrictive space in which the protagonists nervously tramp back and forth. The whitewashed walls provide a particularly fitting background for the outstanding black-and-white photography. The predominant close-ups and medium close-up shots of the protagonists, their abrupt dialogue and frequent outbursts are interspersed with flashback reminiscences to intimate moments (sexual affairs, taking meals with the family) and scenes alluding to the massacre (a silent group of people crowding on the shore of the frozen river, distant noise of shooting, men in underwear taken on a path on the ice to the place of execution that remains unseen). The narrative cuts between the conversations in the cell and flashbacks chronicling human degradation in the pogrom, and, like the consciousness of the protagonists, the camera persistently shies away and avoids showing the killings directly.

One of the inmates, formerly a commanding officer of higher rank (Zoltán Latinovits), rushes to express his moral indignation at the actions of the soldiers. His wife was apparently killed by mistake in an operation that he supervised; he now lives in a state of infuriated and antagonistic denial. During the course of the film, a reliable reconstruction of what happened to the wife can be gradually pieced together: how her husband left her alone when he sent her to be evacuated with two other women and several children she was trying to protect, how she was detained by mistake and went to her death out of solidarity with the friends she would not be able to save. Yet, the details remain blurred and it never becomes clear if the woman mentioned in the discussions related to different stages of the massacre was actually the officer's wife or in fact someone else. One thing is certain: everybody has guessed what happened to the officer's wife and the only one for whom the truth is unacceptable, who still persists in denial, is her husband. He has the nightmarish knowledge of having taken the wrong action, of being guilty without being prepared to acknowledge his own, albeit indirect, part in his wife and son's deaths. He is no longer simply a perpetrator but also a traumatised victim. The inevitable realisation of the monstrous truth turns him violent; he assaults and probably even kills the inmate who admits having witnessed the execution of the woman who may have been his wife.

It is a grim post-factum reconstruction revealing the horrible rationality of the extermination process. 'At naval college', one of the men remarks, 'ice-blasting was studied as the most peaceful subject.' Yet here these same naval college graduates are shown using hand grenades to blow up a hole in the ice and then widen it with small spades, while civilians silently crowd on the shore, awaiting the procedure to end so that they can be disposed of (shot and thrown into the icy waters). The dialogue of the military men is technical, matter-of-fact, interspersed with expressions such as 'lend a hand', 'the work must be done' and 'the scum must be dumped'. A recurring shot gazes at the wide hole in the middle of the ice: an innocent sight which is now endowed with the horrific subtext of human annihilation.

In an uncustomary exchange between superiors and ordinary soldiers, the men correct each other's memories, driven by the need to provide self-justification. In the process of hearing these overlapping, yet differently remembered, accounts, a more or less coherent narrative of the horrible event can be constructed. It transpires that some of the victims in Novi Sad were killed simply because they witnessed the massacre, but the inmates recall situations involving people that they sent to death and would have made good witnesses to exonerate them now. The flashbacks reveal numerous scenes of civilians crowded around town, waiting to be processed, transported (and disposed of). Patrols are shown terrorising the city at night, looting and vandalising. Everything is permissible and no one is accountable. In one of the most depressing scenes of the film a patrol rushes into the bedroom of a family in the middle of the night and sends the husband to fetch *pálinka* from the neighbours. The wife is left alone in bed, sheltering two small children with terror in her eyes. 'Her breasts were protruding', one of the men comments, 'so this was her luck', alluding that others were not so lucky in that night of rape and death.

The greatest achievement of *Cold Days*, however, is its representation of the responsibility that is shifted between these men, each one of whom is an essential link in the chain of the massacre. The film superbly illustrates how talking about the massacre proves more painful for the perpetrators than the actual slaughter. The time is spent in mutual accusations: they all know they are guilty, but each one of them tries to attribute more guilt to another. There is a

Figure 15: Some of the victims in Novi Sad were killed simply because they witnessed the massacres: Kovács's *Cold Days* (1966).

general reluctance to face responsibility: 'What could I have done?'; 'I did not want to know anything of this.'

'How did I end up among these murderers?' shouts the senior officer abruptly and offensively, as if he belongs to some other, morally superior category. Technically, he is correct in pointing that he has not stained his hands; he has only been giving orders. For him those of lower 'field' ranks, the corporals, are murderers (and executors). But they soon bite back, saying that they executed (his) strict orders.

Each of the men pushes aside the issue of responsibility and denies complicity; they avoid facing the horrendous moral implications of the mass murder they have perpetrated, opting instead to recycle ad nauseam their memories of the icy January weather: 'my feet were so cold'; 'my toes froze'. The references to the physical duress they experienced while carrying out the hideous assignment clash with those elements of the flashback-reconstruction that remain unspoken of, clearly revealing the process of readjusting remembrance.

Munk's *Passenger* also examined the process of readjusting memory, issues of guilt and remembrance, and the ways perpetrators construct a morally acceptable post-war account of their crimes. At the time of his premature death in 1961, Munk had completed the shooting of the *Passenger* but had not edited the footage. It was known that he was not happy with certain scenes and was planning to re-shoot. The film was completed by a group of Munk's collaborators led by Witold Lesiewicz and released to international critical acclaim in 1963, two years after the death of the director. One of the main aesthetic decisions in completing the film had been to structure the main present-day narrative framework in a series of stop-motion photographs, similar to the approach used by Chris Marker in *La Jetée* (1962), and to only have acted sequences for the camp flashbacks, thus enhancing the avant-garde look of the film.[18]

The plot of the film is fairly straightforward. In the 1950s, a German Latin American émigré, Liza, is seen aboard a trans-Atlantic liner approaching Europe. This is her first visit since the war; she has recently married and is returning with her husband. A young woman, whose face brings a host of memories from the past to Liza's mind, comes on board at Southampton. Liza is terrified; she thought that the woman – Marta, a former concentration camp prisoner – was dead. The presence of the passenger forces Liza to tell her husband a past secret: she admits to having been a supervisor at Auschwitz during the war. She claims, though, to have helped people, even trying to save this woman's life. In the course of the film, Liza's recollections of the past are played out twice, in two very similar yet crucially different versions – the first is the story she gives to her husband, the second one is the account she keeps to herself. At the next port of call, Lisbon, the mystery passenger simply disembarks. Unlike in Liliana Cavani's *Il portiere di notte/The Night Porter* (1974) no encounter between former inmate and supervisor ever takes place. The two women never confront each other and it remains unclear if this was the real prisoner from Auschwitz or not. The presence of the passenger is only important because it triggers Liza's memory.

The two versions of Liza's story are fairly similar on the surface: in her role as a camp supervisor, she tries to be good to the prisoners, yet she cannot afford to be too nice because it is her job to be tough. Yet she develops some sort of a relationship with a 'pet' prisoner, Marta, whose fiancée Tadeusz is also in the camp.[19] Liza tries to help them stay in touch, but because they do 'foolish things' (attempt to organise resistance), Tadeusz is taken away to the death block. Liza is then transferred and never knows what happened to Marta. Up until the encounter on the ship, she thought that Marta had shared Tadeusz's fate.

The second recollection tells the same story, but shows more aspects of the inhumane camp reality, revealing cracks in Liza's first version, suggesting that she was not as supportive to Marta as she has claimed. Yet Liza is once again vindicated – no wonder, it is she who tells the story. The most shocking element of her account of the camp, however, is the twisted logic she uses to refashion the nature of the relations between Marta and herself: she, the supervisor, sees herself as a vulnerable victim, endangered by strong-willed prisoners such as Marta. It is a remarkable reversal of roles, revealing the oppressor's speculative ways to present oneself as the oppressed. 'She wanted to destroy me', Liza insists, trying to justify the logic of preventive aggression and conceptualise herself as the weak and vulnerable one in a relationship of uneven power. Even though a helpless prisoner, Marta has a private life and is loved, something that Liza is denied and dearly misses. For her birthday, Marta receives a bouquet of flowers, but nobody remembers Liza's birthday. Liza claims she felt humiliated and had her dignity challenged. Her patronising of Marta points to deeply problematic moral propositions: Liza actually blackmails Marta by bringing her together with fiancée Tadeusz and expects her trust and unconditional gratitude in return, while thinking of herself as Marta's charitable benefactor.

Reportedly, Munk was particularly interested in the logic of perpetrators. The proposition of reversed power relations in *Passenger* suggests a paradox: in an effort to justify her actions, the perpetrator transforms the relationship from one of power dependency into one of personal struggle between equally strong and free-willed individuals. Having presented the power mechanics of the relationship as one of equals, the perpetrator can (as Liza does) claim to be 'disappointed' and 'offended', feelings that then sufficiently entitle her to destroy the victim. Whenever she is 'disappointed', Liza can punish, whenever 'offended', she has the licence to send someone to death.

Pursuing a rationally detached Brechtian approach, Munk opts to invite viewers to draw their own conclusions regarding the moral ambivalence of Liza's presumed guilt and redemption. He presents a clear case, asking us to decide if power relations can be conceptualised through moral categories. Liza's monologues contain constant references to ethical concepts such as dignity, moralilty and humiliation. Is she seeking for some kind of forgiveness

Figure 16: In a paradoxical reversal of morality, the perpetrator transforms the relationship with the victim from one of power dependency into one of personal struggle between equally strong and free-willed individuals: Munk's *Passenger* (1961).

from Marta? Is she creating a moral alibi for herself? Is there place for moral discourse in these relationships of extreme adversity?

Passenger is a film that presents a harrowing picture of the camp's reality. On the ocean liner Liza reads a homemaker's magazine, yet as soon as she closes her eyes nightmarish visions from Auschwitz rush into her mind: death is part of the everyday; a dead man's hand hangs over the edge of a cart full of other dead bodies; there is a scene where naked prisoners are made to run to exhaustion in the middle of the night, surrounded by overseers and barking dogs. Many elements give a panoramic overview of the reality of the camp – from the hypocritical behaviour of an International Red Cross commission to the Kapo who is relentless when she crushes an attempt to save a Jewish child but sobs in despair over the murder of her dog. Yet Auschwitz is not presented as a simple catalogue of horrors; rather, it is depicted as a 'humanised' camp, where prisoners are exposed to concert music and where children are escorted to the gas chamber in an orderly fashion, as if taken from one classroom into another.

The most important achievement of *Passenger* is the way the two-tiered remembrance structure is revealed during the course of the film. When discussing her past, it becomes clear that Liza is able to distinguish and move between the two levels of her memoir: she knows very well which one is publicly acceptable, and which one provides the moral justification she needs for her own peace of mind. This suggests, however, that beyond the two levels that Liza is prepared to 'replay' there may be more, deeper layers of this same narrative, other accounts that she would never pronounce or admit, even to herself. First there is the 'acceptable' narrative that can be offered to others. Then there is the flexibly readjusted narrative (allegedly more truthful and already not publicly spoken) that was strictly for private use, aimed at justifying and securing the comfort of Liza's consciousness. But can this second version be deemed the definitive one? Beyond these two there may be a third horrifying version, or maybe even more layers, casting a thick shadow of doubt over the chance that truth could ever be known; all that can be known are adjusted narratives of the past. By comparing the differences between the first and the second version we can draw our own conclusions and compose a picture of what the imaginable deeper layers could be like.

Films like *Passenger*, *Cold Days* and *Diamonds of the Night* rely on the extensive use of flashback references. It is interesting to see how the chilling rationalisation and justification of perpetrators' memories (moving between denial and rational explanation) differ from those of the victims' terrorised minds (mostly playing out in traumatised daydreaming). The perpetrators can face events and stolidly consider them, they can think the unthinkable and imagine the unimaginable. The victims cannot.

Small Individuals, Big Ironies

Roberto Begnini's acclaimed Holocaust comedy *La vita è bella/Life is beautiful* (1997) made critics query the moral acceptability of laughter in the context of the unspeakability linked to the terrifying perception of the Holocaust. In the course of the discussions, writers made references to somewhat forgotten films about the period that had also relied on laughter, such as Lina Wertmüller's *Pasqualino Settebellezze/Seven Beauties* (1976), and some went as far back as to remember Charlie Chaplin's classic *The Great Dictator* (1940). As had often previously occured, East European Holocaust films were not remembered; not intentionally, of course, but simply because, as already noted in chapter one, they remain little known even among critics and scholars who otherwise claim an extensive cinematic education.[20]

Yet humour has been widely used in the region's cinema in representations of the anti-Fascist resistance and the Holocaust in films that received many international awards and were well noted at the time of their release.[21] The quasi-comic situations in these films usually rely on the inherent discrepancy between the small-scale ambitions of the protagonists and the large-scale processes in which this same protagonist becomes enmeshed, usually by accident.[22] Thus, these films can be seen as a variation of the 'burden of history' theme: like Munk's *Eroica* and *Bad Luck*, they are structured on the same premise of juxtaposing a small and insignificant protagonist against the large ironies of history.[23]

People in Czechoslovakia seem to be particularly sceptical of the issue of heroism and have traditionally mocked the belligerent rhetoric of nation-building. It is an attitude that can be traced back to the mockery of Habsburg bureaucracy during the First World War found in the Czech national literary classic, Jaroslav Hašek's anti-war satire *The Good Soldier Švejk*.[24] Operating on the premise that war and big political shifts are an adversary to the common folk who only want to enjoy a pint of beer in a quiet pub corner, the focus of Czech cinema has traditionally been on the pragmatic manoeuvring of individuals trying to side-step great historical undertakings wherever possible, who nonetheless end up in the centre of action because they happen to be at the crossroads of history.

Elmar Klos and Jan Kadár's *Obchod na korze/A Shop on the High Street* (Czechoslovakia, 1965. a.k.a. *Shop on Main Street*) is probably the best cinematic study of moral ambiguity and indecisiveness to result from such a stance. A new pro-Nazi government comes to power in Slovakia and the local thugs who support them suddenly rise to public office. A relative of the simpleton Tono is appointed as the town's superintendent, and in his turn he appoints Tono to be the new owner (or 'Aryan supervisor') of a shop run by an old Jewish widow.

Figure 17: Ida Kaminská in Klos and Kadár's *A Shop on the High Street* (1965).

It soon becomes apparent, however, that the enterprise makes no profit what-soever. The unexpected rise in social position is an important leap forward for Tono, yet he cannot bring himself to take over the shop; instead, he begins to help the old lady who is oblivious of the growing anti-Semitism and takes a friendly attitude to Tono's shy attention, which leads to a string of humorous misunderstandings. Finally, with the deportation of the town's Jewish com-munity, Tono can no longer postpone the choice as to which side he is on. In a somewhat reluctant and bumbling manner, he tries to protect the old Jewish woman in a showdown that brings them both to a tragic end. Starring Ida Kaminská as the old Jewish shopkeeper and Jozef Króner as Tono, it is the story of a brave coward, an ordinary Slovak man whose indecisiveness can be seen as a source of moral redemption.

The tragi-comic encounters of the 'small' individual with history were further developed in one of the masterpieces of Czechoslovak New Wave cinema: Jiří Menzel's *Ostře sledované vlaky/Closely Observed Trains* (1966, a.k.a. *Closely Watched Trains*) is yet another story where accidental heroism is perpetrated by an insignificant person. Based on the work of writer Bohumil Hrabal, the reputed master of this subtle humorous worldview, the film tells the story of a young station master, Miloš Hrma, who becomes an unlikely resistance hero during the Nazi occupation of Czechoslovakia. Miloš is more preoccupied with controlling his burgeoning sexuality, losing his virginity and overcoming his tendency for premature ejaculation than with politics, yet as a sideline to these personal problems he becomes involved with resistance activity. At the end of the film, he carries out an important and dangerous assignment but comes to a tragic and unnecessary demise. His death, though, is much more accidental than heroic, suggesting that heroism is not always the outcome of consciously cultivated moral growth.

It is precisely this demystification of heroism, this representation of historical process through ordinary personal experience, which makes these films so subtle and durable. They are still of interest today, with a human appeal that goes far beyond their socio-historical context. *A Shop on the High Street* and *Closely Observed Trains* are tongue-in-cheek stories that seem to focus more on petty personal concerns, yet it comes down, once again, to the intersection of individual fate and history, reflected in the quasi-comic absurd demise of their lovable protagonists.[25] With their finely crafted humour, *quid pro quo* misunderstandings and scattered sexual references, the films perfectly reveal the atmosphere of small Central European towns at times of duress.

There is also Frank Beyer's *Jakob, der Lügner/Jakob the Liar* (GDR, 1974), based on Jurek Becker's novel, yet another film that elevates an ordinary protagonist to heroism. In this case, the focus is the protagonist's courage to dare using his sense of humour and his imagination in a situation that should diminish him.

Figure 18: Vlastimil Brodský in Beyer's *Jakob the Liar* (1974).

Jakob Heym (played by remarkable Czechoslovak New Wave actor Vlastimil Brodský) is a member of the Jewish community in a Polish ghetto whose inhabitants expect to be transported to the death camps any day. They all live an isolated existence, cut off from the rest of the world, and have no information on the war developments. One day Jakob is caught supposedly breaking the curfew and has to report to the Gestapo headquarters. There he hears on a radio that the Soviet troops are advancing. Since a mistake has been made and there has been no breach of the curfew he is released. However, Jakob's ghetto peers do not believe that the inspiring news could have possibly been received in such an implausible way. Insistent that the Russians are only kilometres away, Jakob tells a lie to persuade people to believe the truth: he has a hidden radio. The information has an unexpectedly uplifting effect on his comrades, and Jakob realises that if he went on pretending to have more good news, this could have a great healing effect on the depressed and suicidal members of the community. Jakob is soon plagued day and night for more news on the Red Army's progress. He initially resists, but the pressure is so great that he fabricates stories, first to stop people from pestering him and later to try and boost the morale of the ghetto; he thus becomes an accidental hero, fabricating outrageously contrived news reports about the advances of the allied forces and an approaching liberation. The effect of his stories, however, is short-lived as no liberation takes place and the ghetto is indeed deported.

Telling lies in the name of a higher (ultimately moral) truth elevates the ordinary protagonist to a heroic status. Like *A Shop on the High Street* and *Closely Observed Trains, Jakob the Liar* retains the primacy of ethical concern: in this case, the moral dilemma of whether it is justified to tell lies for a higher moral objective.[26]

Faced with the great ironies of history, the small individuals of these important war-themed films continue the tragi-comic view of the 'burden of history'. So it seems appropriate that this view is described as 'paradigmatic' for the discourse on history that unravelled in the region. As Hegyi has observed:

Bitter irony, black humour, morbidness, and self-tormenting, almost masochist self-mockery are not only typical phenomena of Central European culture, but at the same time act as paradigmatic strategies designed to make the frustration and long-term lack of perspectives more bearable (2001: 43).

Totalitarianism's Moral Damage

Throughout Eastern Europe, Stalinism coincided with the early years of state socialism, a period referred to as 'totalitarianism' in chapter one (1949 to 1956); thus Stalinism and totalitarianism were often seen as synonymous. Associated with brutal repressions, staged trials, unexplained disappearances, forced labour camps, personality cults and an overall moral decline, the late 1940s and the early 1950s are seen as the darkest period in the more recent history of these countries. It was a period of extreme duress, abounding with situations where the moral capabilities of individuals were greatly tested. The complex ethical dilemmas that people faced during this period explain the great attraction of cinema to plots from the 1950s. It is no wonder that many of the films that focused on this gloomy period were censored, even if they did not engage in direct indictment of the regime but relied instead on (sometimes) cryptic allegories. The subject matter of totalitarianism has been treated differently over time; depending on the political climate at the time of a film's making, their stories differed, reflecting not only the period that the film was supposed to depict but also the prevalent perception of this period in public discourse. Works from the 1950s, for instance, often glorified socialist construction while remaining oblivious of the repression, the trials and the camps. From the late 1960s through to the mid-1980s, an array of films attempted to tackle the overbearing moral crisis of this depressing and compromising period. Even though they had to engage in an on-going cat and mouse game with censors, film-makers were allowed to investigate the moral devastation left by totalitarianism; this was thus the period during which the best anti-totalitarian films were made.

Towards the end of the 1980s and in the early 1990s, film-makers finally had the chance to revisit the 1950s without the need of parabolic plots. Many felt compelled to tell the straightforwardly depressing stories of people whose lives were destroyed by Communist persecution. Films about camp experiences and other aspects of deprivation and humiliation proliferated. Unfortunately, however, many of the more recent films did not go much deeper than offering factual correction of historical record – the story could finally be told as it was. Other preoccupations had taken over the public's mind and the wave of films about the 'true' record of totalitarianism failed to provide any remedy to current identity concerns, and soon lost impetus. In addition, the characterisation and plotlines of many of these films rarely managed to rise above the level of cliché. In the 1950s, there had been scores of films glorifying the Communist hero resisting the sinister capitalist and fascist powers. This time around the stories would be of innocent and helpless people victimised by brutal and amoral Communist villains. Previously, those endowed with political power and controlling all possible forms of redress were capitalists and their henchmen, now they were Communists.

As a result, the films made in earlier periods (the late 1960s to mid-1980s) are more worthy of discussion. Their narratives revolved around individuals, chronicled their fates, and explored the ways totalitarianism affected the minds of ordinary people. Although characters perished along the way, the focus was not so much on the death of the protagonist, but on moral devastation; physical destruction was seen as a logical extension but the stress was on the individual's moral demise.

None of the main protagonists die, for example, in Jaromil Jireš' *Žert/The Joke* (1969), and yet this film is seen as one of the finest works exposing the moral degradation endorsed by totalitarianism. In a flashback that takes him back to the 1950s, the protagonist accounts how a simple political joke, related to the authorities by a former girlfriend, ruined his professional future. Many years later, he has the chance to take his revenge – not on the authorities (who are off limits, of course) but on a friend who had denounced him earlier. He tries to get his own back by seducing the friend's wife, but the retaliation backfires because their marriage has been a sham for many years. A real political confrontation can never take place; it is all reduced to twisted inter-personal relations, leaving a bitter aftertaste – even intimate associations are marred by political opportunism encouraged by the regime.[27]

Andrzej Wajda's richly textured and complex *Man of Marble* is the anti-totalitarian film that has received most international acclaim and is credited with pioneering a whole series of films focusing on the ethical dimension of representation and remembrance. It is a film about memory and historical record, exposing people's resistance to look back and confront the awkward silence that surrounds the period of Stalinist repression. The film takes place in contemporary setting in the 1970s and features a young film student, Agnieszka

(Krystyna Janda), who becomes interested in an intriguing newsreel footage which has never been screened: the portrait of a young man, seemingly a Communist hero of some sort, is being taken down from a façade where it had been part of a line up of several portraits. Why is this particular one being removed? Who is this 'fallen idol'? Agnieszka wants to know more: who was this man and why was he 'removed' from history? She decides that this will be the topic of her diploma film and launches her own investigation; she meets with a number of people (and manages to get some interviews on tape), visits museums and finds forgotten footage from the period.

The inquiry focuses on the question of what happened to bricklayer Mateusz Birkut, a shock worker from the 1950s and one of Nova Huta celebrated builders, whose cherished image can be seen in old news reels from the archives. There is also a 20-minute 'documentary' about Birkut's much-praised work ethics, in which his 'proletarian personality' comes across as an epitome of the elevated spirit of the 1950s.[28] He seems to have been the perfect hero of the Socialist Realist paradigm. As Agnieszka will soon hear, a prosperous film director who 'discovered' Birkut and made him the perfect propaganda hero of socialist construction describes him as his 'biggest coup'. Why then is Birkut's marble statue kept behind locked doors in the museum basement today? Why has the story of his later life (the one after the portrait has been taken down) not been documented and why are people awkward and reluctant to talk about it?

Agnieszka believes that if she finds answers to these questions and manages to make out the logic of Birkut's symbolic 'deletion' from the public mind, she will be able to put to the test some more general hypotheses about the

Figure 19: Jerzy Radziwiłowicz in a mock propaganda documentary in Wajda's *Man of Marble* (1976), a milestone film protesting the distortion of historical record.

doubtful moral condition of the society she lives in. The story of Birkut's demise – accident, personal injury, jail term, growing record of political dissent and ultimate death in the context of later worker's protests – gradually emerges in a number of interviews using extended flashbacks to the past: from the officials who first elevated him and then betrayed him, to the friends and family who abandoned him at a time when his excessive idealism was no longer in line with the prevalent pragmatic approaches of later years.

Wajda's preoccupation with totalitarianism in *Man of Marble* is not so much with the 1950s period. His main concern is with the contemporaneous take on the totalitarian past: with the adjustment of memory to fit post-1950s developments, the abuse of historical record and the inconsiderate disposal of the agents of certain strands of social life, once this specific angle of the country's social past is no longer deemed appropriate and needs to be forgotten. The hushed protest of his protagonist, Agnieszka, is against the manipulation of memory and the distortion of historical record, against the unwillingness to confront the past and acknowledge the abuse suffered by people.

There were also other films directly aimed at exposing the inhumane nature of the period. The nightmarish story of Ryszard Bugajski's *The Interrogation*, for example, recounts the experiences of a young woman (also played by Krystyna Janda) who is arrested one night and then kept in jail and tormented for years without it ever becoming clear on what charges she is being kept. Having suffered extreme humiliation and abuse at the hands of her captors, at the end she is simply let go – released due to a change in the political climate after Stalin's death – again without explanation or apologies. The protagonist survives, but her life is ruined, her personal story serving as an allegory of the individual's destruction by the brutal police state.[29]

In Hungarian cinema, the 1950s have naturally been the subject of intense attention by film-makers, given that Hungary lived through the shattering events of 1956. The best films about the period offered psychological explorations of the ways Stalinism affected the state of mind of ordinary people.[30] Sometimes, however, directors opted to treat the period's problems with the means of political ridicule, as seen in Péter Bacsó's work, a director whose sarcastic view of the reality of state socialism is something of a personal trademark.[31] Bacsó's *The Witness* was a biting satire of the absurdities of the socialist system of the 1950s and a mockery of totalitarianism in Hungary. The name of the protagonist, Jószef Pelikán, has since become a synonym for a naive victim of the Kafkaesque bureaucratic machine.[32]

One of the most important Hungarian films on totalitarianism, Pál Gábor's *Angi Vera* (1978), is set in 1948, the year of the so-called 'amalgamation', the coercive co-optation of all liberal parties under the Communists. It is the story of a young nursemaid, Vera Angi, an orphan of working-class background, who is chosen to receive special political training. Vera ideally fits the template for new cadres that the Communist Party is looking to promote – ignorant

Figure 20: Bascsó's *The Witness* (1969): a biting satire of the absurdities of the socialist system of the 1950s.

but willing to learn and eager to comply. She soon learns to denounce the untrustworthy and to report on the politically deviant, and is so diligent in doing it that she even renounces the married colleague with whom she has an affair, thus causing the man's political demise. Rather than challenge the morally crippling environment, Vera loses her sensitivity in favour of total devotion to the party line. She rejects human warmth, friendship and love, and becomes the system's willing role model.

Angi Vera is a subtle study of personality formation in a society that demands conformism and has banned individuality in principle. Here, personal politics are treated as an extension of party politics. The individuals who are in the centre of attention are concerned with survival and are prepared to adjust by swiftly changing allegiances. They are constantly on the alert, which is illustrated particularly well in a story that is structured around depressing Party meetings shown as the formal 'moment of truth' where everybody's personal life is subjected to harsh scrutiny and self-criticism is demanded. Meant to incite constant feelings of unspecified guilt among the attendees, the meetings are the main tool for cultivation of uncritical conformity and are detested by most ordinary people. They are, however, regularly attended by high-placed Party comrades and make a thriving ground for Vera and her type.

With its exploration of suppressed sexuality and numerous references to a deprived childhood, *Angi Vera* is a finely crafted psychological study of an individual in a constraining social context, and it is ultimately the society that is indicted for turning the protagonist into a politically correct monster. Lajos Koltai's exquisite cinematography stresses the relationship between public and private by juxtaposing extreme close-ups and scenes of mass gatherings. The grey, dull light of winter afternoons amidst cold landscapes justifies the choice of subdued colours that work greatly to enhance the message of alienation and constraint.

Like *Angi Vera* and *Man of Marble*, the best films set in the 1950s do not deal directly with the overwhelming Stalinist coercion but rather explore a variety of individual reactions to the awkward historical moment when politics becomes so overwhelming that its repercussions are felt in every single aspect of a person's life. They often rely on plotlines structured around a coming-of-age point of view and offer fine studies of personality formation in a society that demands conformity.[33] A good example of this approach is István Szabó's psychological study *Apá/Father* (1966). The film uses an adolescent's point of view and traces his attempts to reconstruct the image of his late father. While the viewers understand that the father has been an ordinary medical doctor, the teenage son, living in the 1950s, constantly transforms the memory of the father adjusting it to the range of positive social roles sanctioned by Stalinism (from an anti-fascist fighter to a great materialist scientist). In a series of fantasy flashbacks that give the story an added complexity, the son keeps distorting the image of the 'real' father and substituting it for the 'desired' one, thus effectively trying to enhance his own self-esteem.[34]

Totalitarianism took away the right to private life from the individual; everybody's personal life had to be political and politicised – as seen in films like *The Joke, Man of Marble, Angi Vera* and others. It was this suspension of the private in favour of an imposed communal interest that ordinary people in the region found particularly difficult to live with. However, whenever the official ideology tried to make the politicised concept of communal interest the substitute for concern over personal welfare, the response of narrative arts (cinema included) was to pay more attention to the individual. Moral issues were at the centre of interest yet again. Shown in an everyday context, these concerns became an underlying interest for many seemingly apolitical views of contemporary topics. As we will see in chapter five, however, the aversion of these films to politics was in fact a strong political statement in itself.

CHAPTER FIVE

State Socialist Modernity:
The Urban and the Rural

The Greyness of Everyday Life

One of the consequences of Cold War isolationism was that the artistic and moral concerns of film-makers working within the Eastern Bloc often contrasted with those of their Western counterparts. As Andrzej Wajda put it:

> Films made in Eastern Europe seem of little or no interest to people in the West. The audiences in Western countries find them as antedeluvian as the battle for workers' rights in England in the time of Marx. Thus our efforts here in Eastern Europe have nothing to show audiences in the West who look upon the world they live in as permanent [...] And that is a pity, for I am certain that those concerns are not ours alone but apply to the world at large, or will in the very near future. (1986: 131–2)

Wajda is quite right: to many viewers in the West the East European concerns appear limited to the monotonous East Central European existence of depressed protagonists leading controlled lives associated with the overwhelming greyness of landscape and urban milieu. The imagined vision of the whole region was of a squalid place where the sun never shone and everything was dreary, colourless and claustrophobic. There may be plenty of sunshine in Budapest and Prague, in Kraków and Bratislava, but it was the desolate perennial rainfall of Béla Tarr or the prefabricated tower blocks of Kieślowski that came to stand for the region in its most recognised representations, and it was the association with greyness that supplied this cinema's specific atmosphere and mood.[1]

This vision of metaphoric 'greyness' has been powerfully asserted in the films about life under state socialism. Hungarian, Polish, Czech and Slovak film-makers regularly chose such tones to create their gloomy images and project their own realities. It was life that was supposed to be grey and colourless, monotonous and dull, murky and ominous. It was the colour of life in the dimly lit corridors of inefficient bureaucratic institutions and at the dusty construction sites of oversized enterprises and junkyards, in the Communist penalty colonies and in the shadows of monstrous complexes of apartment buildings.[2]

Here we will look at the diverse range of these films to explore how and why, though conscious of the 'greyness', East Central European cinema nonetheless came to display a paradoxical aversion to straightforward critical social realism. First, we will consider the basic differences in the political agendas of socially conscious film-making east and west of the Iron Curtain. In a social context where state socialist ideology would not leave much space for individual privacy, film-makers vigorously asserted the right of the individual to be indifferent to politics. Thus, many of the films that address contemporary topics were intentionally apolitical examinations of existential concerns rather than works of critical social realism. Having set the context, we will look at some specific features of Czechoslovak New Wave cinema.

Then, in separate discussions, we will explore the various approaches to representing village life and the interactions between the dominant ethnic groups and the Romani minority, in both cases remembering issues such as the discourse on modernity and patriarchal society. Finally, we will trace the main characteristics of the 'cinema of moral concern' and attempt to explain why a director like Krzysztof Kieślowski, who was not one of its original or main proponents, comes to be seen today as the best representative of this film-making tradition.

In the course of all these investigations, we will come to see how the rights and wrongs of state socialist society, while recognised as important, once again served as a backdrop for ethical and existential investigations, and how the interest in intensely personal experiences also marked the best works of East Central European cinema.

Apolitical Political Cinema

During the decades of state socialism, the concerns of film-makers in Eastern Europe differed from those of their West European counterparts. Europe, of course, was seriously divided and up until the mid-1970s the artistic exchanges between the two camps were minimal. Directors on opposite sides of the Iron Curtain worked in different political settings, and reacted to different political events, which respectively defined their distinct ideological agendas.

While in 1968, for example, many directors in Western Europe made films that reacted to the student protests and other social upheavals of the time, this was not really matched by a significant similar wave of films from East Central Europe.[3] Such divergence in interest is not particularly surprising, given that the Eastern Bloc countries had a whole set of socio-political concerns of their own at the time. In the West, 1968 is mainly remembered for the powerful student protests. In the context of East Central Europe, however, the most important event of 1968 was the suppression of the Prague Spring and the Soviet-led Warsaw Pact invasion of Czechoslovakia.

While progressive West European film-makers were busy exposing the faults of capitalism, their counterparts in the East were engaged in subverting state socialism. While left-wing West Europeans explored capitalist social inequality, poverty and the marginalisation of the working class, in East Central Europe the concern was rather to expose the wrongs of imposed egalitarianism. In addition, the East Central European take on social concerns found expression in a more anguished and sometimes paranoic view of social process, quite different from the more balanced, analytic and relaxed take on the same issues found in West European cinema. Given that the intellectual exchanges were kept to a minimum, this discrepancy in agenda did not come across loud and clear, and in the public perception left-wing film-makers from the West continued to be closely associated with East European film-makers.

Even though many of the leading East Central European directors would identify Italian Neo-realism as a key artistic influence, only a few of them would confess to the outspoken Marxism found in the work of a director like Vittorio de Sica, for example, whose proletarian-minded films like *Ladri di biciclette/Bicycle Thieves* (1948) and *Miracolo a Milano/Miracle in Milan* (1951), or the later socially conscious *Ieri, oggi, domani/Yesterday, Today and Tomorrow* (1963) were admired but not imitated. Even more, it is difficult if not impossible, to point to East Central European equivalents of the British 'kitchen sink' social realism of the 1950s and 1960s or to the work of those Western European directors (like Costa-Gavras, Ken Loach, Rainer Werner Fassbinder and Bertrand Tavernier) who, while very different from each other, all shared a commitment to outspoken left-wing film-making.

In their quiet resistance to the imposed politicisation of the personal, East Central European directors were much closer to another type of West European film-making, best represented by the films that Michelangelo Antonioni made in the early 1960s (*L' Avventura/The Adventure*, 1960; *La Notte/The Night*, 1960; *L' Eclisse/The Eclipse*, 1962; *Il Deserto rosso/The Red Desert*, 1964), all atmospheric works that focused on intensely intimate existential dramas often evolving within the confined space of a couple or a small circle of friends. Another immensely popular and influential film was the equally atmospheric *Un homme et une femme/A Man and a Woman* (1966) by Claude Lelouch. Many of the East Central European films replicated these and other introspective dramas of personal traumas and adjustments which, while accounting for the social and the political, would be focused mostly on existential issues of love and separation, loss and recovery, loneliness and togetherness. The general influence of the French Nouvelle Vague and Jean-Luc Godard in particular is also of importance.

Well aware of the excesses and the dangers of totalitarianism, film-makers saw the making of 'apolitical' films as a matter of priority. The films that they opted for would often be about disturbances of intimate relationships rather than heroic confrontations and class struggles; they would focus on ordinary everyday life and thus, in the context of imposed excessive politicisation of the personal domain, deliver a covert political statement. Their 'apolitical' cinema was, in fact, profoundly political.

As early as the 1950s, the resistance to the politicisation of everyday life was manifested in films that quietly opposed the prevailing tendency to attribute economic failures to sabotages and external conspiracies rather than to domestic management weaknesses. Fábri's *Életjel/Fourteen Lives* (1954), for example, told the story of a group of trapped miners but, in contrast to the Party line, did not attribute the disaster to sabotage. A similar point was made by Andrzej Munk in his *Man on the Track*.[4] The film focused on the inquest into the death of a retired track engineer and revealed how the people who are asked to give evidence do so by uncritically bringing in their personal backgrounds and ideological interpretations. Károly Makk's *Megszállottak/The Fanatics* (1961), a film dealing with the irrigation problems in a village, was equally sceptical about harsh ideological classifications and bureaucratic leadership. At a time when 'sabotage' was the miracle buzzword used to explain away every glitch in management, these films made the clear point that in an excessively politicised environment it was easy to see conspiracies while remaining in denial about one's own organisational shortcomings.

Towards the early 1960s, directors began making 'existential' films with contemporary themes that circumvented the expected political commitment by simply failing to stress the concrete socio-political framework. An early example of the trend was Jerzy Kawalerowicz's *Pociąg/Night Train*, for example, a crime film that concentrated on the relationship of a man and a woman who meet accidentally on a train. *Nóż w wodzie/Knife in the Water*, Roman Polanski's only Polish-made feature, is another good example.[5] It dealt with a marital crisis triggered by a couple's encounter with an attractive young vagrant. The film focused on the intensely personal dimensions of the story, leaving the drama to unravel largely independently of the socio-political specifics of place and time.

Before embarking on the historical-ethical explorations that were discussed in chapter four, Miklós Jancsó made *Oldás és kötés/Cantata* (1963), a similarly intimate film about the mid-life crisis of a doctor in his late thirties, played by one of Hungary's best-loved actors, Zoltán Latinovits. Even though it contained plenty of political references to concrete historical memory, the legacy of Jewishness and the relationship between generations, *Cantata* was much more an 'existential' film which, once again, focused on personal identity issues. Likewise, István Gaál's *Sodrásban/Current* (1963), a film about the traumatic mourning of several teenage friends over a drowned comrade, was an equally 'apolitical' work. It told a story that could have happened in any country but the fact it happened to be taking place in socialist Hungary made little difference to its deeply personal theme. Evald Schorm's existential exploration *Návrat ztraceného syna/The Return of the Prodigal Son* (1966) was very much a Nouvelle Vague work that focused on a suicidal young man and his difficult relationships.[6]

It is in the context of this quietly subversive line of apolitical existential film-making that the masterpieces of the Czechoslovak New Wave came about.

The Czechoslovak New Wave

Most Czechoslovak New Wave films deal with contemporary themes (*Closely Observed Trains* is one of several notable exceptions). More importantly, they were internationally recognised and acclaimed, a recognition that came along with the 1960s endeavour of the country to transform the social system and emancipate itself from the grip of the Soviet Union. By that time, the faults of totalitarianism were clearly identified by reform-minded Czechoslovak politicians who called for 'socialism with a human face'. The narrative conceptualisation of this 'human face' was largely fleshed out in the films of the period, some of which even pre-dated the Czechoslovak socialist humanist slogans.

Many of the directors who worked in Czechoslovakia during this period were related to the New Wave movement in one way or another. Thus it is difficult to strictly define who 'belongs' to the group and who does not. An omnibus film directed by several FAMU graduates in 1965, *Perličky na dně/Pearls of the Deep*, is considered to have been a manifesto of the movement. It included shorts by Věra Chytilová, Evald Schorm, Jiří Menzel, Jaromil Jireš and Jan Němec.[7] Besides them, however, the Czechoslovak New Wave is closely associated with the work of directors such as Miloš Forman, Vojtěch Jasný or Ivan Passer, actors such as Vlastimil Brodský and Jana Brejchová, screenwriters such as Esther Krumbachová and Jaroslav Papoušek. The most important defining characteristic of the group's film-making is the specific style. True, the films of the Czechoslovak New Wave covered widely diverse stylistic ground, including absurdist parabola (*Až přijde kocour/Cassandra Cat*, Vojtěch Jasný, 1963), Surrealism (*Mučedníci lásky/Martyrs of Love*, Jan Němec, 1966) and Dadaism (*Sedmikrásky/Daisies*, Věra Chytilová, 1966), as well as films that developed the cinematic means of representing fantasy and magic (*Rozmarné léto/Capricious Summer,* Jiří Menzel, 1968; *Valerie a týden div/Valerie and Her Week of Wonders,* Jaromil Jireš, 1970).[8] If we seek to identify the unifying features of this film-making, it appears that the most specific manifestation of the Czechoslovak New Wave style can be reduced to an idiosyncratic combination of several characteristics. These include the interest in contemporary topics (often tackled with documentary authenticity), the subtle humour (often bordering on the absurd), the use of avant-garde narrative and editing techniques (often deployed with astonishing persistence) and the attention to psychological detail (often better revealed in explorations of interactions within a group rather than in studies of individual protagonists).

This discussion will focus on three select aspects that are key to recognising the group's achievements: their attentive attitude to documentary authenticity, their subtle self-reflexive sense of irony and their appreciation of the aesthetic quality of the absurd.

One of the best combinations is found in the films of Miloš Forman. Starting off in the early 1960s, Forman's main interest was the changing Czech society where modern and traditional lifestyles could be seen existing side by side, occasionally in amusing incongruity. Letting the camera observe

Figure 21: Modern and traditional lifestyles exist side by side in Miloš Forman's *Competition* (1963).

Figure 22: The hilarious scene of a 'singles' matching party involving female factory workers: Forman's *A Blonde in Love* (1965).

everyday situations, Forman showed these two sides of Czech life in perceptive documentaries which, as has been the case with many other classical examples of the documentary genre, contained re-enacted elements and focused respectively on a rock music contest and on the rehearsals of a traditional brass band (*Konkurs/Competition*, 1963; *Kdyby ty muziky nebyly/If There Were No Music*, 1963).

Forman soon turned his sharp eye for detail to features where he went on using the amateur actors he had discovered while filming documentaries.[9] He retained his interest in ordinary people's lives and developed his ability to discover the amusing and the absurd in their day-to-day situations. Forman's first feature film, *Black Peter*, follows a teenage protagonist who, fresh out of high school, takes up his first job as a shop assistant. The boy's main concern is how to approach a girl at the dancehall, yet he has to sit at home and listen to his father's wisdom about life. With the help of cameraman Jan Němeček, Forman manages to achieve a remarkable balance in the film between some scenes that convey fine psychological detail and those that track the movements of a crowd, a skill that became a trademark of his later work.[10]

Forman's next film, *Lásky jedné plavovlásky/A Blonde in Love* (1965, a.k.a. *Loves of a Blonde*), is a timeless comedy, a superb achievement in the main because of the apprehension with which the director conveys the comic subtext of situations involving ordinary exchanges, particularly in the brilliant opening sequences. The unforgettably hilarious scenes of a 'singles' matching party involving female factory workers and army reservists (also discussed in chapter six) have been identified by various film-makers as some of the best moments ever filmed. Beyond the psychologically subtle and richly detailed opening, the plot is straightforward: after a one-night stand a factory girl from the provinces arrives in Prague to claim a more permanent place in the life of an unsuspecting, philandering piano accompanist who still lives with his parents. The subtly humorous scenes featuring the girl's encounter with the pianist's parents carry a psychological truthfulness which is rare in cinema.

For his next film, his last to be made in Czechoslovakia, Forman modified his humour along the lines of other New Wave directors (such as Němec and Chytilová) to get much closer to the absurd and the satirical. *Hoří, má panenko/ The Firemen's Ball* (1967) does not focus on a central protagonist but relies on a series of quasi-absurd situations. The members of a provincial fire department are to celebrate their honorary 86-year-old boss's birthday by holding a party at the town hall. Besides the traditional dance and raffle, the firemen are planning to stage a beauty pageant. Only nothing works out quite as they have imagined: the (fairly plain) contestants they select for the beauty contest are not so keen to appear in swimsuits, the raffle prizes keep disappearing mysteriously, and on top of everything a devastating fire breaks out.

The director is at his best in masterfully tackling the awkward group dynamics in *The Firemen's Ball*; the scenes of many people dancing and subsequent turmoil are unsurpassed. More importantly, however, the film fruitfully draws together the plain funny and the absurd. The result, no wonder, comes across as a biting satire on inept social organisation and mismanagement. Indeed, this is the way *The Firemen's Ball* was perceived by the authorities at the time, as a suggestion that the men in charge are not only incompetent to run the show but are not even capable of taking care of their own line of business. The film was co-produced by Italian Carlo Ponti; viewed as a subversive assault on Communist administration, it was banned. The director emigrated shortly thereafter.[11]

Forman's combination of innocuous tongue-in-cheek humour, found in his endearing comedies, and mockery of institutional ineptness, revealed in his socially pointed satires, also characterises the work of other directors in the group. One of the finest Czechoslovak New Wave comedies to combine both aspects is Ivan Passer's *Intimní osvětlení/Intimate Lightning* (1966). The action takes place over a weekend during which a thirty-something old bachelor-musician from the city and his modern girlfriend visit a fellow student who has, after graduation, retired to his native small town where he lives with his parents, wife and kids. The visit provides ample opportunity for collisions on issues of lifestyle and world-view. But no crisis ever erupts. There is no denial that the low-brow routines of the provincial friend (angling, afternoon naps, liqueurs after dinner, and devotion to greasy foods resulting in a growing waistline), punctuated by fleeting musical moments on Sundays, give him a comfortable, cosy and relaxingly undemanding existence. The urban friend, who publicly subscribes to a different set of ideas about living, is repelled but also strangely attracted to this quiet descent into provincial snuggery. Nothing can be further apart than the cutting-edge swing and the low-brow pragmatism that mark the opposite poles of this encounter. Yet, the two lifestyles never really clash, leading to an ending that leaves an aftertaste of bitter irony.

One of the main qualities of Czechoslovak New Wave humour is its emotionally cohesive power, which is clearly felt in the films of Jiří Menzel, whose *Closely Observed Trains* has already been discussed. Like Forman and Passer, Menzel also made quietly subversive films that looked at present-day realities. One in particular – the bittersweet comedy *Skylarks on a String*, which was completed only after the crushing of the Prague Spring – was at that time perceived as dangerously subversive and shelved.[12] It was released to international acclaim only in 1990. The film tells of a group of women serving prison terms for having tried to defect to the West. As part of their 'socialist re-education' the inmates are made to spend their days labouring in a junkyard which becomes the site of lively interactions with a group of dissident male intellectuals who are also sentenced to hard labour, and also the young innocuous guard. The viewer witnesses a series of endearing and amusing events that take place in the lives of these (and other) marginalised characters. Like other New Wave films, *Skylarks on a String* evolves around group dynamics rather than a single protagonist and relies more on recreating a subtly comic atmosphere than telling a complex story.

In the best tradition of Kafka (who, like most Czech film-makers, was also a citizen of Prague), many critiques were aimed at the excessive paranoia of surveillance and control that had the tendency to take absurd proportions. Though the list of films that fall into this category is longer, the two to highlight first and foremost are Jan Němec's *The Party and the Guests* and Karel Kachyňa's *The Ear*. Unlike other films, *The Party and the Guests* and *The Ear* were not so preoccupied with specific social events but rather relied on parabolic associations and hints of the specifically perverted reality of totalitarianism as a system diametrically opposed to the 'laissez-faire' attitude: here everything was forbidden unless explicitly permitted.

For his surrealist study, *The Party and the Guests*, Jan Němec gathered together a number of well-known Czech intellectuals. The acting they were required to do for the film was fairly straightforward: on a sunny day, during an out of town picnic a group of friends are apprehended by a mysteriously inquisitive man (and his strange entourage) who starts asking them suspicious questions, alluding to some unspecified guilt. As time goes on, the man's behaviour becomes more and more inscrutable and the situation more and more cryptic, given that no misdeeds are ever identified and it all evolves around elusive hints of culpability. The friends are invited to attend a 'party'

Figure 23: Jan Němec's *The Party and the Guests* (1966): scrutiny of impulsive conformism instigated by autocratic control.

and are taken to a nearby lakeside location where a banquet is set up and where they have to mingle with more secret police members as the 'hosts' are finally identified. It is an absurd situation which leads to a wide range of reactions among the friends. The film's set-up provides an excellent opportunity to study the disoriented reactions of individuals in a controlled environment where no reliable hints are given of what might represent desirable behaviour. The situation is masterfully constructed and offers a perfect opportunity to scrutinise the impulsive conformism instigated by autocratic control. The pervasive sense that even breathing could constitute a misdemeanour was one that free-thinking intellectuals often lived with under state socialism. The film can be seen as an allegory of other aspects of social conformity, however, and its reading should not only be one of inherent critique of the controlling Communist regime. Even though he cautions against hasty conclusions of mutual referencing, Peter Hames (2001) notes that *The Party and the Guests* has been compared to Buñuel's surrealist masterpieces *El Ángel Exterminador/The Exterminating Angel* (1962) and *Le charme discret de la bourgeoisie/The Discreet Charm of the Bourgeoisie* (1972), both black comedies challenging the absurdity of social confines and priggish compliance.

The other 'absurdist' masterpiece of the Czechoslovak New Wave, Kachyňa's *The Ear* is a satire of an ambitious Party official who has recently moved up to Prague from provincial Olomouc. Returning from an official function late one night to the residential villa to which he is assigned, he and his wife discover that their keys have disappeared, the electricity has been disconnected and a suspicious car is parked nearby. Once they manage to get themselves inside and start moving in the dark they realise that the house is bugged; its shadowy candle-lit claustrophobic interiors take on absurd Kafkaesque dimensions. They realise how vulnerable they are; their anxiety is enhanced by flashbacks to scenes from the party earlier that night during which they are informed in whispers of the 'removal' of the husband's immediate superior. In the house, the husband hastily tries to get rid of some documents by stuffing them into the toilet bowl. The wife's bickering and accusations of opportunism lead to an outburst of domestic abuse. Expecting that he will be taken into custody at any moment, they are terrified by a ring at the door and cannot relax even after they realise it is just a group of drunken friends bringing back their lost keys. In the morning the husband prepares for his arrest, but a phone call informs him that he has been appointed to take over the Ministry. It is a political context, then, in which promotion and arrest are equally likely developments.

The Ear is a classic study of paranoia triggered by social insecurity. By far surpassing the concrete Eastern Bloc targets of its critique, it remains one of the best cinematic texts on the psychological effect that the torment of Big Brother-type surveillance has on people.

The Prague Spring was short-lived, brought to an abrupt end with the brutal Soviet-led intervention in August 1968. In the aftermath of these events, during the so-called 'Normalisation' process, many of the Czech and Slovak New Wave films made around the mid-1960s and thereafter were banned as particularly subversive, even though, as noted, their main strength was laughter over pragmatism and social clumsiness. Some of the New Wave directors emigrated (Forman, Passer, Němec, Jasný), and those who stayed had difficult careers ahead.[13] Some of those who stayed (Menzel, Kachyňa, Jakubisko) managed to make seriously dissident films that, though not released at the time, had a significant impact later on; many of the Czechoslovak New Wave directors became involved with dissident organisations like Charter 77 and other civil initiatives.

Village Life: Patriarchy in Crisis

The relationship between the urban (associated with modernity) and the rural (associated with patriarchy) as two quintessentially different lifestyles in constant tension has generally been explored in the context of the discourse on modernity. While industrial development in the region under discussion led to the growth of cities, villages and small towns continued existing as a parallel (albeit ailing) mode of communal organisation. Consequently, film-makers' interest in village life persisted. One could see numerous films that represented the village as an idyllic sphere where community life is sweetly preserved but also films that offered serious critique of the stubborn residues of a paternalistic system. There were also films dealing with the difficult years of the village during and after the wars and with the period of forced collectivisation in the 1950s. Other 'village' films scrutinised the incompetent administration of state socialism that led to the destruction of many positive features of traditional life. Industrial growth in the 1960s and 1970s had led to the desertion of villages and to massive village-city migrations that were explored in the so-called 'migration' films. Last but not least, some of the most interesting films presented the village as a bewildering and self-contained parallel world, without many communicative exchanges with the outside.

The latent tensions between city and village have been a source of ongoing interest for film-makers. One of the best examples of such interest is Wajda's *Wesele/Wedding* (1972), an adaptation of Stanisław Wyspiański's classic play that works as a treatise on the relationship between peasant folk, nobility and urban dwellers, directly subverting the traditional class structure and setting the stage for new social tensions. Set at the turn of the century, the plot revolves around the provocative decision of a radical intellectual who ventures into marrying a village girl. Further variations of the complex relations between allegedly sophisticated city folks and idyll-loving rural inhabitants can be seen in Wajda's *Brzezina/The Birch Wood* (1970, based on Jarosław Iwaszkiewicz) and in Zanussi's *Życie rodzinne/Family Life* (1971). Even though these two films differ in plotline and setting, in both an intellectual urbanite is forced to make tough choices between urban and rural values, once again problematising the underlying tensions between village and city cultures. (Coincidentally, the lead roles in all three films is played by Daniel Olbrychski.)[14]

Figure 24: Daniel Olbrychski in Wajda's *Wedding* (1972).

The heritage aspect of village life has been a permanent subject for film-making in the region, with works such as Jan Rybkowski's adaptation of Władysław Reymont's *Chłopi/The Peasants* (1973), an epic of village life in nineteenth-century Poland. However, there have also been films exploring the severity of patriarchal society, as seen in the Hungarian *Árvácska/Nobody's Daughter* (1976), directed by László Ranódy and based on the novel by Zsigmond Móricz. It is a film of striking contemporary resonance, chronicling the mistreatment of a seven-year-old orphan girl who suffers physical and mental abuse and denigration in a string of foster homes.

Only a revised inclusive picture of European cinema of the 1970s could pay adequate tribute to these films by making sure that they are recognised as equally important as the much better-known Italian works on village patriarchy such as *Padre Padrone* (Paolo and Vittorio Taviani, 1977) and *L'albero degli zoccoli/The Tree of Wooden Clogs* (Ermanno Olmi, 1978).

Even earlier, though, East Central European film had explored tensions at the crossroads between patriarchy and the socialist rush for collectivisation of agriculture. Set against the backdrop of rural Hungarian life after the Second World War and featuring traditional country fairs and folk dances, Zoltán Fábri's *Körhinta/Merry-Go-Round* (1955) tells a lyrical love story of star-crossed lovers who want to marry against the will of the girl's land-owner father. A breakthrough indictment of patriarchy, *Körhinta* was among the first films that looked into the controversial years of collectivisation, a period also featured in Ferenc Kósa's *Tízezer nap/Ten Thousand Suns* (1965) and revisited by Fábri in his *Twenty Hours*. Later, Hungarian film continued using the village setting as a backdrop for exposing the overwhelming bureaucracy that plagued state socialist (mis)management of the village, as seen in well-known political satires such as Peter Bacsó's *The Witness* and László Vitézy's *Vörös föld/Red Earth* (1982).

One of the most important village films of this category is the highly personal *Všichni dobří rodáci/All My Good Countrymen* (1968), for which the Czechoslovak New Wave director Vojtěch Jasný won the best director award at the Cannes Film Festival. Taking place in a Moravian village between 1945 and the late 1950s, the film tracks down the complex changes in the relations between the villagers as shaped by Communist intrusion on their small, close community. Aside from being a multi-faceted portrayal of the difficult period of coerced collectivisation and the concurrent moral degradation, *All My Good Countrymen* is also a rich and psychologically satisfying film about free will, ethical choices, betrayals and revenge, uneasy loves and friendships, guilt and repentance, faith and superstition. Zoltán Fábri's *Hungarians* (1978), a village saga set earlier (at the time of World War Two), is similarly structured and, little wonder, focuses on remarkably similar visuals: fields and forests, women and men in black against a background of whitewashed walls of village homes and churches. Once again, it revolves around a close-knit community of extended village families whose lives are affected by the adverse experiences of volatile and violent politics and war.

In some of the other village films, the stress remained on the mutually empowering co-existence within the community where everybody knows everybody else and where people are inclined to turn a blind eye to the little oddities of their neighbours. These are films displaying special appreciation of the disappearing small-town universe as a community where traditions are nurtured, where patriarchy is often intact, where reputation easily falls prey to ill-intended gossip, and where hard labour is everyday reality. These collective portrayals of charming (but now lost) communal life in small towns and villages sometimes relied on idealised representation: this is the case, for example, in the strikingly beautiful and highly stylistically crafted but excessively idealised *Perła w koronie/Pearl in the Crown* (1972) by Kazimierz Kutz. Though very different in tone, Jiří Menzel's endearing *Vesničko má středisková/My Sweet Little Village* (1985) also belongs in this category.

Cities in East Central Europe are generally small, a fact of particular importance which accounts for the specific provincial mentality and gossipy view of life that is depicted so well in the films of the Czechoslovak New Wave. Very different from the urban culture in the West, towns in East Central Europe were habitually unfamiliar with the checkered mappings of the urban territory through class and function, with its divison of inner-city problem at the core encircled by rich and poor suburbs. The reality of city life in East Central Europe is of a small town with a 'petit bourgeois' feel and a high street where people go to stroll after early dinner. It is not possible to understand Czechoslovak New Wave cinema without taking this provincial mentality into account.[15]

It may be easier to place the 'village' films in a wider European context by using another classification of 'village' plots and distinguish between those 'migration' films that feature the escape from the village towards the city from those that revolve around 'back to nature' plots of return to tradition and family roots. The 1970s saw many of the first type, with films chronicling the gradual desertion of villages and the migration of younger people towards the cities.[16] Plots that presented village life as a solution to the pressures of urban life continued to be popular throughout the 1990s.[17]

There are also those deeply pessimistic yet remarkable films that depicted the village as an isolated and bleak parallel sphere. One such piece was Slovak Dušan Hanák's *Obrazy starého sveta/Pictures of the Old World* (1972, but not shown until 1988). An avant-garde documentary shot in black-and-white and making extensive use of stop-motion photography, the film chronicles the daily lives of lone elderly villagers discussing in a series of interviews issues that vary from domestic animals to astronaut Yuri Gagarin and space travel. Young people have deserted the village but the peasants who are left behind compensate for the loss of tradition in society with youthful spirits and a good sense of humour, showing they are quite conscious of the maverick position they occupy between tradition and modernity.

At the other extreme, presenting the village as a desolate territory diametrically opposed to any enlightenment, the Hungarian director Béla Tarr radically subverts popular idyllic concepts of the rural. The village in his 450-minute black-and-white *Sátántangó/Satan's Tango* (1994) is a terrain that consists of crumbling walls and muddy roads scattered with cowpats. Tarr shows a depressed community whose alienated inhabitants are forced into unwanted togetherness, which carries over into a routine of drunken copulations and brutality. It is a depressing picture but also unforgettable viewing, a challenging statement on the human condition.

Romanies: Little-known Neighbours

Ethnically, linguistically and religiously diverse, East Central Europe is inhabited by various minority groups. Slavic-speaking Serbs live in East Germany, Hungarians inhabit Romania, Slovakia and Serbia, there are Ukrainians in Poland, and so on. The history of these groups' interactions with the main ethnicity, however, has not always been easy and the relationship between various ethnic groups in the region has been characterised by latent suppressed tensions. Distrust of the 'other' has regularly been stronger than tolerance, and in many cases groups have co-existed without really interacting, constantly suspicious of each other and often unable to overcome long-standing prejudices about a 'foreign' group, even if its members may have inhabited the region for as long as the 'locals'. Sometimes the dominant ethnic group, seeing itself as marginalised and oppressed within a wider European context, has held minorities responsible for various difficulties (as seen in the periodic resurgence of anti-Semitism, for example).

Cinema has usually been interested in exploring instances of potentially (or actually) adverse relationships between ethnic groups. Traditionally exploring the most important minorities of the region, the Jews and the Gypsies (Romanies), film-makers have displayed a different approach to the representation of each of these groups. The cinematic exploration of the Jews, both in feature and documentary film-making, is mostly linked to the Holocaust experience, and only a few films have looked into the authentic culture of the group. Whenever they have, it has been within the considerate but limited framework of doomed and mistreated people.[18]

This is not the case with the Romanies. Rather than being given the chance to portray themselves, the Romany people have routinely been depicted by others. And while there may be many films featuring Romanies, only a small number of those explore the troubled relationships between the dominant ethnic group and the minority. Such is the case, for example, with two of the subplots of Jiří Menzel's *Skylarks on a String* (1969), one featuring the playful wedding of a young Czech policeman to an untamed Gypsy bride, the other presenting the extremely problematic case of paedophilic abuse of a Romani teenage girl perpetrated by a city official and mutely endured by her family.

Only in select cases is the impeded mechanics of inter-ethnic interaction the centre of attention, and as a rule these are films that look into the limited sphere of singular personal relationships (suggesting that those are not the norm but a deviation). A version of inter-racial romance narratives, these features usually rely on a story that revolves around a pure and spontaneous liaison between a Romani girl and a boy from the dominant ethnic group (or vice versa) whose relationship quickly gains mainstream disapproval and comes under attack.

Out of many examples, for our puroposes here we will focus at one, Dušan Hanák's *Ružové sny/Rose-Tinted Dreams* (1976). The story is about the tender love affair between Jakub and Jolanka, a nineteen-year-old village postman and a young working Romani girl from Slovakia. They often take off to the forest on his bike for long romantic afternoons, and easily earn the disapproval of the Slovak villagers, the boy's parents and her fellow Romanies, who do not want a Romani woman mixing with a *Gadjo* ('foreigner' or non-Romany). After a series of bittersweet and endearing episodes between the lovers, Jakub is challenged to defend his love and beaten up. The couple are forced to escape to the city where they soon grow tired of resisting the disapproval they encounter at every turn and where the first cracks in their relationship appear. Jakub gradually succumbs to stereotypical views of the Gypsies; he is passive and cannot decide to commit to Jolanka at a moment when she is under pressure to marry one of her own (to which she eventually consents).

In an everyday tragedy these romantic lovers will part, each one of them suffering quietly and preserving the tender dream-like memory of kisses and hugs in a sunny forest meadow. The clash of the communities that co-exist in self-imposed isolation, the unspoken but pervasive intolerance, the prejudice of the Slovaks and the stubborn dignity of the Romanies are all depicted with the subtle tender attitude inherited from the Czechoslovak New Wave.[19]

The significant cinematic interest in the Romanies has repeatedly raised questions of authenticity versus stylisation and of patronising and exoticising. Even when genuinely concerned with the Romani predicament, film-makers have exploited the visual richness of their excitingly non-conventional lifestyles. Often allowing for spectacularly beautiful magical-realist visuals, the films featuring Romani have used recurring narrative tropes. Virtually every 'Gypsy' film from the region has relied on at least several of these motifs: passionate and self-destructive infatuations (often accompanied by suitably passionate Gypsy music); 'feast in time of plague' attitude (visually enhanced by scenes of dancing); astonishingly mature and strong-willed street-wise (often teenage) protagonists; complex patriarchal power structures within extended families; mistrust of outsiders; coerced urbanisation, forced integration and imposed conversion away from semi-nomadic lifestyles. Combined in one, the rough realism and the excessive exoticism seen in a range of films, the cinematic celebrations of freewheeling Romanies are best understood if considered in the context of the broader preoccupation with marginality that has traditionally been a concern within East European film.[20]

The Cinema of Moral Concern

The cinema of moral concern, yet another important current within East Central European film, is usually associated with the names of Polish film-makers – Zanussi, Wajda, Holland, Kieślowski, Falk. If one looks more closely, however, one can find similar trends in the cinemas of most countries in the region from the 1970s and the first half of the 1980s.[21]

These were the autumn years of state socialism, 'unlovable but livable', as some have aptly described what others have termed 'goulash communism'. The promised prosperity had not materialised. No drastic changes of any sort were expected, and it was difficult not to slip into conformism unless one chose to become a dissident. The routines of this 'normalised' environment of stagnated socialism brought about indifference and moral insecurity. In Poland, there was a growing social discontent, particularly over the worker's prosperity that was promised but never materialised. The strong workers' movement entered a unique interaction with the intelligentsia that took the shape of the trade union Solidarity. Several turbulent years of strikes and showdowns with the government forces led to the 1981 imposition of martial law, which lasted until 1985 and was ultimately the main symptom for the general weakness of the system of state socialism.[22] The cracks in the system were growing deeper and the cinema of moral concern played an important role in all this.[23]

The unease about obscured moral sensitivity had become an overwhelming preoccupation for film-makers in East Central Europe. Particularly worried about the adjustment of state socialism to the rules of controlled consumerism, they began making films that revealed a depressing reality governed by elaborate bureaucratic machinery. The cinema of moral anxiety did not reveal a system of sinister political machinations (like that exposed in the context of New German Cinema by directors like Fassbinder, von Trotta and Kluge) nor a panorama of corruption and Mafia-perpetrated and politicians-protected violence of the kind seen in films made in various parts of Western Europe around the same time (for example the Italian cinema of Francesco Rosi or Damiano Damiani). The moral anxiety did not engage in direct political critique, yet the screen images of dull routines it relied upon carried encoded dissent that was equally powerful. Film-making became an oppositional activity, as it exposed the crisis of the regime by showing the stagnating lives of small people. In these films, the protagonists' existences are bogged down by petty squabbles at work and the struggle to acquire the means to afford a one-bedroom apartment or a used Trabant or Fiat Polski.

Krzysztof Zanussi's 1970s work is probably the most typical of 'the cinema of moral concern', consisting of films on contemporary themes, mostly shot on a low budget and often with a cast that segued from one film into another. The focus was on issues such as the difficult reconciliation of career success and durable friendships (*Struktura kryształu/The Structure of Crystals*, 1969), the conflict between modern and patriarchal, independence and family commitment (*Życie rodzinne/Family Life*, 1971), the identity quest leading to conscious acceptance of responsibilities (*Iluminacja/Illumination*, 1973), the mid-life crisis (*Bilans kwartalny/Quarterly Balance*, 1974), and trauma and loss (*Constans/The Constant Factor*, 1980).[24] By the end of the 1970s, Zanussi's view was becoming more and more politically pointed, which is particularly evident in his films that take a critical stance on conformity and moral compromise such as *Barwy ochronne/Camouflage* (1977) and *Kontrakt/Contract* (1980).

All films of the 'moral concern' cycle focused on problems arising at the intersection of personal interest and socio-political demands. The stress was usually on the personal and particularly on the moral dilemmas that came along with the need to correlate the individual interest with the social one. A commonly shared view among the film-makers of this time was that no moral-ity existed independently from a given historical time and space. Thus the political context had an important role to play, ultimately as the common trig-ger for most of the moral dilemmas played out in the films. The subtle (though sometimes overt) tensions between personal and political took central stage in films such as Wajda's *Man of Marble*, *Dyrygent/The Conductor* (1979), *Bez znieczulenia/Rough Treatment* (1979), and *Man of Iron* where the stifling politi-cal environment was identified as the main factor which defined the personal choices of the protagonists, be it in regard to love affairs, marriage, divorce and even suicide.

Since 1989, along with the disappearance of the immediate social issues addressed by the cinema of moral concern, there is a dangerous tendency to overlook these films and to play down their importance. They should not be seen, however, just as a semi-forgotten chronicle of the 'grey' times of state social-ism. They represent one of the most important periods in East Central European film and contain elements that, having undergone certain modifications and adjustments, significantly influenced contemporary European cinema.

This is well illustrated by the career of a film-maker such as Krzysztof Kieślowski.[25] He began as a Zanussi epigone and until the mid-1980s was one of the several representatives of the cinema of moral concern (along with Holland, Falk and Kijowski) but then went on to become one of the most widely acclaimed Polish film-makers and by far surpassed the popularity of his mentor, thus giving the cinema of moral concern a powerful continuation on a higher level.

Following his start in documentaries in the early 1970s, Kieślowski made several features that can be described as typical representatives of the 'moral concern' cycle: filmed in the vein of documentary realism, dealing with everyday issues and displaying explicit political commitment. His debut feature *Blizna/Scar* (1976) chronicled the attempts of a small-town community to resist an unwanted industrial development and prevent a feared ecological disaster. The film foregrounded the moral drama of its protagonist, an executive who, after extenisve litanies, forfeits the prospects of personal advancement for the sake of the higher common good. In its message, *The Scar* was in many respects reminiscent of the tone and the work ethic concerns of the enormously popular 1974 Soviet drama *Premiya/Bonus*.

Amator/Camera Buff (1979) was a fine psychological study of the manipulation of an individual, once again replaying leading themes of the 'moral concern' strand, such as conformity and compromise. The film, featuring director Zanussi in a cameo role, tells the story of an innocuous working-class amateur film-maker (the remarkable Jerzy Stuhr) who is at first encouraged by the management to film scenes at his place of work but soon thereafter realises that he has filmed certain scenes that are not to the management's liking. Having created an accidental record, he soon becomes a nuisance to those who would prefer the instances of mismanagement to remain undocumented. In many respects, the situation is reminiscent to the set-up of Antonioni's

Figure 25: Jerzy Stuhr as the innocuous amateur film-maker in Kieślowski's *Camera Buff* (1979).

Blowup/Blow-Up (1966) where an inadvertent photograph triggers a whole series of adverse events, yet the message here is more politicised and should be viewed as a continuation of the concern over the socio-historical dimension of documentation and witnessing as seen in Wajda's *Man of Marble*.

Przypadek/Blind Chance (1981) had an original narrative structure that revolved around three equally plausible and yet irreconcilable imaginary scenarios of the life of a single protagonist (Bogusław Linda). With emphsasis on the political, the central tenet of the film was that it takes very little (such as an accident or a chance encounter) to completely alter the course of life, to become either a political dissident or a conformist Communist functionary. Beginning with the same event (running after a train that is leaving the station), each one of the three different versions of the protagonist's life led to the same ending (the protagonist dies in an airplane crash), thus questioning the existence of 'fate'. *Blind Chance* is said to have inspired some more recent and more personally focused films such as Peter Howitt's *Sliding Doors* (1998) or Tom Tykwer's *Lola rennt/Run Lola Run* (1998).

Bez konca/No End (1985) dealt with trauma and mourning and depicted the depressing reality of political harassment and a corrupt judicial system. Set during the martial law period, the film's plot follows a young recently widowed woman (Grazyna Szapolowska). Her dead husband's ghost claims a durable presence in her everyday life, while she tries to go on fighting a political case the husband could not complete. It is a film about grief and coming to terms with life after loss which extended the narrative premise of the classic Brazilian adaptation of Jorge Amado's *Doña Flor e seus dois maridos/Doña Flor and Her Two Husbands* (1976) and can be seen as a predecessor of other well-known films on mourning such as *Ghost* (1990) and *Truly, Madly, Deeply* (1991) as well as the more recent French *Ponette* (1996) and *Sous le sable/Under the Sand* (2000). Compared to all these deeply personal films, however, *No End* has a much stronger engagement with a difficult socio-political environment, in this case that of Poland under martial law. Kieślowski subsequently returned to the theme of mourning and loss in his *Three Colours: Blue*; remaining engaged with social concerns (in this case Europe's unification) but on a lesser scale, his focus primarily on the personal.

Around the mid-1980s, Kieślowski claimed he had begun to grow tired of being a politically committed director. The moral choices that the individual faced in the context of resisting Communism, Kieślowski explained in later interviews, were somehow too simple (see Stok 1993). He felt he was growing more interested in general existential issues that were located beyond the limiting scope of politics.

It was with *No End* that Kieślowski started to move away from concerns with the overwhelming bureaucratic routines of state socialism and chose to focus instead on aspects of destiny, transcendence and reincarnation. There were two important factors that made *No End* the film that marked the beginning of the director's metamorphosis. This was the first film co-scripted by Krzysztof Piesiewicz who then became Kieślowski's permanent writing collaborator (both were credited with the scripts for *Dekalog/The Decalogue*, 1988; *La double vie de Véronique/The Double Life of Veronique*, 1992; *Three Colours: Blue, White, Red*, 1993/1994/1994). It was also the first film that, alongside documentary realism and political conflict, featured a transcendental trope – the continuous presence of the dead husband's ghost in the life of the protagonist.

By the time he worked on his made-for-television series *The Decalogue* (1987–88), Kieślowski had lived through a period of self-reflexive appraisal and had transformed himself from a film-maker preoccupied with socialist politics into one concerned with universal ethics. He had come to realise that the problems faced by people trapped in state socialism did not profoundly differ from the more general moral questions he had sensed when travelling in the West. With life opening up for people in East Central Europe, it was possible to see that in both the East and the West people could be equally trapped in the anxieties of everyday living and distressed survival. Wajda's view that people on both sides had different concerns no longer seemed to hold true for Kieślowski. In his own words:

> I'd already started to travel abroad a bit by this time, and observed a general uncertainty in the world at large. I'm not even thinking about politics here but about ordinary, everyday life. I sensed mutual indifference behind polite smiles and had the overwhelming impression that, more and more frequently, I was watching people who didn't really know why they were living. (in Stok 1993: 143)

So Kieślowski began making films with a more universal message that reached out further than the direct social criticism of his earlier work. Stylistically his films also changed and he started paying more elaborate attention to music, colour and camera angles.

The Decalogue was the first manifestation of this transformation. Still set in a grey Warsaw housing estate,[26] the series dealt with issues of God's will and wrath, of right and wrong, of illness, loneliness, betrayal, rudeness, mid-life crisis, life and death. The two best known parts of *The Decalogue*, five and six, were also released in independent screen versions. The austere plot of *Dekalog 5: Krótki film o zabijaniu/A Short Film About Killing* (1988) tells the story of a troubled protagonist who plans and cold-bloodedly executes a meaningless murder of a randomly picked victim; he strangles a taxi driver. We never fully understand the exact reason for the killing, although it is suggested that it may be connected to an unrelated deep psychological trauma that the young murderer suffered. He is apprehended, tried, sentenced to death and executed. Shot with a yellowish lens that slightly distorts the perspective, and told from the point of view of the novice lawyer who is appointed to defend this clear-cut case, it is a film that raises serious doubts about the effectiveness of capital punishment without being gratuitously lenient to the perpetrator of the gruesome crime.

A timeless treatise on the issue of capital punishment *A Short Film About Killing* delivers, together with Gianni Amelio's *Porte aperte/Open Doors* (1990), one of the strongest cinematic arguments against the death penalty. The seven-minute violent scene of the killing is juxtaposed to the equally violent scene of the lawfully sanctioned execution. Watching the details of the murder is painful but so is observing the preparations for the carefully organised execution; both are presented as everyday activities in the business of killing people and disposing of their bodies. It is not reduced to an indictment of a particular political system; the issues are universal.

Equally acclaimed at the time but of lesser importance now (particularly because some of its central motifs were recycled in the director's later work) *Dekalog 6: Krótki film o miłości/A Short Film About Love* (1988) tells of a voyeuristic loner who grows possessed with his free-spirited neighbour (Grazyna Szapolowska) and obsessively follows her life in the apartment building opposite his through a telescope. Developing motifs of such classics of 'voyeurist' cinema as Hitchcock's *Rear Window* (1954) and Michael Powell's *Peeping Tom* (1960), yet closest in spirit to Patrice Leconte's atmospheric *Monsieur Hire* (1989), the film revolves around troubled communication and a subtle power struggle; it is no wonder then that it all ends in bitter confrontation. Like *A Short Film About Killing*, this much-admired part of *The Decalogue* is, once again, a study of universal issues of alienation and the boundaries of privacy.

In the early 1990s, Kieślowski began to make films that were financed internationally, with the backing of French producer Marin Karmitz who pulled together funding from various French sources, and distributed successfully by companies such as Artificial Eye in the UK and Miramax in the US. In these films, Kieślowski departed even further from the documentary realism of the cinema of moral concern in his quest to explore existential and universal themes. In *The Double Life of Veronique* he explores rebirth, premonitory signs and transcendental affinities. In the films of the *Three Colours* trilogy he continued developing the themes of *The Decalogue* and focused on fearful, uncertain and lonely post-traumatic recovery (*Blue*), existential tensions of double-crossing schemes and personal revenge (*White*), and attractions ruled by providence (*Red*). While the plots of *The Double Life of Veronique* and *Three Colours: White* were still linked with concrete social processes taking place in Poland, the other films reflected the concerns of people in Europe at large. The protagonists of these films lived in a state of moral unease and not because of overwhelming social demands or externally imposed limitations on their creativity. The director emancipated himself from the dominant materialist view, so his protagonists were no longer reacting to the immediate triggers of their concrete social surroundings. Now he let them be led by the immaterial will of a superior being.[27]

Figure 26: Krzysztof Kieślowski: his transcendental and philosophical stance influenced the direction of European cinema in the 1990s.

Unlike the typical 'moral concern' directors who continued making films that responded to immediate political events, Kieślowski went one step further and rejected politics in his own way by becoming the ultimate 'apolitical' director. Like the 'moral concern' directors, he initially subscribed to the view according to which social context defined people's subjectivity and behaviour. Now, however, he no longer wanted to see the individual as an endlessly malleable entity, mirroring society and politics.

Kieślowski had made his most daring political films at home, in the face of Polish censorship, but only gained international visibility after he started working in France, recycling motifs found in his early work and receiving wide exposure and acclaim. Looking in retrospect at the process of Kieślowski's 'emancipation,' Andrzej Wajda made an important observation that gives us a clue to understanding Kieślowski's success:

> During the slow collapse of communism, when other artists and film-makers in Eastern Europe were struggling, Kieślowski was the first to look beyond the immediate horizon. [...] When we were lost and confused during martial law, he alone knew which path to follow. [...] Most of our films were in one way or another political. We were trying to relate to society and history. He chose a different way – a psychological, meta-physical way – of dealing with contemporary life. (in Macnab 2002: 6)

In further attempting to identify the winning ingredients in Kieślowski's film-making recipe, Derek Malcolm pointed to 'his ability to transcend naturalism and push inwards towards the metaphysical' (2002: 18). Back in the 1960s, Antonioni had influenced East Central European film-makers in their move to be 'apolitical'; in the 1990s Kieślowski's transcendental and philosophical stance was to greatly influence the direction of European cinema.

PART THREE

FILMS AND FILM-MAKERS

OVERVIEW

The films and film-makers that have been discussed so far address the core of East Central Europe's leading cultural concerns. Yet there is a vast range of films and film-makers that have not yet been touched on, most of which belong to what are known as 'popular genres'.

Indeed, the 'popular' films have been consistently ignored and still remain neglected by scholarship today. One reason is that these genres do not fit easily into the generally accepted reputation of this region's cinema – preoccupied in the main with ethics, history and politics. International distribution and promotion also has much to do with this. The 'popular' films rarely play at film festivals and are hardly promoted internationally by national cultural centres which prefer to program 'serious' cinematic works. Unlike these 'serious' films that are believed to be the essence of East Central European film, the popular genre films are sidelined because they take different approaches and sometimes display different aesthetic concerns.

To ignore part of the cinematic legacy is to see only half the picture. First of all, here we have a significant body of surrealist works, as well as the widespread interest in magic realism, both in narrative and pictorial representation. Examples of surrealist films by Has and Jakubisko have already been discussed but there are many more that need to be considered in a concise study that would explore the phenomenon across the region rather than in the context of national traditions (as it has been done so far).[1]

A second investigation should also be launched into the range of films celebrating heritage and folklore, and the numerous adaptations of fairytales. Many of those were made for children and clearly with mass audiences in mind, yet displayed great artistic achievements. When working on these kinds of projects, directors could freely engage in experimentation with the form and could pay elaborate attention to style.[2]

A third range of 'popular' films would include the stylistically diverse area of films devoted to the artistic heritage, mostly biographies of composers, painters and writers.[3]

Yet another largely unexplored genre is science fiction.[4] The situation is also similar with films belonging to the genres of horror and erotica; while it is possible to quote some very interesting examples, they remain largely unknown.

The action-adventure genre flourished in post-Communist times, as we will see in chapter seven. Yet films of that genre were also made before 1989, and an investigation into the politics of these productions would be particularly welcome.[5] Many of these films were made for the more popular medium of television, and many were set in the context of the anti-fascist resistance during the Second World War. Further neglected genres include the enormously popular crime, mystery and spy dramas.[6]

The comedy genre also requires further exploration. Many comedies were made and released, but only a few are remembered and known beyond the boundaries of the respective countries. In all likelihood, this is because not all humour is universal. What is perceived as funny in one context may be barely understood in another, and it is not by chance that only a fraction of the numerous French, Italian or German comedy blockbusters do well internationally. Many of the Czech, Polish and Hungarian comedies were preoccupied with the mockery of communal life and the absurdities of the dysfunctional economy, often satirising the conditions that led to blossoming petty opportunism among ordinary people.[7]

It would take another book to cover all those diverse films and film-makers, and to pay adequate attention to all these neglected strands of East Central European film-making. Here we will cover only some of these genres, looking into two areas that supplement the better known historical and political dimensions of East Central European film-making. The first is the issue of women and film; the second is the generational change in post-Communist cinema.

CHAPTER SIX

Women's Cinema, Women's Concerns

Women in East Central European cinema

State socialism maintained elaborate policies designed to secure gender equality. This, however, did not significantly change the situation of women in film-making, who were traditionally marginalised and had fewer chances to become directors. Still, women were actively involved in film-making in various other capacities – as screenwriters, set and costume designers, actresses, film critics, and, occasionally, as directors of photography. Despite their limited number, female directors managed to make films addressing all the major women's concerns: restricted opportunities, abusive relationships, unwanted pregnancies, single parenthood and the glass ceiling.

The Hungarian director Márta Mészarós is probably the most productive and best-known figure among the region's women film-makers. She came to feature films after graduating from Moscow's VGIK in the mid-1950s and then pursued a career in documentaries; her feature film debut was made at the age of 37.[1] Dealing exclusively with the problems affecting women of various generations, Mészarós' filmography includes over 25 feature titles, made in Hungary, France and Canada. In traditionally low-key plotlines she tackles questions of motherhood, adoption, marriage, the generation gap and victimisation. Her fragile heroines spend many rainy afternoons inquiring about severed family ties, often returning at night to cold rooms in orphanages and dormitories; they explore the painful vulnerabilities of human sensuality, frequently through stubborn introverted struggles for love. The tensions between the imposed routine of compulsory communal settings and the individual's pensive craving for privacy involve the exploration of various social problems such as drug addiction, hidden unemployment, incest and rape. Mészarós' work also includes fine explorations of eroticism and women's sexuality, nurturing friendships, loneliness and aging. An intellectual director, whose best films are shot in black-and-white, she has often been classified as a feminist film-maker, a qualification which she rejects.

Other active women directors from Hungary are Lívia Gyarmathy, who has made films focusing on social issues and inter-ethnic relations, and Judit Elek, director of a historical drama centred on a woman (*Mária-nap/Maria's Day*, 1983) and of films exploring various dimensions of anti-Semitism (*Tutajosok/Raftsmen*, 1989; *Mondani a mondhatatlant: Elie Wiesel üzenet /To Speak the Unspeakable: The Message of Elie Wiesel*, 1996). Women-directors of the younger generation have also been active. Ildikó Enyédi first came to prominence with *Az én XX. Százado/My Twentieth Century* (1989), a black-and-white stylish feminist treatise about the interplay of history and personal fate. In the 1990s, Enyédi made several films that confirmed her as an original and innovative figure within European film-making. Ildikó Szabó has worked mostly on contemporary topics, and has shown a persistent interest in Romani-related themes or sub-themes (*Gyerekgyilkosságok/Child Murders*, 1993; *Csajok/Bitches*, 1995; *Chacho Rom*, 2001). Of this generation it is Ibolya Fekete, however, who enjoys the widest recognition beyond Hungary. A 'late bloomer', she made her first feature, *Bolse vita/Bolshe Vita*, only in 1996 at the age of 45, and her second one, *Chico*, at the age of fifty in 2001. Both received deserved international acclaim for their originality.

The leading female figure in Czech cinema is Věra Chytilová – known best for the avant-garde *Daisies*, the story of two rebellious and subversively destructive girls – who is often quoted as a classic example of a feminist film-maker, having mostly made films focusing on gender relations.[2]

Chytilová's unique approach has been variably described as 'post-modernist [...] playfulness' (Bird 2002: 1) or 'more ironic and distanced than respectful' (Radkiewicz 2002). In addition, she has been spoken about as a 'dadaist' rather than a feminist film-maker (Eagle 1991) for her extensive use of fragmented narratives, her tableaux-like settings showing naked bodies involved in beach games and surrounded by her favourite trademark backgrounds with displays of apples and cut newsprint, familiar from the time of *Daisies*. Critics have noted her radically subversive attitude to traditional ideas of gender appropriateness and have classified her as an outspoken anti-patriarchal activist. It has been difficult for male critics, in particular, to swallow some of the extreme situations

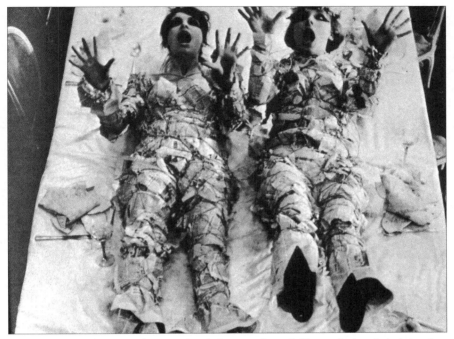

Figure 27: Chytilová's avant-garde *Daisies* (1966): the story of two rebellious and subversively destructive girls.

in her films, often showing women acting aggressively and disrespectfully towards men, as seen in her classic *Daisies* and, particularly, in the recent *Pasti, pasti, pastičky/ Traps* (1998).[3]

Two other women of Chytilová's generation need to be mentioned here. Screenwriter Ester Krumbachová, one of the most important figures of the Czechoslovak New Wave, wrote scripts for many of the prominent avant-garde and surrealist features.[4] Director Drahomíra Vihanová routinely suffered censorship problems, and even though she had made her debut in the 1960s, she was only able to work again in the 1990s (Slovak documentary film-maker Kamila Kytková had very similar experiences). A member of the next generation, Zuzana Zemanová has made several features in the 1990s. Working in the comedy genre, young director Alice Nellis proved to be as good as her male counterparts in delivering the subtle Czech humour with her *Ene bene/ Eeny Meeny* (2000). Slovak director Eva Borušovičová also belongs to this younger generation.

Holocaust survivor Wanda Jakubowska was the female doyen of Polish film-making. Her best-known film is *The Last Stage* (1948), a personal account of women's lives in concentration camps, one of the earliest Holocaust films to be internationally acclaimed and distributed. Even though most of Jakubowska's work is closely associated with the clichés of the Socialist Realist paradigm, the interest in her work was recently revived and her films were featured at many international film festivals throughout the 1990s.[5] Ewa Petelska often worked in tandem with her husband, Czesław Petelski, and directed many historical features. Other important women directors in Polish cinema include Barbara Sass, director of *Bez miłości/Without Love* (1980), *Debiutantka/The Debutante* (1982) and *Dziewczęta z Nowolipek/The Girls of Nowolipki* (1985) and the younger Magdalena Łazarkiewicz, director of *Przez dotyk/By Touch* (1985) and the adolescent drama *Ostatni dzwonek/The Last School Bell* (1989). Both have displayed a continuous commitment to making films about women, and their works are particularly interesting within the socio-political context of the 1980s.

The career of Pole Agnieszka Holland, who has been working predominantly in the West since the late 1980s, is a story of talent and ambition led by the imperatives of success. In Poland, she directed some remarkable films of the 'moral concern' strand, and a key subversive feature exposing the moral faults of Communist ideology (*Fever*, 1981). She was also active in screenwriting (having worked on Wajda's *Rough Treatment* (1979) and *Korczak* (1990), and on Kieślowski's *Three Colours: Blue*) and in acting (in Bugajski's *The Interrogation*, 1981, for instance). Her early work presented sensitive female protagonists (for example in *A Woman Alone*, 1981) but the director

Figure 28: Wanda Jakubowska's *The Last Stage* (1948): a survivor's account of women's lives in a concentration camp.

did not pursue the representation of women as a special interest, even though she created fine female portraits in her German *Angry Harvest* and American *Washington Square* (1997). After emigration, Holland continued working very actively; her career is an example of overcoming unfavorable marginalisation through exceptional motivation, hard work and talent. [6]

The work of Dorota Kędzierzawska including *Devils, Devils, Wrony/Crows* (1995) and *Nic/Nothing* (1998) has enjoyed a considerable international acclaim. Most recently, the names of younger female directors have been in the focus of attention, such as Urszula Urbaniak (*Torowisko/The Junction*, 1999) and actress-turned-director Krystyna Janda (*Pestka/The Pip*, 1995).

Reluctant Feminists

Film-making by women represents a different kind of sensitivity. If you interpret my films as strictly political, you will see that I approach power relations differently from the way they are portrayed by male directors. Not because my films are necessarily better, or theirs worse, but because they are different. [...] What I want to work for is to help women become conscious of their being, the essence of their womanhood: this is what I want to express in my films, to make them aware of their own female personalities. (Márta Mészáros, in Portuges 1993: 130–1; 133)

Although these statements, as well as her entire oeuvre, appear to conform to feminist thinking, Márta Mészáros has vigorously refuted the 'feminist' label and repeatedly insisted she is not a feminist (see interviews with Portuges 1993). Similarly, other leading female directors from the region have distanced themselves from 'feminism', a situation that leaves us facing the curious phenomenon of clearly committed feminist film-makers who are nonetheless reluctant to be seen as such.

These women's dissociation from what was publicly believed to be 'feminist causes' deserves special consideration. The reluctance appears to be a reaction to the somewhat aggressive importation of Western feminism in the immediate aftermath of 1989. Feminist ideology explained most women's problems with the male-dominated patriarchal culture. Under state socialism, however, both men and women shared common problems; they were both on one side, facing the same 'enemy' embodied by the adverse social system, which was proving insensitive to the needs of the individual, was disrespectful to privacy and thus regularly destroying people's intimate relationships. Placing the emphasis on men as representatives of patriarchy would inappropriately divert the attention of film-makers from where they believed the focus of their critical attention should be (on concrete social issues, and not on abstract patriarchy) and would unnecessarily add another tension (between men and women). It was the unspoken consensus that it was not patriarchy but the social system that was ultimately to blame. Hence, even though much of the film-making by women in the region would undoubtedly qualify as 'feminist', female directors have often publicly dissociated themselves from what feminism was perceived to be.

In addition, women intellectuals were sceptical about uncritically adopting the categories of a discourse that had developed in a different social setting. According to feminist author Slavenka Drakulić (1991: 123–33), for example, Western feminist critiques tended to impose a ready-made template over a reality that did not easily fit into the framework they could offer. The problems of East European women, emerging from behind the Iron Curtain, she insisted, were not identical to those of women in the West, and the differences needed to be accounted for. While Western feminism was more worried about domestic violence, abuse, rape and the glass ceiling, the leading concerns in the former Eastern Bloc were the legacy of state socialism and the manipulation of women's voices within the public sphere. In the aftermath of Communism women's exclusion from public life was rapidly defining a new range of problems specific to the area: growing unemployment, loss of social benefits, and closure of women-focused social programmes (Funk 1993). It was in order to recognise these specific needs that many outspoken women from the region displayed reluctance to the imported 'feminist' cause that appeared rooted in a different set of problems.

In a move typical of this attitude, Chytilová has dismissed journalists' questions on the issue of her feminism as 'pointless and primitive' (Connolly 2000: 3). Evidently, even though her work clearly belongs to the feminist strand, the director did not want to be regarded as blindly committed to any identifiable feminist cause. Indeed, her 'feminism' could be seen as more complex than a simple engagement with the political causes of the day; it is a feminism found more in images than in spoken words. Still, she has never really cared to articulately explain where she stands on these issues.

Yet another variation of the reserved stance on feminism that East Central European female film-makers have taken is the one of Hungarian Ibolya Fekete. When asked why she prefers to focus on men in her films, she said:

> Normally, the female film used to be concerned with the so-called 'female issues'. I was accused of not being a real woman because I wasn't dealing with these things. [...] I understand women, what they do and why they do it. But I don't really know why men are doing what they are doing. What is their motivation for acting that way? (Clark & Federlein 2002)

It is true that in her films Fekete has focused on men rather than women, and she is quite articulate on the reasons why this is the case. A truly liberated female film-maker should not need to limit herself to the women's domain, especially if men appear to her a more challenging and interesting territory. Women are surely as capable of creating fine cinematic portrayals of men as male directors, and male directors have created female portrayals for decades; so why wouldn't women venture in exploring men's experiences and concerns?

Ultimately, however, the issue of 'reluctant feminism' remains unresolved, at least for the time being. It was Anikó Imre who brought to my attention a further dimension to this issue which may indeed contain useful clues for extending this investigation. In considering the fact that it is certainly problematic to assert that Márta Mészarós or Věra Chytilová are feminist given their explicit insistence to the contrary, Imre maintained that we need to keep in mind that the very concept of 'feminism' means very many different things for different constituencies at different historical moments. On the one hand, a certain consensus about 'feminism's' meaning is always taken for granted: these film-makers are feminist because they provide sensitive portrayals of female characters and typical women's troubles. On the other hand, Imre noted, these directors' refusal of the 'feminist' label should not be seen as the result of a simplistic, demonised understanding of a limited, liberal-activist feminism. Another possible explanation would be that it is also be the result of these female directors' implication, whether acknowledged or not, in an oppressive patriarchal-nationalist social reality. And indeed, it is more often than not that some of the female representations and the representations by female directors that we analyze here turn out to be allegories of specifically masculine themes and causes, thus suggesting unspoken endorsement of nationalist patriarchal causes (as seen in the excessive use of the mother figure as nation-symbol, for example).[7] Indeed, it may well be that the need for thinking East Central European cinema 'outside' of the boundaries of Europe, Imre noted, is felt most clearly in the discussion of this 'reluctant feminism' issue and the corresponding investigation of representations of various feminine themes. This is especially evident in those instances where female and feminine representations are radically cut off from any sort of budding consciousness, and are most often appropriated in the service of the national cause.[8]

When investigating these issues, we need to bear in mind that some of the finest portrayals of women in East Central European cinema have come from male directors who, in most cases, are not explicitly concerned with feminist ideology and who, furthermore, often use female images as allegories of the respective nation. In Hungary, for example, they are found in the work of directors such as Károly Makk (for example *Macskajáték/Cat's Play*, 1974 and *Egymásra nézve/Another Way*, 1982), Péter Gothár (*Ajándék ez a nap/A Priceless Day*, 1979), or János Rózsa (*Vasárnapi szülők/Sunday Daughters*, 1979), and in Poland in the early work of Krzysztof Zanussi (*Quarterly Balance*, 1975). This discussion will examine the way cinema in the region has presented women's concerns by using examples not only from films made by women but also from films made by men. Looking at the representation of communal confinement, women's solidarity, loneliness, motherhood and sexuality we will identify the discourse in which the social and gender limitations faced by women have been explored. The focus of attention will be on the plots and specific thematics that seem to be most representative of East Central European cinema. One such aspect is the preoccupation with women and history, most often used to deliver serious social criticism of certain adverse periods.

Women and Stalinism: Mothers of Missing Children and Children Looking for Mothers

Extending the 'burden of history' attitude, in many films family drama was used to comment on historical fate, usually by depicting the adverse effect of history on the family and intimate relationships within it. The interest in women's fates comes within a concrete socio-historical context; the woman is shown against a certain historical backdrop, which determines the direction of her actions and often limits them. Traditionally positioned against history, the female protagonist most often has to struggle against a fate that is imposed from the outside, usually in order to shelter her children from a destructive force that endangers the family entity. This is clearly visible in those films that focus on the relationship between mother and child in the period of Stalinism.

Typically, the focus is on strong women as mothers. The husband-father is usually missing, presumably taken away, and often appearing only in dreams (a classic example is Andrei Tarkovsky's *Zerkalo/Mirror* (1975), but also films by Márta Mészáros, Kieślowski and others). Mother and child are left alone to struggle in a crippling social setting. Finding a substitute father or starting a new family in not a solution; even if a supportive partner was there things would not be profoundly different; the problems are seen much more as social rather than personal ones.[9]

Within the template of Socialist Realism, mother and child would share the same ideological beliefs. In times of revolutionary struggle, they would be on the same side of the barricade, witnessing the triumphant arrival of the new times. The classic example of this type is found in Vsevolod Pudovkin's *Mat'/Mother* (1926), based on Maxim Gorky's 1906 proletarian novel; David Bordwell categorises this film as a 'prototype' of Socialist Realist film-making (1993: 200). In this film, the mother, a typical product of patriarchal society, is initially opposed to the revolutionary activities of her son. Gradually, however, she grows class conscious, joins the revolution and becomes a leader. The famous ending – the mother carrying on the flag of revolution – was one of the key propaganda images of Soviet cinema.

By the time Poland, Hungary and Czechoslovakia were 'assigned' to the 'Soviet sphere of influence' after the Second World War, the Soviet model of state socialism was already sufficiently compromised. In addition, the early years of state socialist rule in the region are associated with the period when the pattern of Stalinist purges was imported from the Soviet Union. Communst rule was more or less coerced on people in the region; those who dissented became victims of the purges, and those who opted to remain in silent disapproval witnessesed a string of false trials and political incarcerations. It was a process of forced social 'transformation' that could not be openly spoken about; the means with which Communism was imposed were to be deleted from the annals of history and only the record of its final triumph was permitted to stay on record.

Film-makers were unable to tell the story as it was, but wanted to. The only way to depict the wrongs of the period was by exploring the private arena where the repercussions were reflected, focusing on cinematic plots in which the family and the private individual were positioned against politics. These were stories of families ruined by the 'revolution', of mothers forced to give away their children and of children whose mothers are taken away. The plots ultimately recycle the same indictment: one of the deepest consequences of Stalinism is the destruction of the sacred relationship of mother and child; the nurturing function of motherhood could not take place within the context of the absurd and irrational society of the early 1950s. By making this statement over and over again, by reiterating it through a variety of plots, film techniques and approaches, film-makers indicted Stalinism's inhumanity.[10]

The protagonist of the Hungarian film *Szerelem/Love* (Károly Makk, 1971), played by the legendary Lili Darvas, is a fragile old lady in her nineties whose days on Earth are numbered. She lives in seclusion, with no idea what is going on outside the walls of her home and surrounded by the memorabilia of her Austro-Hungarian youth. Her son is imprisoned by the Stalinists, which she is not supposed to know. Her daughter-in-law (Mari Törőcsik) lies to the old lady, making her believe that the son is away in America, involved in making movies. During her visits, the daughter-in-law 'reads' to the old woman imaginary letters from the son. The scenes of letter reading are interspersed with the old woman's flashback visions and dream-like reminiscences of her missing son's childhood and adolescence, all scenes carrying the specific flavour of glorious imperial Austria-Hungary. The son has been taken away and will not be back before her death; the only private encounter between mother and son that can still take place is the mother's daydreaming. With its cinematic and psychological subtlety, *Love* is simultaneously one of the finest treatments of the bond between mother and child as well as an indictment of Stalinism.

Janusz Zaorski's *Matka Królów/Mother of Kings* (made in Poland in 1983 but only released in the late 1980s) also critiques Stalinism by looking into the damaging effects it has on a family. Teresa (played by Magda Teresa Wójcik) is a widow who struggles to raise several sons through the difficult years of the Second World War. Having managed to bring the four boys up on her own, she lives on to see them destroyed one after another in the 1950s. Each one of them is ruined in a different way: one becomes an amoral conformist, another is deprived of chances to grow in society and a third falls into petty crime. The favourite son becomes a Communist activist but then falls victim of the purges in the early 1950s. Kept in jail without being formally charged he dies during an interrogation. His wife, herself a Communist, cannot believe that the Party would destroy him so easily: 'Nobody is in jail without reason', she says, 'there might be crimes my husband has committed that we do not know about.' The mother's attitude is different: she will do her best to help her son, unconditionally. All her efforts are of no avail. In one of the key scenes of the film, we see the mother waiting at the bottom of the staircase at a government office to be received by a highly placed acquaintance. He never comes, though, and she remains there waiting, staring at Stalin's portrait at the top of the stairs: an allegory of ordinary people's deprivation in the face of totalitarian hierarchy. The story of the powerless protagonist of *Mother of Kings* is, once again, the story of a mother whose child is taken away by an unjust and adverse social system.

In Bugajski's *The Interrogation*, a newborn child is taken away from the mother. The protagonist, Antonina (Krystyna Janda), is another victim of the Stalinist terror of the early 1950s. She is kept in jail for several years without clear charges or trial. In the course of her ordeal, she is impregnated by one of the prison guards who has a strange affection for her. A baby girl is born, but, after a short period of mothering in the prison's infirmary, it is taken away from Antonina. Only three years later, after she is finally released, Antonina is able to find her daughter in an orphanage; mother and child are reunited. Stalinism has taken away everything but this child she never planned for. For Antonina, the hope of motherhood, after all other hopes have been abandoned, comes as compensation. But can it be a fulfilling solution to the moral devastation and desperation the protagonist was forced to undergo? Will she be able to invest this forced motherhood with a new meaning?

In many of these films mothers see their children taken away. In others, it is the children who suffer the loss of their mother to an adverse social reality. This is, for example, the defining theme of Márta Mészáros' autobiographical 'Diary' films where the loss of mother is closely associated with the inhuman Stalinist regime: *Napló gyermekeimnek/Diary for My Children* (1982), *Napló szerelmeimnek/Diary for My Loved Ones* (1987) and *Napló apámnak, anyámnak/ Diary for My Father and Mother* (1990).

Mészáros' father was a Hungarian sculptor and an outspoken Communist sympathiser. In the 1930s, the family had moved to the Soviet Union, and shortly thereafter the father fell victim to the Stalinist purges. The mother died a few years later, during the war. Tracing the time from the director's adolescent years (the time of her return to Hungary) to her later twenties (including the period of studies in Moscow), the films of the 'Diary' feature finely crafted dream sequences and flashbacks enhanced by an exquisite black-and-white photography. The memories of the lost mother and father appear in a lighter tone than the overall dark grey that refers to the austere grim reality, associating the longing for lost parents with sunshine and calmness.

The first instalment of the series deals with the legacy of Stalinsim most directly. Here the orphaned Juli, the adolescent protagonist, is shown returning to Hungary after the war. She is entrusted to Magda (a relative who has been too busy to have children of her own) who enjoys the privileges of a highly placed Communist official. Magda is not loved, but this is not a concern for her; she prefers to know that everyone fears her. She plans to raise Juli the way she sees fit for the Communist future, disregarding Juli's growing resentment.

Even though the power-play develops within the realm of a personal relationship, the uneven struggle between Juli and Magda takes on an allegorical meaning. Juli's resentment of Magda's intense, inconsiderate and imposing 'motherly' interest stands in for the attitude of ordinary people to the political regime. Magda is directly associated with Stalinism: she plays 'Suliko', Stalin's favourite song when her comrades are visiting, she accepts the offer to become a prison guard, and she likes to wear uniforms. She is seen exercising her power at home in one of the key episodes of the film, when she makes Juli take off her boots and enjoys watching the girl kneeling in front of her.

Magda's lack of femininity is juxtaposed with the pervasive dreamlike visions of Juli's mother, whose idealised fragility ultimately overpowers Magda's strength

Figure 29: In one of the key episodes of the film, Magda makes Juli take off her boots and enjoys her power: Mészáros' *Diary for My Children* (1982).

even though it is only an imaginary presence. It is the eternal search for the lost motherly warmth that is the main predicament of Mészarós' protagonist. Inter-cutting contrasting images of daily life with dreams and visions of memories about the mother represents the symbolic struggle between the missing real mother and the imposing step-mother.

Juli's coming of age is associated with an evolution towards the rejection of Stalinism, accomplished only in the final part of the trilogy. But if July is meant to stand in for Mészarós, there are some questions to be asked here. Mészarós was an offspring of a Communist family; her parents believed in the same ideals that Stalin did. Juli's (and perhaps Mészarós') denial of Stalinism should then logically lead to rejecting her missing parents' Communist beliefs altogether (and thus to disrespect the memory of the parents). The director, however, does not reach such an extreme collision point; she never accepts that the orphaned feelings that Stalinism creates may be associated with the utopian Communist dream of her parents; the first is exposed as anti-human while the latter remains unquestionably good and humane. Ultimately, Mészarós' choice is to preserve a somewhat idealised vision of the Communist ideal and indict only Stalinism as its perverted extreme version.

Communal Confinement

With the industrial growth of the early 1960s, significant numbers of women entered the work force. Many took jobs in plants having moved from smaller towns or villages, where they could exist independently and leave patriarchal lifestyles behind. The lives of these women – typically working in factories and living in dormitories – became the topic of numerous films made in the 1960s and 1970s. Rather than glorifying these new developments, however, cineastes proved to be critical of the adverse effects of progress. In some places the migration had resulted in a disproportionate concentration of women and had affected the local demographics; the new way of life appeared more confining than liberating. One of the earliest films focusing on the personal discomforts of communal life was Forman's classic comedy *A Blonde in Love* (1965).

The premise of the story is one of demographics. In a provincial Czech town, girls far outnumber boys; there is a large shoe factory, employing mostly women. Girls do not want to stay since they have no real chances of getting married so the factory's director makes arrangements that army reservists come to town for a night out with the girls. The arrival of the army men, many of whom are middle-aged and married, cannot provide a miraculous resolution to the mating crisis (and the story of the film is soon taken to Prague where the protagonist ends up chasing the good-looking pianist with whom she has had a one-night stand). Yet the encounter between the reservists and the factory girls gives rise to a number of humorous situations, explored with great subtlety by the director. As testified by film historian Antonín Liehm, the film had an impact on the social policies of the region:

> When [*A Blonde in Love*] was released, the Ministry of Light Industry began to howl. The authorities claimed they were already having enough difficulties recruiting girls to work in these factories and now, after we had shown the situation on the screen in such a dismal light, nobody would want to take such a job. [...] The noisy protests tapered off after a while; but as the weather got warmer, a funny thing happened: hundreds of boys began to head for Zruč to spend Saturday and Sunday there. [...] The movie was like a big classified ad announcing that there were hundreds of boy-starved girls in Zruč. (1975: 67–8)

A Blonde in Love was a comedy, but it tackled a serious problem: one of communal confinement experienced by large numbers of women entering the labour force in the newly industrialised cities across the region. Forman had used this macro-sociological development as a backdrop for his fine psychological study of interpersonal relations.

For other film-makers, however, the focus remained more concerned with the social dimensions. A range of low-key dramas from Hungary, Poland and Czechoslovakia made between the late 1960s and the mid-1980s presented a damaging picture of the alienation resulting from the new social realities.

Some of Márta Mészáros' early films represent this strand in East Central European cinema the best. Her films are no longer about the relationship between the sexes as in *A Blonde in Love*; Mészáros' attention is much more focused on women's quiet plight for recognition, on their silent struggle for legitimation and right of privacy. As Catharine Portuges has noted, Mészáros' women were 'at odds with social convention', questioning 'the constitution of the self in East-Central Europe which has favoured group identity at the expense of the individual' (1993: 126). Mészáros knew how to show the confining nature of imposed communal space, and positioned her protagonists against it in a difficult and sometimes desperate search for privacy. In Mészáros' debut feature, *Eltávozott nap/The Girl* (1968), there is a scene from a girls' orphanage: in a typically egalitarian festive meal for their 'graduation', the girls all get the same plate with the same food on it, the same kiss, and the same amount of love from the people who run the place. The protagonists in *Szabad lelegzet/Riddance* (1973) are young female factory workers who share a room in a dormitory, all equally deprived of better chances, and all struggling to free themselves from the communal life they have taken on.[11] Juxtaposing such scenes of communal confinement with scenes of private intimacy is Mészáros' key narrative technique. She balances the mass scenes with intimate ones, usually showing a woman searching out for 'a room of one's own', for some little space where at least some privacy would be granted: taking a walk, showering, or simply looking through the window to winter trees with freezing sparrows.

Mészáros' subtle critique of the communal confinement of state socialism is the best-known example for such socially critical cinema. However, there are numerous other films that have explored individual tragedies triggered by imposed compulsory communal settings. They all show women destined to spend their lives desperately craving for privacy, inhabiting a variety of ghetto-like surroundings, ranging from reformatory schools (for example, in Hunagry, János Rózsa's *Vasárnapi szülöki/Sunday Daughters*), orphanages (in Czechoslovakia, Filip Renč's *Requiem pro panenku/Requiem for a Maiden*, 1991), jails (in Poland, Wiesław Saniewski's *Nadzor/Surveillance*, 1985), factory dormitories (in Poland, Barbara Sass's *Without Love*), hospital wards (in Poland, Magdalena Łazarkiewicz's *Przez dotyk/By Touch*), to work places of feminised occupations, such as schools and nursery schools (in Hungary, Péter Gothár's *Ajándék ez a nap/A Priceless Day* and István Szabó's *Édes Emma, drága Böbe – vázlatok, aktok/Dear Emma, Sweet Böbe*, 1992). Differing in details, all these films nonetheless focus on serious social problems such as addiction, neglect, unemployment, incest and rape. All explore individual trauma caused by the coercive setting of communal life.

Sunday Daughters, János Rózsa's shattering film of teenage girls confined to a correctional establishment for juvenile delinquents, opens with raw interview footage from a series of brief encounters with the inmates. The opening sequence gives no indication which one of these troubled teenagers will be the focus of the story, allowing Rósza to suggest that they all have individual stories worth telling. Blurring the boundary between documentary and fiction (the young delinquents play characters similar to themselves) helps the director draw attention to the grim reality of the protagonist's struggle for self-determination. Skilfully using this seemingly detached documentary style, relying on grainy interview footage, the director creates a moving portrayal of emotional trauma and rejection.

Gothár's *A Priceless Day* looks at another dimension of the same plight for self-determination. This time around it is literally about the struggle for personal space. The protagonist, Irén, works at a day-care centre staffed by women. Her lover is married to one of the other teachers and everybody at work knows about the affair. Irén cannot even make a personal phone call without being watched by a dozen curious eyes. She cannot afford to be with her lover, as she has no dwelling of her own; she cannot even be by herself if she wanted to. She needs to get a flat, a realisation that defines her struggle for privacy and will soon become an obsession: 'If I get this flat', Irén says, 'I will ask nothing more of life.' In order to fulfil her trivial dream she is prepared to enter into a number of dubious deals and engage in hard and dirty bargaining. The 'priceless day' of the title is the day when she finally gets access to the dwelling. She has secured access to the apartment at the cost of entering unwanted relationships and making questionable compromises, so it comes as no surprise that soon thereafter she is left disappointed and disillusioned.

Many more films, made mostly in the 1980s, but also in the 1970s and the 1990s, could be discussed here. Taking place around various communal premises, they all focus on female protagonists involved in drunken revelries behind locked doors, unwanted pregnancies and attempted suicides, and all offer complex and moving portraits of young women driven towards despair by a cruelly monotonous routine.

But why always women? Why female dorms, girl's orphanages and feminised spaces of toy factories or nursery schools? Why not military reservists, barracks, male factory dorms, and settings that men are confined to? Why not films like *Full Metal Jacket* (Stanley Kubrick, US, 1987) or *Scum* (Alan Clarke, UK, 1979)? It seems this has something to do both with the unstated sanctions of film under Communism and the unspoken general gender conventions. On the one hand, depicting the plight of women would somehow fall among the permitted themes of state socialism. If the story was about men it could be seen as a direct indictment of the social system; as long as it was about women, it would not come across as direct social criticism or a revolt. To tell stories of female communal confinement meant to practice social criticism and still avoid an open confrontation with the regime. The fact of the relative safety associated with the treatment of female themes, however, only confirms that state socialism had not gone far enough in abandoning widespread gender conventions. As in the West, women's concerns here were traditionally relegated to the 'private' sphere (as opposed to the 'public' one). The equality between men and women, even though an officially declared goal (and a proclaimed achievement) of socialism, was still a distant prospect.

In Search of Privacy: Loneliness, Betrayal and Solidarity

While most of the films discussed here approached the issue of communal confinement in a similarly critical manner, directors differed in the way they viewed women's chances in the search for privacy. One can distinguish three main interpretations. First, according to some, the only alternative available to those women who react adversely to the communal society is loneliness. A woman may be an accomplished professional or may have achieved a high social standing; nonetheless, she remains alone in her personal life. Second, there are films that cast a sceptical look at female friendships, ultimately questioning the ability of women to be loyal and genuinely supportive of each other. At the opposite end of the spectrum, a third range of films asserts the union of two women as an act of genuine solidarity that creates a universe of self-sufficiency and offers an alternative to the alienating communal space of state socialism. There are several examples that illustrate each one of these approaches.

Loneliness

Even women who are among people may be lonely, and it is this existential loneliness, persisting in the intimate corners deep below the façade, that female film-makers have done so much to explore. It is the kind of suppressed loneliness that is a continuous interest for female (Mészáros, Holland) and male (Zanussi, Kieślowski) directors alike.

The protagonist of Márta Mészáros' first feature, *The Girl*, is raised in an orphanage. As soon as she comes of age, she undertakes a painful search for her biological mother who has brought her to life only to reject her. When she finds the mother – who turns out to be a peasant woman, committed to her other children and family, reluctant to admit she has had a child out of wedlock – the girl realises she is more alone then ever. It is too late, and life has taken its toll; mother and daughter can no longer bond. The girl remains as alone as she was at the onset.

The atmosphere of Mészáros' subsequent films is permeated with this same loneliness, marked by existential fear and insecurity. The encounter of two women, each one of whom is lonely in her own way, is the theme of her *Örökbefogadás/Adoption* (1975). Loneliness is also the leading motif of *Kilenc hónap/Nine Months* (1976), the quasi-documentary report of the lonely pregnancy of a young woman (remarkably played by Lili Monori). Mészáros' protagonists are often shown spending time alone. They may be strong and independent but, when alone, it is revealed that, like others, they also suffer emotional trauma and struggle for personal space. A trademark image for the director is to show the protagonist taking a shower alone, watching water run down her body, a rare intimate moment of privacy.

In Agnieszka Holland's shattering *A Woman Alone*, the loneliness comes hand in hand with misery and social indifference. The protagonist, Irena, is a plain-looking single mother in her thirties who works for the post office and lives on the brink of poverty.[12] On top of that, as if fate is conspiring against her, everything that can go wrong does: she loses the chance to get a better job; a recently deceased aunt leaves her in debt. With prospects getting grimmer every day, Irena is driven to desperation; she gives up on her son and takes him to an orphanage. She will try to get back on her feet before being able to take the boy back. Irena has met a young handicapped and equally marginalised man, Jacek, with whom she has a romance of sorts. They make a botched robbery attempt and end up in despair; as an act of mercy killing, Jacek smothers Irena with a pillow.

A Woman Alone is a film of grim realism that looks at a weak and helpless protagonist left alone to face a hostile world. Every step she takes deepens her isolation: the shattering scene when she leaves her boy in the orphanage is the moment when she cuts the final tie that links her to this world. From there on she becomes a stray tragic character who is doomed to die.

Figure 30: Maja Komorowska, a Zanussi actress.

While Holland's view of the loneliness of her protagonist is clearly reinforced by anger at a society that fails individuals, Zanussi's 1970s films also look at lonely women, but focus more on the existential dimension. A representative example is *Quarterly Balance*, which tells the story of another woman in her late thirties, Marta (Maja Komorowska). She is happily married, has a nice child and good office job, and on the surface everything is going just fine. Marta feels suffocated by the monotonous routine and has all the symptoms of a mid-life crisis. She starts an affair with a friend, an energetic man who comes across as very different from her balanced and ultimately boring husband. But is this a real passionate love or simply a romantic detour in the face of approaching old age? There are many scenes when Marta is shown alone in silence, thinking, reflecting on whether she should leave her husband: Marta sailing, Marta drinking tea at home, Marta on a windy beach. Even if she left her marriage, what would this change for her? The affair and the family is only part of her life. She is a professional woman who cannot simply escape her place in society; she may leave the husband but there are mounting problems at work (the quarterly balance suggests that a colleague has been embezzling funds), she will have to go on. The pressures at work mount; she grows impassionate with her lover, fights with him and insults him for no apparent reason. Later on she embarks on more affairs, but soon, disillusioned, comes to the realisation that these are not a solution to her loneliness. Her child is alienated and is now closer to the father. The crisis in the relationship with the husband deepens, and yet in the end Marta surrenders and returns to him. She comes to terms with the alienation that bothered her so much at the outset, and perseveres with work and the family. Deep inside she may still have rebellious inclinations and may not be reconciled, yet she accepts the reality and enters the next stage in life.

It is important to note that the protagonists of these films are always working women – be it in professional or lay occupations. It is almost impossible to find films about the loneliness of the woman confined to the home; the neurotic housewife of Cassavetes' *A Woman Under the Influence* (1974) is not the type of female character encountered in East Central European cinema. Ultimately, the message of these films is that even the working woman, one who presumably has a role equal to men in the social world at large, is equally lonely and disoriented as the woman confined to the family setting. State socialism claimed to have provided adequate socialisation for women, yet this did not appear to solve women's existential problems.

Betrayal

The accomplished professional woman in the centre of many films from the 1970s and the 1980s, however, was often presented as selfish and incapable of genuine love. She was ultimately alone in all relationships, by her own choice. She was often shown as incapable of sincere female friendship and loyalty, thus suggesting that relationships between women are based on betrayal and mutual mistrust rather than gender solidarity.

The protagonist of Barbara Sass' *Without Love*, Ewa, is an aspiring journalist of ruthless ambition. Her realism borders on cynicism; she is fully aware of her good looks and exploits her sex appeal in affairs that help her professional advancement: 'The main thing in life is to live', she says, and she has got 'to have it all at any price.' One day, Ewa is asked to write about the life of female factory workers. She approaches the assignment in a street-wise manner by using a chance acquaintance, a victimised young woman called Marianna. The resulting sensational reportage paints Marianna's life in excessively grim colours, and presents a picture of drunkenness and promiscuity in the workers' dorms. Marianna is offended, while Ewa claims she has exploited her in order to help others in the same situation. She even helps Marianna to move out of the dorm and passes some nice clothes on to her. Seemingly acting out of female solidarity, Ewa's actions are clearly dictated by shallow careerism.

Sass is clearly sceptical about Ewa's morality and loyalty to women. Ewa routinely ignores her daughter, and her masquerade of impenetrability renders her unsympathetic. Because she has suffered from trusting men in the past, she now does not want to depend on anybody. It is Ewa's inconsiderate struggle for independence that, the film suggests, is at the root of her questionable ethical motives. She is, indeed, an independent and strong working woman; but the director clearly indicates she disapproves of this kind of strength.

Another film from around the same time, Ryszard Bugajski's *Kobieta i kobieta/A Woman and a Woman* (1980), deals with the relationship of two active professional women. In the first part, their friendship is put to a test, they argue and separate. Ten years later life brings them together again; each one has grown into a strong and experienced executive woman. However, professional and personal conflicts erupt again and yet another collision is unavoidable. Thus, while women may be trying to be friendly and even forgiving, the film seems to suggest, it is nearly impossible for them to be loyal to each other; female friendships are always marred by opportunism and shaky moral foundations.

Łazarkiewicz's debut drama, *By Touch*, is also ambiguous about the chances of genuine female friendship. The film features two women sharing a small hospital room, surrounded by an atmosphere of sickness and death; many scenes show them staring through the window into the foggy day outside. One of the protagonists is the beautiful Anna (Grażyna Szapołowska), a former ballerina who has a loving husband and a child. She is gradually dying from cancer of the uterus and has now suffered a miscarriage.[13] The other one is an almost autistic teenage girl with a shaved head, an incest victim who has had an abortion and suffers from post-traumatic stress syndrome. The women befriend each other; the girl starts telling her story to Anna, gradually recovers and returns to normal life. While the beautiful Anna fades away, the girl, who has identified with her, takes over Anna's child and, after her death, more aspects of her life. Reminiscent of Kieślowski's later style, *By Touch* is shot through a blue filter, and changes into colour only towards the end. The bluish tint prevails also in the key scene, where the camera focuses on the hands of the protagonists, stretching towards each other and touching. The touch of the two women appears as a vow of loyalty. And yet, while seemingly believing in the strength of female solidarity and mutual support, Łazarkiewicz shows the bond of the two women as ultimately destructive: one of them has to perish for the other one to thrive.

Solidarity

For other directors, the encounter of two women can turn into a strong alliance helping them to resist the rough and unfriendly reality. Such is the union of the two teachers in Szabó's *Sweet Emma, Dear Böbe*, for example, or the improbable friendship between Irén and the wife of her lover in Gothár's *A Priceless Day*. Women bond as part of their resistance to communal confinement and, within these friendships they finally become subjects of their own relationships. Sometimes such unions of two women are seen as a spontaneous creation of a private universe, a world of complete sufficiency and spiritual satisfaction.

Makk's *Another Way*, for example, is one of the rare films dealing with the issue of same sex love, looking at the relationship between two female journalists working in Stalinist times. In a plotline that goes far beyond exploring their strong physical attraction, the director focuses more on the staggering limitations imposed upon the journalistic profession and on the social and political repercussions that their affair leads to.[14] Makk lets his protagonists show their affection in public, thus provoking widely accepted social conventions. He wants to suggest that to become real, the union of women needs to endure the judging gaze of strangers. Only when tested in this way can women assert that they can meet each other's needs.[15]

The director who believes most in the power of female solidarity, however, is Mészáros. In her classic film *Adoption*, she explores the gradual bonding of two women. Anna is a teenage girl neglected by her youngish biological parents, who has run away from home and taken a factory job. Kata is in her forties, a lonely woman who works at the same factory, and who gives Anna shelter and emotional comfort. The two women's relationship soon becomes like that of loving mother and daughter, a symbolic temporary 'adoption'.

The film looks into a fragile but deeply satisfying union, which has come into being as a result of the suppressed emotional struggle each one of these women has been undergoing, a union richly permeated by intimacy. Shot in black-and-white, the framing and use of camera movement in the film help to reinforce this constructed intimacy and raise the relationship of the two women above any heterosexual interests. There is a scene when Kata and Anna are shown sitting at a table in a restaurant, being watched by a group of men at the bar. The camera starts with a medium-close shot of the two women, and then repeatedly pans back and forth between them and the men who watch them. The emotional bond and mutual absorption of the two women is projected onto the space that now becomes impenetrable for the men. The juxtaposition of medium-close shots of Anna and Kata with long shots from the perspective

Figure 31: Katalin Berek in Mészáros' *Adoption* (1975).

of the intrusive male patrons suggests that their bond is simultaneously strong and vulnerable. The display of the women's intimacy is intentional, but not meant to be challenging. It is not meant to attract attention; it is not extroverted. These two women do not care anymore about the male gaze, they are not like the women on display in *A Blonde in Love*, who are willing to be objectified and obtain legitimisation through dance invitations. In *Adoption*, the male gaze is pushed back by an invisible wall of self-sufficiency and solidarity. The women's union is impenetrable since it is legitimised from within.

The two women are together only for a while. Anna gets married, mostly because she wants to be independent; it is hinted, however, that her new independence is elusive and she may be bound for trouble with the new husband. Kata adopts a baby girl, whom she is determined to raise on her own. Their union is no more, but has been a deeply fulfilling experience for both, having helped them to come to terms with their identities.

Sexing-up the Post-communist Woman

In post-Communist times, the representation of women in East Central European cinema has undergone substantial changes. First and foremost, one observes astonishing sexism which accompanies a great emphasis of women's sexuality and less attention paid to the social problems faced by women.

One of the biggest ironies of this transitional social environment seems to have been translated to the screen: sociologists have noted that the situation of women in the aftermath of state socialism has barely improved; many writers have discussed examples which show that women's social position has, in fact, worsened, and that gender inequalities are on the increase (Einhorn 1993; Berry 1995; Gal and Kligman 2000). New problems such as growing unemployment, pay inequality, overwhelming feminisation of certain sectors and the exclusion of women from others have been reported, and various benefits and rights, previously in place, have been cancelled. Having seen many of their earlier social privileges scrapped, women have largely been losing out in the new developments.

In addition, there is an overwhelming fascination with sexuality across most mainstream media. The coverage of women by the thriving tabloid press has been more than problematic. (One can regularly stumble across reports about women who have not only enjoyed being raped, for example, but have eventually even married the assault perpetrator.) It may be tempting to see this obsession only as a compensatory 'catching up' after the years of state socialism when open discussion of sex-related matters was more or less absent from the public sphere. It seems that the explanation should rather be sought, however, by recognising the growing importance of simple market forces: sex and violence sell.

While films made during Communist times would regularly feature scenes depicting intimacy, representing explicit sex was usually taboo, and sex was off limits in the context of print and broadcast media. The import of Western publications, even of the more innocent *Playboy* variety, was illegal. In its place developed a context in which the semi-naked women smiling from the pages of smuggled Western magazines not only helped to satisfy suppressed user desires but also functioned as one of the most effective strands of Western propaganda.

Over a dozen years into the democratic transition, it is difficult to avoid sex even in the remotest corners of East Central Europe. The overall 'tabloidisation' of media across the region today is compounded by a boom in indigenous and imported pornographic publications, a whole range of which (from straightforward erotica to hard-core magazines) are openly sold in every kiosk.[16]

All these transformations take place within a context of absent regulation (or lacking enforcement where regulation is in place) and an absent political will to tackle problems that adversely affect women. At the same time, increasingly there are groups of women who are acutely aware of the difficult situation and attempting to organise themselves in order to resist it. The growth of such groups is accompanied by a process of establishing women's studies programmes at universities across the region. Even though today feminists are more active than before, their voices remain quite isolated and prove unable to counter the growing social marginalisation and compulsory 'sexing-up' of women. As far as cinema is concerned, the situation is not much better, given that veteran feminist directors like Chytilová or Mészáros have been so articulate in rejecting their feminist roots (and even though each one of them released several films devoted to women's issues, these have been works that have not managed to gain the critical acclaim earned by their earlier works).

Overall, the number of films featuring complex and psychologically plausible female characters has been on the decrease since 1989. The best women's films of post-Communist times seem to be made by members of the younger generation, such as Dorota Kędzierzawska (who tackled the sensitive theme of motherhood and of abortion in *Nothing*) and Urszula Urbaniak (who looked into issues of chances for women in *The Junction*).[17]

The most popular films of the post-Communist period, however, the comedies and action-adventure releases, present women in a different light. Yesterday's overworked factory dorm girls become today's sex-kitten playmates, regularly cast as constantly horny creatures mostly interested in playing out their erotic fantasies and in entering new sexual relationships at any time of day or night.

In Róbert Koltai's Hungarian comedy *Sose halunk meg/We Never Die* (1993), for example, one of the traditional film settings – a train travelling through the countryside – is transformed into a terrain for the exciting sexual adventures experienced by an insipid uncle and his nephew: while the uncle moves to a neighbouring compartment to indulge in the pleasures of love-making with a young woman, the teenage nephew undergoes a sexual induction with a nymphomaniac lady. Many other recent films rely heavily on a similar celebration of promiscuity. The message is: real women want to have sex all the time.[18]

The men, on the other hand, are all lining up to cater to these women. Sexual relations between mature men and 'hot' teenage girls are a fixture in these cinemas, and the sexual advances are most often made by the women. In the Polish film *Kolejność uczuć/Sequence of Feelings* (Radoslaw Piwowarski, 1992) an aging actor has a sexual affair with a teenager, and in the box office hit *Psy/Pigs* (Władysław Pasikowski, Poland, 1992) the protagonist, a former police officer, picks up a former teenage prostitute from a home for juvenile delinquents. She definitely does not intend to return to the streets, yet as soon as she is out of the 'establishment', she makes sexual advances to her rescuer.

Thus, in post-Communist cinema, women are rarely given more complex social roles than being preoccupied with extra-marital affairs and a variety of other sexual adventures. This approach to women's representation and sexuality is doubtlessly offensive and often humiliating. It does not seem, however, that there has been much public outcry against these films, celebrating 'femininity' as their authors would claim. For the time being it appears that the best works of East Central Europe's feminist cinema are strictly those made in the past.

CHAPTER SEVEN

East Central European Cinema Since 1989

The Industry

The pattern of changes in the economy of the media and cultural policies after the end of state socialism has been similar throughout all East Central Europe. Film industries underwent volatile structural changes and were subjected to often contradictory undertakings in administration and financing. Initially there was crisis, which found expression in crumbling production routines, an abrupt decrease in state funding, a sharp increase in unemployment among skilled personnel, and a considerable, yet temporary, decline in documentary and animation output. There was also a concurrent crisis in distribution and exhibition. Earlier concerns over freedom of expression rapidly vanished, taken over by worries over the emerging constraints of the market economy. Financing for film production was to change profoundly, shifting from the unit-based studio system to producer-driven undertakings. The involvement of national television networks in film production and exhibition became of vital importance, alongside the international co-production funding and the expanding sector of private financing. The scarce state subsidies, competitive in some countries or automatic in others, were turning into a hotly contested territory.

The drop in film production was most significant in the early 1990s. After the initial disarray, however, previous output levels were restored in most countries. In the dawn of the twenty-first century, the production cycle is in a process of stabilisation, reinforced by the introduction of new legislation and well-regulated funding mechanisms.[1]

Year	Hungary	Poland	Czechoslovakia	
1988	20	34	58	
1989	15	23	70	
1990	23	27	62	
1991	19	no data	17	
1992	22	21	15	
1993	16	21	20	
			Czech Rep.	Slovakia
1994	20	no data	19	2
1995	no data	23	23	3
1996	15	17	20	2
1997	23	20	20	2
1998	24	14	14	1

Table 2: Number of films produced annually in East Central Europe, 1988–1998. Sources: *Encyclopedia of European Cinema* and *Media Salles* National Reports 1999 (http://www.mediasalles.it).

The most problematic aspect of the crisis was that for a while film-makers seemed to be losing their domestic audience. The centralised control over distribution and exhibition networks as well as over television had made it easy to keep the audience compact and taste niches in cultural consumption had been largely disregarded.

In the early 1990s, however, viewers could no longer be taken for granted and film-makers were faced with accelerating audience segmentation. The years when people would go to the cinemas to see national film productions seemed to have passed. Film-makers had trouble identifying whom they addressed in their works. If they tried to appeal to the volatile mass taste, they had to put up with the overwhelming competition of imported mass culture. If they decided to address a more sophisticated audience they were unable to reach it, as in an underdeveloped market economy distributors and exhibitors were not interested in researching and targeting scattered pockets of potential viewers. The presence of national productions in the domestic 'top ten' charts varied.[2]

The abolition of the centralised management of culture divorced film production from exhibition and distribution, and earlier distribution networks were ruined before new ones had come into being. Most of the new private distributors who emerged subsequently chose to abide by market rules and rather than play the losing card of domestic productions opted for Hollywood box office winners. Although well-received at festivals, productions carrying an East

European label continued to be considered hard sells at film markets. In such a distribution context, East Central European cinema was left on the margins of the international image markets; in the 1990s, the numbers of East Central European films distributed internationally reached a record low.[3]

So, just what has changed in the years since 1989? What have the film industries done in response to the shift to a market economy, which has affected every aspect of the motion picture industry?

With the advent of market criteria, fundraising efforts concentrated on finding alternative sources – from the emerging private sector, from international film funding bodies, from various co-production agreements with European and American partners (see Iordanova 2002a). The share of international subsidies for film-making increased as the concept of 'national cinema' gave way to the concept of a 'new European' one.

After 1989, along with the crisis in national film production routines, the exchange mechanisms within the Eastern Bloc came to an abrupt end. Film-makers from each one of the countries in the region turned to the West as the only desired partner.[4] The reasons were twofold – economic and political. In strictly economic terms, the distinction between the capitalist economies of West European countries and the transitional economies of East Central European ones translated into a relationship of 'haves' and 'have-nots', and the monies needed to keep culture, a sector of a secondary economic importance, going could only come from the West. Politically, reorientation to the West was now on top of the agenda for all the former Eastern Bloc countries, and collaboration with Western countries was highly desirable. Former partnerships from within the region were quickly abandoned and new alliances were sought.

Most studios were partially or fully privatised and started competing with each other in attracting foreign film crews to shoot on location – a race in which the Barrandov film studio in Prague stands out as the undisputed winner.[5] A range of new small production companies proliferated, competing for the business of Western runaway feature and advertising productions. Since becoming a definitive hot spot for Hollywood runaway productions, Prague has been a booming film-making centre, yet Barrandov has become prohibitively expensive for a number of Czech film-makers (who make their small-budget productions elsewhere). It is expected, however, that with the Czech Republic's entry into the EU in 2004 (and the likely rise in prices to West European standards), Hollywood's interest in Prague will sharply decrease. There have already been public discussions on the possible move away of this thriving but 'portable' industry; the move may be enhanced by the flooding of the city in the summer of 2002.

In the aftermath of the 1989 'velvet revolutions', the film distribution networks of what used to be the Eastern Bloc rapidly disintegrated, and were, by the end of the decade, replaced by a more or less uniform system of Western-controlled subsidiaries. The well-integrated and centralised vertical distribution networks of state socialism were ruined and promptly replaced by a new two-tier system, consisting of a well-integrated vertical system for Hollywood products and a poorly co-ordinated horizontal system for domestic and European films. The entry of Hollywood distributors took place mostly via West European subsidiaries, but occasionally also directly. There has been significant growth in newer forms of distribution, such as video, DVD and the cable/digital market. While the region's distribution carries an overwhelming percentage of Hollywood fare (currently varying between 80 and 95 per cent of the market share of cinematic distribution in the region), the distribution of East Central European features in the West and within the region is extremely limited.

Exhibition practices have also changed. The centrally-run system of state-owned theatres was abolished and is being replaced by private cinemas, and, most recently, by newly built foreign-owned multiplexes. There are clear-cut distinctions between art-house cinemas and mainstream chains. The outlets belonging to mainstream-orientated operations strictly follow box office indicators, even though the steadily growing ticket prices and the mushrooming of video stores have sometimes led to an overall drop in admissions. Some countries have attempted to counteract the growing Hollywood dominance by imposing quotas or by charging surtax on ticket prices that would help subsidise domestic production.

The transition coincided with a clearly articulated period of insecurity in West European film production and distribution practices and policies. Studying the industry transformation in the region is a chance to dissect some of the deeply seated general problems of the European audio-visual landscape. At the same time, it gives a clear indication of the range of disparities within the West's cultural policies, by showing the deep split between European and North American approaches to cultural production and consumption.

The dynamics of international trade in canned images directly reflects the international distribution of power and the struggle for control over certain territories (even when these are defined in purely cultural terms). While a few decades ago the cinema industries in the countries of the Eastern Bloc were thought 'immune' to international commercialisation trends (Mattelart *et al.* 1984), today the picture has changed dramatically. The current position of East Central Europe's film industries within the New International Division of Cultural Labour (Miller *et al.* 2001), is one that needs to be explored in greater detail than can be afforded here.[6]

Generations

Transformations in the production and distribution system brought about an increased consciousness of the generational split in film-makers' ranks. Some film-makers of the generation, born in the 1920s and 1930s, proved unable to adapt to an environment where the rules were changing, and were forced to quit active film-making.[7] Others, such as Kutz, Menzel, Hanák and Jakubisko, had difficulties securing financing and only made one or two acclaimed films. Yet a third group, which comprised of auteurs such as Wajda and Zanussi (and Mészáros, Jancsó and Szabó to a lesser extent), managed to capitalise on their high-profile position and to make even more, or bigger, films than before, even though securing financing also cost them a considerable effort. However, some of these directors barely managed to match their own artistic achievements and made films that ranked below the standards set in their earlier work (like Jancsó, Chytilová, Mészáros). Directors such as Jakubisko and Zanussi made several films each, but were genuinely acclaimed only for one: Jakubisko for *Nejasná zpráva o konci světa/An Ambiguous Report About the End of the World* (Czech Republic, 1997) and Zanussi for *Życie jako śmiertelna choroba przenoszona drogą płciową/Life As a Fatal Sexually Transmitted Disease* (Poland, 2000). With an Academy Award for lifetime achievement in 2000 and several well-publicised films in the 1990s, Andrzej Wajda proved to be the ultimate survivor and should probably be seen as the most successful director of the older generation.

The film schools in the region (most notably the ones in Prague and Łódź), continue putting out new professionals who are entering the film-making industry in the 2000s. These young film-makers start working under the new production and distribution conditions and one would expect them to be better adapted to the changed situation. Like the directors of the older generation, however, the younger ones have managed to play the system with varying degrees of success.

Jan Svěrák is probably the most successful new film-maker from the region, not only in the Czech Republic but also internationally. Less than a decade after his graduation from film school, Svěrák had established himself as one of the most versatile directors and a leading figure of the younger generation of Czech film-making (which also includes Vladimír Michálek, Petr Václav, Petr Zelenka, Jan Hřebejk, David Ondříček and Saša Gedeon). He is certainly a film-maker of considerable business skill, who knows that securing international distribution is of equal importance to obtaining production financing.[8] Two years younger than Svěrák (both born in 1967), FAMU graduates Jan Hřebejk (*Divided We Fall*) and Petr Zelenka (*Knoflíkáři/Buttoners*, 1997), are en route to follow in the footsteps of Svěrák's success. They seem to continue the landmark black humour of the Czechoslovak New Wave.

While we may not be able to match Svěrák's international success story with examples from Hungary and Poland, both countries have had some fairly successful film-makers that emerged in the 1990s. Among other relatively new directors (such as Ildikó Szabó, Zoltán Kamondi, Tamás Tóth) Ibolya Fekete has managed to establish herself as one of the most original directors working in the region. With only two features to her credit (*Bolshe Vita*, 1996, and *Chico*, 2001), she has revealed an excellent ability to pin down some of the most important

Figure 32: Jan Svěrak: a director of talent and considerable business skills.

social problems affecting the region today: economic downfall, migrations, political disorientation, civil conflict and war.

A new generation of directors works in Poland as well. The so-called 'Young Wolves' – a group led by Władysław Pasikowski – enjoy the biggest commercial success, mostly working in the action-adventure genre and making films catering to mass-market tastes. A very different and particularly important director of the new generation in Poland is Jan Jakub Kolski. Having managed to release a new film almost every year since his debut in 1991, by the early 2000s Kolski had more than ten titles to his credit. While critics have noted that his work is somewhat uneven, all his films are characterised by a unique magic realist vision that seeks out and transposes the poetic value of nature, village life and peasantry, as seen in films such as *Pogrzeb kartofla*/*Burial of a Potato* (1991) and *Jańcio Wodnik*/*Johnnie the Aquarius* (1993). The sense of miracle, everyday magic and closeness to nature are leading elements of Kolski's work that make him one of the most original film-makers currently working in Poland.

The directors of the middle generation, positioned between the veterans and the newcomers, have not been as highly visible. Many of them began work in the 1980s, and the highlight of their careers coincided with the restructuring of the early 1990s; some were adversely affected by the transition. Yet there have been success stories as well: the work of actor-turned-director Jerzy Stuhr

(Poland) or of directors Robert Gliński (Poland), Béla Tarr (Hungary) and Péter Gothár (Hungary) has been internationally acclaimed. Members of this generation who had made successful popular hits in the 1980s, such as Juliusz Machulski (Poland) and Péter Tímár (Hungary), managed to continue making quality films of mass appeal and released even more box office successes.

An important extra dimension of the generational transformation is found in the changing migratory patterns of film-makers. In line with increased global migrations, today's movements of cineastes are not only more intense, but also no longer following the one-way path to the West. While many East Europeans rushed to the West, many young Westerners moved eastwards.[9] In addition, many of the émigrés returned after decades in the West, some permanently (Jan Němec), some for engagement with specific projects and ventures (Skolimowski, Forman, Polanski).[10]

The 1990s witnessed a number of border crossings in all spheres of cultural production. Nowadays, the movement of film professionals is more intense than ever, and with cross-border financing for film, more and more of them work internationally. Migration to the West is no longer about creative freedom but more a matter of resourceful convenience.[11] Today's film-makers can go back and forth as they wish, and are permitted to work both at home and abroad – a luxury which was not available to the typical East Central European émigré intellectual of the Cold War era. They are no longer exiles, and not even émigrés, but members of a transnational film-making group. Their movements, directly reflecting the intensifying migratory dynamics and the transnational essence of contemporary cinema, make it necessary to re-evaluate the concepts of belonging and commitment to a national culture, to reflect new paradigms of creativity as defined by globalisation and a culture of co-production.[12]

Themes

To claim that a new, profoundly different profile of East Central European cinema has emerged since 1989 would be an exaggeration. While the industry structure continues to change, earlier thematic concerns persist and there is continuity in topics and style. Privately financed heritage blockbusters have taken the place of state-financed historical super-productions. Gangster action adventures and post-totalitarian comedies have begun to fill the void left by the disappearance of partisan action-adventures and the comedies of state social-ism. Films focusing on the drab everyday life and moral frustration of post-Communism have replaced the dramas focusing on the depressing everyday life and moral discouragement under Communism itself. The cinematic image of the destruction of the Berlin Wall that became synonymous with the new era was widely used in documentaries and features, and so were the images of formerly glorious monuments that have now been laid to rest in sculpture cemeteries.

Over a decade into the transition, it is impossible to claim (as some tried in the early 1990s) that the old film culture has been destroyed and has now been replaced by ruthlessly triumphant commercialism. In spite of commercialisation, all cinemas in the region have continued to make the same type of films they were making before, releasing films that still deal with issues of national history, heritage, the Holocaust and war. Even though the growing dependence on market forces may have damaged art cinema, film-makers have continued making art films and continue moving within the same thematic areas discussed thus far. The traditions of lyrical cinema, Surrealism, magical realism and experimental avant-garde animation are alive and well. Numerous festival awards for films from East Central Europe counter-balance the still popular belief that this cinema is undergoing a major crisis.

Looking more closely at the specific thematic, genre and stylistic developments of the period since 1989, several thematic areas stand out:

- In what can be seen as a continuation of the socially critical tradition of the 'cinema of moral concern', there is a range of new films that focuses on immediate social issues, often reflecting the drab post-Communist reality and evolving around gloomy and grotesque images of transition.

- Continuing the tradition that focuses on subtle psychological portrayals of individuals, there is a range of new psychological dramas that deals with an individual's difficulties in social adaptation and living with a life-long trauma.

- Continuing the existential strand of earlier film-making, the international art-house film-going audience still regularly has the chance to admire fine and often gloomy existential explorations on enduring issues of destiny, death, distress and disorientation.

- Continuing the tradition of historical film-making, East Central European cinema persists in producing a range of films that focuses on very similar historical experiences and concerns. Most often, historical film-making concentrates on episodes from two world wars, the Holocaust, the Stalinist period, as well as certain glorious moments in national history.

- Continuing the tradition of films featuring village life and paying tribute to the rich folklore and heritage, a number of new films look into the politics of ethnic identity. The focus is on the past and present relations of various ethnic minorities (Jews, Romanies) and on the patriarchal structure of life in small isolated communities.

- Continuing earlier trends in entertainment-orientated film-making, the output in popular genres such as comedy, romantic comedy, action-adventure, thriller, crime drama and horror is growing.

- Reflecting the increasing awareness of changing geopolitical realities, a range of films looks into issues of contemporary migrations and new identities.

These areas will be further discussed in greater detail below.

Post-Communist Drabness

Communism came to an end, but many people across the Eastern Bloc were not prepared for the change. Even though they had eagerly awaited the 'velvet revolutions' and welcomed them, they had not fully anticipated the practical dimensions of the transition, and did not realise that it may lead to a change in their day-to-day experiences and may have a knock-on effect on their established working and domestic routines. While many of the old problems were swept away, a range of new social problems were experienced, unforeseen complications by many who had operated within the idealised image of Western prosperity.[13] Governments needed time to master the sweeping changes, social institutions to adjust to the transition, and people to find a new place in the constantly changing environment. Yet everything had to happen here and now.

The contradictions of the social 'order' that immediately followed the demise of the Communist system had a profound effect on everybody's personal lives, and were adversely experienced by many individuals. From a storytelling point of view, the time was extremely rich. Film-makers reacted by making films reflecting the difficult and often distressing events that were evolving right in front of them. The economic and social chaos sometimes led to extreme and overwhelming situations and the creation of films that presented a dark and uncompromising picture of depressing and demoralising experiences lived by protagonists faced with the mighty sweep of historical change. This body of work dealt with gloom and despair, with disoriented people undergoing extreme experiences unable to find a solution and who often ended in self-destruction. Extensively written about and discussed by international critics, these works were referred to by the Russian term *chernukha* (films with a 'black' viewpoint).

They dealt with new social problems – prostitution, for example, was tackled in a number of films (with variations of male prostitution as seen in the Czech films of the Polish-born director Wiktor Grodecki).[14] Other subject-matters included human trafficking, the trade in body parts, the raise in domestic violence and alcoholism, or the extreme confrontations of aspiring honest entrepreneurs with ruthless loan sharks.

Many of these films were satires, as it seemed that satire was the most adequate tone which would reflect the situation. The protagonists of these films encountered a variety of improbable characters that had sprung up with the advent of the post-Communist transition, formerly ordinary people who have turned into caricatures of themselves, responding either to economic pressures or unexpected fortunes they did not know how to manage. Besides the key presence of the 'nouveau riche' protagonist (usually Russian, with solid past KGB connections, now involved with international underground trade and business networks), the satirical menagerie of 'new' post-Communist types included 'down-sized' Soviet diplomats trading in Kalashnikovs, small-time smugglers, pimps, prostitutes, go-go dancers and Rambo-like paratroopers of all nationalities. Thematically, these films touched on almost all contemporary concerns in the region: troubled vernacular economies, travel restrictions, forced economic migrations, black marketeering, violence, crime, nationalism, racism and growing disparities within their once egalitarian universe.[15]

As far as style is concerned, for the most part these films rarely offered an original cinematic approach, and in all likelihood will not leave a lasting trace in the annals of cinematic art. When discussing the *chernukha* films, critics have repeatedly noted weaknesses in dramaturgy; they tend to tackle too many themes (ultimately, aspects of the general theme of social chaos and disorientation), and often feature too many protagonists and subplots. Film-makers have often rebuffed these critics by referring to the difficult situation within the film industry: as they face enormous challenges in securing financing for their films, they claim, it takes them longer to ensure that they can indeed work on the planned project. So, when they come to make the film, they simply take the chance to cover all the problems that have concerned them over the years it has taken to secure the financing. In such volatile industry conditions, it is never clear if they will be able to make another film.

Subtle Psychology

The tradition of subtle psychological film-making (Kieślowski, Fábri, Gaál, Passer, Mészáros), where the focus is on the individual and the social backdrop is present but not stressed, was kept alive throughout the 1990s and into the 2000s. Some examples of the genre include the Slovak *The Garden* and the Hungarian *Child Murders*, both films appreciated regionally. More recently, however, films of this category have been acclaimed at leading international venues, with a series of festival awards for Saša Gedeon's *Návrat idiota/Return of the Idiot* (Czech Republic, 1999) and Robert Gliński's *Cześć Tereska/Hi, Tereska* (Poland, 2001). Paying meticulous attention to psychological detail, both films explore the difficult socialisation of sensitive young people in rough environments of limited possibilities. *Return of the Idiot* looks at the uneasy readjustment of a young man who has suffered mental illness and is now trying to reintegrate with society. *Hi, Tereska*, shot in gritty black and white, is a harrowing everyday-life drama. It is centered on a teenage girl whose prospects are already bleak at the age of fourteen, and who comes from a working-class family that can barely provide material or moral support. Tereska's mother hurriedly enrolls her in a vocational school for seamstresses while trying to maintain the illusion she is helping the girl to fulfill her dream to one day become a fashion designer. As soon as this is arranged, the mother largely ignores her, having transferred all her clumsy attention to a younger sister. Shy and insecure, Tereska does not have much choice but to mingle with the street-wise teenagers from the school or the 'associates' they pick up who often ridicule her; her only friend is a handicapped man whose friendship soon turns into unwanted sexual interest. Her life seems fated to end in tragedy. *Hi, Tereska* is a film that continued the well-established tradition of film-making that portrays the existential dimension of everyday life as conditioned by social constraints.

Another remarkable film is *Przypadek Pekosińskiego/Story of Pekosiński* (Grzegorz Królikiewicz, 1993), a subtle existential feature about the crippling effects of childhood psychological trauma. Here, continuing the fine tradition of semi-documentary approaches, a handicapped lonely old man, Bronisław Pekosiński plays himself and tells of his life by appearing (stuttering and leaning on his cane, barely able to move his numb limbs) in re-enacted episodes from his childhood, teenage years and youth. Thrown as a bundled baby out of the window of a concentration camp transport, Pekosiński's earliest traumatic recollection is the reminiscence of his fall on the potato heap, a flashback that is repeatedly reproduced in the film. Marked by trauma, Pekosiński keeps repeating that he does not know his real name, for it has never become clear whose child he was; all his life he continues searching for his long-lost mother. It is a life that is split between triumph and tragedy. As a child, his soul is a battleground for the clashing Catholic Church and the Communist pioneer organisation; as an adult he descends from his status as a chess genius to becoming a helpless alcoholic subjected to domestic violence. Continuously fixated on the riddle of his identity and experiencing himself as a lost child, the weak Pekosiński perpetually falls between two stools, always used and manipulated, always trying to please everyone.

Existential Concerns

Existential concerns have informed some of the best-regarded film-making from East Central Europe. Take the work of Zanussi, Makk, Mészáros and Schorm, but most of all, that of Kieślowski. The films that Kieślowski made in France in the early 1990s continued themes that he had been developing earlier in Poland, particularly in *The Decalogue*, a project which had marked a major change in his interest: from social to more existential concerns, issues of fate, pre-determination, destiny, life, love and death. Kieślowski's *The Double Life of Veronique* and his *Three Colors* trilogy became some of the most discussed and internationally appreciated works of the 1990s precisely because of their empahasis on existential issues, over and above social and political preoccupations. Some of Kieślowski's critics declared his departure from social commitment to be a major weakness and blamed him for his newly found abstract humanist (read by some as devotedly Catholic) stance. However, it was a different strand of morally concerned film-making, one that had left the social determinants of morality aside and was now focusing more on transcendence and universal ethics.

Kieślowski's untimely death in 1996 prevented him from making more films of this type, but he left behind a number of unrealised screenplays, many drafted in collaboration with his regular scriptwriting partner, Krzysztof Piesiewicz. Around the time of Kieślowski's death Polish actor Jerzy Stuhr (who himself had acted in some of Kieślowski's films) turned director and made several films that shared the sensibility of the director. In 2000, he released a film that was an adaptation of an unrealised script by Kieślowski, *Duże zwierzę/The Big Animal*, continuing the line of moral concern. The interest in Kieślowski's legacy seems to endure, with several of the unrealised Kieślowski scripts in the making by the German director Tom Tykwer (*Heaven*, 2002) and the French director Eric Zonca. This all suggests that there is a continuing general interest in this universal ethical existential line in film-making.

Some of the recent work of veteran Krzysztof Zanussi also plays along these existential lines, particularly his acclaimed *Life As a Fatal Sexually Transmitted Disease*, even though some of his recent films, as well as his social position, was marked by overt commitment to Catholic causes and can be seen as an extension of a specific Catholic world view and not of universal existential concerns.[16]

The most respected representative of the 'existential' strand of film-making, however, is the Hungarian director Béla Tarr, whose work has been growing in significance on the international art-house circuit. Since the 1980s, Tarr has persisted in working in the same strand of black-and-white cinema, making films about depressed people inhabiting dreary areas drenched in never-ending rain, moving down the streets of unwelcoming industrial towns, between gloomy dwellings and poorly lit pubs (for example *Kárhozat/Damnation*, 1988). Ultimately, Tarr's films make bleak statements about the state of humanity. In the 1990s, he worked on lengthy existential explorations, films like *Satan's Tango* and *Werckmeister harmóniák/Werckmeister Harmonies* (2000). With his specific camera style, extremely long, slow takes of crumbling walls and seemingly dispassionate contemplation of human violence and despair, Tarr belongs to the group of auteurs which today comprises people such as Aleksandr Sokurov (Russia), Theo Angelopoulos (Greece) and Fred Kelemen (Germany). In Hungary, Tarr's work is paralleled by that of György Fehér (*Szenvedély/Passion*, 1998). It is a brand of film-making that relies on slowly moving stories, revealing the overwhelming limitations imposed by destiny and rendering human undertakings questionable and vain.

Historical Film

The engagement with history persisted in East European cinema throughout the 1990s, and historical films were among the most important to be made in the region. Here, it is sufficient to mention again the boom in Polish heritage epics. A prevailing tendency in the Holocaust-themed pictures seemed to be the interest in revisiting the relationship between the victims (Jews) and those of their Gentile counterparts who became involved with helping, be it willingly or reluctantly (as seen in Wajda's *Holy Week* and in Hřebejk's *Divided We Fall*). The persistent interest in the theme is additionally enhanced by the international recognition given to works of art that explore East Central European Holocaust experiences, like the 2002 Nobel prize for literature for Hungarian novelist Imre Kertesz,[17] or the international awards that showered Roman Polanski's Poland-set *The Pianist*, a film that chronicled the experiences of Warsaw ghetto survivor Władysław Szpilman.

However, there have also been a range of other 'historical' films made in the 1990s that cover new thematic ground, two types of which stand out. The early Communist years, formerly off limits for investigation, were now revisited by film-makers determined to bring to light suppressed stories of this dark period. Marking a new trend, some films presented a romantic picture of the Communist period laced with nostalgia.

In the past, films that focused on the shady period between 1945 and 1956 were regularly shelved (for example *The Witness*, *All My Good Countrymen*, *The Interrogation*). Encouraged by the advent of *glasnost* in the Soviet Union, film-makers had started looking at the Stalinist period in the late 1980s, when a number of films were made to reflect on this period (such as *Shivers*, *Oh Bloody Life*). After 1989, it became even easier to revisit the times of repression without restrictions, and to tell the story of forced collectivisation and oppressed intellectuals. As the concern of the drab post-Communist reality soon overtook the minds of people, this strand of historical film-making did not flourish as much as it would have if Communism and *glasnost* had persisted. While some of the films of this genre came across as excessively sentimental, there were others that offered a remarkably skilful exploration of the discrepancy between official record and personal history. *Papierové hlavy/Paper Heads* (1995), a little-seen Slovak film by Dušan Hanák, is one of the best examples. The film is a graphic excursion through Czechoslovakia's post-Second World War history. On the one hand, the director works with extracts of propaganda newsreels and documentaries, showing the advancement and triumph of socialist policies. On the other, the film features numerous personal testimonies given by people who were declared adversaries of the system and were marginalised and suppressed in a variety of ways (tried, imprisoned, violated and tortured). The official footage, usually featuring triumphant masses building the bright communist future, is juxtaposed with even-voiced testimonies delivered by elderly people in medium close-up. Their somewhat monotonous monologues expose the enormous discrepancy between officially sanctioned memory and private remembrance. To portray the 'agents' of the injustice suffered by his interviewees – the Communist *apparatchik*s – Hanák uses a group of men wearing suits and giant papier-mâché masks. Even though some of the masks are reminiscent of Soviet and Czechoslovak officials, these 'agents of history' remain silent and unidentified, a silence meant to hint at the anonymous and alienated manner in which they exercised their power.

The other trend, of 'nostalgia' for the nice calm years of Communism, is revealed best by the success of Péter Tímár's *Csinibaba/Dollybirds* (1997). Working mostly in popular genres, Tímár was widely acclaimed for his privately-produced stylish 'retro' musical set in the early 1960s, which became the biggest box office hit in Hungarian cinema that year. Besides the attractive soundtrack, the production design and the nostalgia motifs of the swinging sixties, the film gave a new interpretation to the spirit of the times, traditionally portrayed as an overtly bleak period (the years after the failed revolution attempt of 1956, which resulted in a Soviet invasion). Tímár's film supplied the 1960s with a new look, building on the easygoing sweet memories of the period. Depicting a carefree existence, *Dollybirds* presented the local pioneer leaders as singing and dancing customers in garden pubs and the Communist *apparatchik*s as aimiable folk who would even attend the neighbourhood transvestite costume contest.

Pleasant and easy to watch, *Dollybirds* is reminiscent of a crossover between the aesthetics of Julien Temple's *Absolute Beginners* (UK, 1986) and the representations of musicians seen in Czech New Wave films like Passer's *Intimate Lighting* or Forman's *Competition*. With its teenage rock band and its use of Western popular imagery, the film was received in a way very similar to Emir Kusturica's debut *Sjećaš li se, Dolly Bell?/Do You Remember Dolly Bell?* (1981), which became a cult feature in Yugoslavia because it catered to the audience's need to 'reclaim' the past from politics and emphasise universal elements (like growing up or falling in love for the first time) whatever the political system.

The retro nostalgia, however, elicited mixed feelings among critics who questioned the use of historical memory (see, for example, Sneé 1998; Stöhr 1998). What was one to make of all this 'nostalgia' business? Was this a true portrayal of life in the early 1960s? Well-known Hungarian films about the same period made by directors such as Fábri, Szabó or Mészáros could have over-stressed the bleak reality of these years, but was not *Dollybirds* going to the other extreme and re-writing history with its emphasis on the swing? And indeed, *Dollybirds*' sanitised approach to the past, reducing references to repressive politics to parody, was symptomatic. The film's politics of remembrance (approaching history as a source of 'retro' entertainment) was particularly problematic. Yet its commercial success clearly indicated that audiences in Hungary had had enough of gloomy and serious stories and now wanted to be entertained. By showing their past as an anthology of sugary sweet memories and stressing the enjoyment and the humour, *Dollybirds* catered to clearly identified market needs.[18]

Minority Groups

Some general areas of interest – social concerns, the preoccupation with history – found expression in a proliferation of films that addressed sensitive social issues by focusing on the life of minority groups. In post-Communist times, the Romani population of East Central Europe was affected by excessive impoverishment and resurgent racism. Some of the worst cases of institutional racism, human rights abuses and violent pogroms have been reported here. The complex social situation of the Romanies in the periphery of today's Europe has been the subject of many international documentaries, expressing concern of their socio-economic conditions and the growing racial hatred they face on a daily basis. These issues have also been at the centre of attention for feature film-makers from the region. The socially critical *Marian* (Pétr Vaclav, Czech Republic, 1996), for example, tells the story of a Romani boy whose life evolves around petty crime and excessive punishment, and takes an inevitable pathway from juvenile delinquency to prison. Equally gritty realities are depicted in a range of recent Hungarian films, often with strong documentary power, such as Ildikó Szabó's *Gyerekgyilkosságok/Child Murders* (1993), János Sászsz's *Woyzeck* (1994), based on Georg Büchner's play, and in Bence Gyöngyössy's *Romani kris – Cigánytörvény/Gypsy Lore* (1997), which follows a *King Lear*-type plot. Yet even though many films tend to sympathise with the plight of the Romanies and question the social framework of minority policies, the exploitation of their free-wheeling lifestyles by mainstream feature film still continues, and the pattern of presenting the interaction between Romanies and '*Gadjos*' within the familiar old clichés is as pervasive as ever.[19] In some recent Hungarian films, for example, such as András Solyom's *Érzékek iskolája/School of Sensitivity* (1996) and Zoltán Kamondi's *Kísértések/Temptations* (2002), the young female Romani protagonists are mostly shown as creatures who are largely defined by the impulses of excessively sensual, obsessive and ultimately destructive sexuality.

The way Romanies are treated in post-Communist cinema, however, does not seem to have profoundly changed yet. The 'new times' were supposed to be characterised by a tendency to make socially conscious feature dramas that would be genuinely concerned with the Romani predicament and would result in films that address head-on the troubled relationship between the dominant ethnic group and this minority. Some recent films did indeed attempt, with various degrees of success, to substitute the excessive exoticism of the traditional

Gypsy plots with rough realism. Others, however, went exactly the opposite way and continued exploiting the exotic image.

The Romani population across the region today may be poverty-ridden and exposed to racist attacks, there may be serious social concerns over the causes of trafficking and marginalisation, yet in many films that use the Romani 'trope' there was no place for melancholy or squalor. Poverty or social exclusion was often seen as irrelevant, and the Gypsy protagonists were frequently shown living in a self-contained universe of celebratory enjoyment. The Romani universe was continuously represented as inhabited by passionate lovers, as a visually sumptuous microcosm of exuberant flamboyance, a kingdom of excitingly contagious lifestyle overtaken by intense vigour and desire for life.

Provided that in post-Communist times cinema is expected more than ever to deliver entertainment that sells, it is unlikely that the socially conscious trend in representing the Romani minority will prevail. 'Gypsy exotica' and 'Romani predicament' films will most likely continue to co-exist side by side, revealing the inherent contradictions of the mainstream nationalist discourse that wants to 'retain' the Romanies as a constantly present part of the nation while at the same time excluding them by reiterating their 'ungrateful' rejection of the 'terms of belonging' they are offered.[20]

The interest in Jewish heritage persisted throughout the 1990s, still mostly within the prism of a Holocaust framework. A number of other films made since 1989 revisited past relations between the dominant majority and minority groups, such as Judit Elek's historical investigation into destroyed Jewish communities, *To Speak the Unspeakable*, where a weary Elie Wiesel is shown returning to the native lands of his Transylvania. Jan Hřebejk's tragi-comedy *Divided We Fall* presented an interesting portrayal of the Holocaust via the interaction between a Czech couple who hide a Jewish camp escapee with the local Nazi representative, a Sudeten German with whom they manage to stay on friendly terms. In a range of quasi-comic situations, the Holocaust was treated as a community affair and race relations were approached as a multicultural idyll: the Jew fathers a baby for the infertile Czech couple while the German helps deliver it.

More interested in the poetics of village life rather than in minorities, the work of magic realist Jan Jakub Kolski should also be mentioned in this context, with his interest in the daily miracles of village life and the idyllic poetics of closeness to nature.[21]

Popular Genres

As already mentioned, it would be incorrect to assert that popular genres did not exist before 1989. In the aftermath of 1989, however, there was proliferation in the production of home-grown variations in the action-adventure or comedy genres that openly targeted (and frequently hit) the box office. These films were

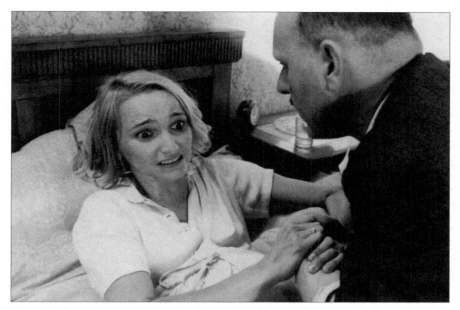

Figure 33: The Holocaust as a community affair: In Hřebejk's *Divided We Fall* (2000) the Czech couple's baby is fathered by a Jew and delivered by a German.

made mostly for domestic consumption and contained a wealth of specific boorish jokes, often understandable only in the concrete national context. The inclusion of brutal violence and graphic sex scenes, allegedly aiming to appeal to mass audiences, became new features of East Central European film. One of the best examples would be Władysław Pasikowski's *Pigs* (1992), a hard-hitting film that not only glamourised the life of a thuggish former secret policeman but cast him as a man of integrity. It enraged the older generation, particularly as it contained a parody of the 1970s workers' protests, specifically as portrayed in Wajda's *Man of Iron*. *Pigs* came to be so popular that it set a specific trend of fast-paced 'boys with toys' films featuring excessive violence and often focusing on the underground world of traffickers, drug dealers and pimps. Pasikowski's approach to film-making was proliferated in the work of other representatives of the 'Young Wolves' (such as Jarosław Zamojda and Maciej Ślesicki) who made a range of overtly commercial films that were patterned as action-adventure or other 'male' genres (see Mazierska 2002).

Another variation of the popular genres is found in the work of Juliusz Machulski, a key box office success story in Poland. After a brief detour into more complexly textured films around 1990, Machulski, a well-known creator of popular genre films, made a triumphal return with his post-Communist action comedy *Kiler* (1997). The film, which is a parody of the action-adventure genre, tells the story of an ordinary cab driver, Jerzy Kiler, who is mistaken for a legendary hitman and gets mixed up in a series of quid pro quos and comic situations revolving around mistaken identity. Similar films are made nowadays also in Hungary and the Czech Republic, usually ranking among the box office hits.

Changing Geopolitics, Changing Identities

For the people of East Central Europe, today's universe is one where old borders crumble and new spaces come into existence. The fall of the Berlin Wall and other turbulent events triggered unforeseen mass migrations and a host of social and political changes. Within the new geopolitical realities, the encounters between East and West were no longer restricted to the European semantic space. The interaction moved beyond the European dimension to a truly global one. Worlds that were unlikely to touch (unless they collided) now interact and overlap. The world is on the move, bringing together Russians and Catalonians, Hungarians and Bolivians, Czechs and Afghans. Alliances and confrontations that were unlikely just a few years ago are now commonplace.

In our times of migrations and radical cultural and historical shifts, comes a restless identity quest. Film-makers' attraction to themes of migration and their interest in people of unsettled hybrid identity suggests a desire to explore new transnational and trans-diasporic interactions.

In 1988, the Soviet presence in the region seemed everlasting, yet it took only a short time for it to become transient. The Soviet military started a reluctant withdrawal early in 1990. This opened up space for an influx of new economic migrants from the crumbling Soviet Union, and today the Russian language is heard all over, in bars and on the streets, at markets and construction sites.

With the withdrawal of Soviet troops and the dissolution of the Soviet Union, film-makers' interest in the Russians intensified, and in the 1990s East Central European films featuring plots or subplots involving Russians proliferated significantly. The films made here subtly (and sometimes quite directly) problematised the traumatic experiences associated with all things Soviet. Instead of taking the chance to articulate the long-standing resentment, however, the tendency was to humanise the image of the Russians. From an impersonal embodiment of an oppressive power, the despised and feared *Homo sovieticus* had now rapidly turned into the ordinary Russian, a vulnerable human being that was susceptible to demystifying scrutiny and pity.

Demonised in a number of films from the late 1980s, in today's East Central European cinema the Russians are being humanised. The subject of the disintegrating Soviet Union itself is treated with a mixture of curiosity and caution; the tyrant has disappeared, leaving behind a nostalgia-filled void. No longer marked by straightforward resentment to the imposed Russian dominance, a range of new films – Jan Svěrák's *Kolja/Kolya* (1996) or Ibolya Fekete's *Bolshe Vita*, to name just two – revealed a mixture of love-hate attraction, or even sympathy and bittersweet longing for the specific Russian kitsch and worn-out revolutionary symbolism.[22]

Kolya, a subtly humorous film – very tongue-in-cheek – revolves around cross-cultural tensions and identities. It tackles the relationship between Czechs and Russians via an unusual situation (an impoverished Prague cellist who resents all things Russian becomes a reluctant guardian to a five-year-old Russian boy) and transposes the tensions between occupiers and occupied onto the realm of personal interaction. The poignant story builds on a comic series of events, a process in which the protagonist's long-standing anti-Soviet sentiment gradually softens to be replaced by a genuine bond with the boy. The cross-cultural appeal of *Kolya* lies in its assertion of personal commitment against all odds. The film-makers favoured personal intimacy over abstract political allegiances and questioned the anti-Russian stance as a deep-seated 'identity' prejudice, thus taking an unusual self-critical stance that facilitated the film's international success.

Subverting long-standing geopolitical stereotypes, Ibolya Fekete's acclaimed *Bolshe Vita* also told a story about Russians and Americans who all end up in Hungary to experience first-hand the lifting of the Iron Curtain. Migrating Russian men experience Budapest's underbelly and explore various dimensions of life in this new post-Communist Babylon. Their life and encounters evolve around 'Bolse Vita', the bohemian bar where the Iron Curtain fall-out is celebrated nightly in a never-ending party, and where former enemies, Russians and Americans, can happily mix as they please.

This specific hybrid essence of post-Communist identities was further problematised by Fekete in *Chico*. In this quasi-documentary feature relying on re-enactment, the forty-year-old protagonist, Eduardo Rózsa Flores ('a Spanish-Hungarian, Catholic-Jew') plays himself and recounts his own controversial litanies. Born in Bolivia to a Latin American mother and a Hungarian-Jewish father, Chico is raised as a dedicated Communist and atheist and grows devoted to the leftist cause after experiencing the violent downfall of Allende's government in Chile in 1973. In his later life, having moved to Eastern Europe (Hungary) as a teenager, he is frequently confronted with the contradictory politics and history of the region; the volatile circumstances turn him into a spontaneous political chameleon. In a prolonged identity quest, he crosses sides many more times. Trained by the KGB and having begun a career in intelligence, he grows disillusioned after becoming involved with international terrorism and ends up fighting on the Croatian side in the Yugoslavia wars of succession. Chico crosses fault lines many times: at one moment in the film he helps a Catholic priest hold a mass in mostly Muslim Albania, and just a few minutes of screen time later we see him praying alongside Orthodox Jews at the Wailing Wall in Jerusalem.

Chico's 'confused identity' is expressed in his unstable national (Bolivian-Chilean-Hungarian), religious (Catholic-Jew, atheist-believer) and political (leftist, terrorist, nationalist) belonging. In a way, he is an opportunist, continuously adjusting to changing circumstances. His switching sides, however, is not led by a mere survival instinct; it is the result of a sincere intellectual quest that weighs major ideologies and currents of thought against each other. As Fekete has noted, a similar crisis of identity is experienced by many in the post-Cold War period. Her focus is thus on the controversial and difficult identity quest that one has to live through when confronted with constantly contested claims on history and with a 'collapse of coherent ideologies' (in Clark & Federlein 2002). Her highly original approach to history and contemporary politics touches on areas of key importance for post-Communist identities; these are the anxieties and the questions that are on the minds of so many East Central Europeans that belong to a generation that has lived through the volatile times of crumbling political systems and transitional worlds.

Resources

The goal of this appendix is to present an overview of some of the most important English-language resources for those who undertake to teach East Central European cinema. Matters such as existing scholarship and availability of video resources will be briefly discussed.

Scholarship

Film scholarship on Eastern Europe in the West does not occupy a particularly prominent position in the context of Western studies into world cinema. Studies on East Central European film did not increase as intensely as one might have expected in the 1990s, particularly in relation to other areas of international cinema, such India, Iran or the Middle East, for example. One possible reason for the low profile may be that most writing concentrates on single national cinemas, and almost none explores the issues regionally, thus failing to note and discuss significant trends. Proponents of the national cinemas approach have expressed scepticism in regard to the 'regionalist' one, claiming that it only makes sense from the point of view of commercial publishers who insist on a 'less ambitious' approach instead (Haltof 2001). While I agree that in certain instances the 'regionalism' has been applied inconsiderately and inconsistently, I would still argue that examining the cinema of East Central Europe in a regional context is a pre-condition for serious academic investigation.

In addition, writers of the younger generation have blamed existing scholarship for being insensitive to general developments in film theory and cultural studies, and for making no use of, or even being 'hostile' to, the frameworks found within the discourses on postmodernism, post-colonialism, globalisation, feminism and queer studies (Imre 1999: 406). While such accusations may be too harsh, it is important to note that there is little interaction between Slavic scholars on the one hand, and media and film scholars on the other. Unlike other modern language departments where a faculty member specialising in film is a fixture, in the field of Slavic studies film is still to be represented adequately on the curriculum, as it has not yet been recognised as an equally important strand of cultural history but is seen as subordinate to literature. More attention to the great cinematic traditions of the region is needed; if given, it may well reinvigorate the interest in Slavic studies in general.

The leading texts on East European cinema were published during the Cold War period, and some are rapidly becoming out of date. The only comprehensive study which approaches the issues regionally is one by Antonín and Mira Liehm (1977), augmented by three collections of essays from the 1980s (Paul 1983, Némes 1985, Goulding 1989) and two reference works from the early 1990s (Balski 1991, Slater 1992). In addition, some very good writing on film can be found in *Cross Currents*, the little-available annual review on Central European culture published throughout the 1980s by academics at the University of Michigan (Ann Arbor) and Yale. Historians and theoreticians of East Central European film in the West include Yvette Bíró, Daniel Goulding, Peter Hames, Ronald Holloway, Antonín Liehm and Graham Petrie, most of whom are still active even though they are either retired or nearing retirement. Herbert Eagle, who has produced some of the most insightful texts on Czechoslovak and Polish film, has published numerous essays in various obscure publications, but his writings have never been brought together in a book, thus leaving a serious gap in the scholarship on film of the region. Scholars who have published important texts during the 1990s include Paul Coates, Andrew Horton, Janina Falkowska and Catherine Portuges. In addition, some well-known Western critical scholars, like Fredric Jameson, David Bordwell and Stuart Hall, have occasionally written on selected topics in East Central European cinema.

A new generation of scholars is about to begin publishing studies that hopefully will offer the much-needed combination of factual knowledge with new theoretical insights. Some of these include Ewa Mazierska, Marek Haltof, Anikó Imre, Andrew James Horton, Jesse Labov, Saša Milić and Bjorn Ingvoldstadt. A positive trend since the late 1990s is the appearance, for the first time, of critical studies that include contributions by Western critics placed side by side with scholars based in Poland, Hungary, the Czech and Slovac republics. The end of the decade saw the publication of a comprehensive book on East German film history (Allan and Sandford 1999), and of *The BFI Companion to Eastern European and Russian Cinema* (2000, the East European part of which was edited by Nancy Wood and myself). Peter Hames, author of the classic study of the Czechoslovak New Wave, is putting together a collection of essays, which will cover a selection of twenty-four key films from the region.[1] An important development has been the appearance of *Kinoeye* (http://www.kinoeye.org), the on-line magazine run by Andrew James Horton, which covers both current film from the region and understudied aspects of film history.

Further Sources

Videos

Only a small fraction of the films discussed here are available in 35mm and 16mm formats. Most are, however, accessible on video and, as of recently, an increasing number of these have started appearing on DVD. Thus, to find a film, the first port of call should be the companies that specialise in art-house cinema on video and DVD. Many smaller companies carry various titles but to keep track of who has what can be laborious. Hence, the best approach is to use a distributor that acts as a clearing-house for other distribution companies.

In the United States, the most important of these is undoubtedly Facets Multimedia (http://www.facets.org) in Chicago. Operating by mail order, their website features a user-friendly searchable database of all titles. Started by Czech-born Milos Stehlik, Facets has done much to promote film from the region by releasing a number of Czechoslovak, Polish and Hungarian features under their own label while also listing films available from other distributors. Facets' extensive catalogue, which is periodically updated (currently in its sixteenth edition), is an invaluable resource for those teaching in the field of film studies. They also occasionally publish thematic catalogues on a variety of topics, such as Slavic or German film.

Many Polish titles are available on video from PolArt (http://www.polart.com), based in Sarasota, Florida. Another distributor of growing importance is Icestorm International (http://www.icestorm-video.com), based in Amherst, Massachusetts. They started off as an outlet specialising in East German films made at DEFA but are in the process of expanding and have plans to release a number of other titles.

In other countries, it is difficult to find a video distributor that has the same comprehensive operation and still remains specialised in the way Facets does. The clearing-house outlets that are accessible in the UK, for example, are not particularly focused on world cinema. Nonetheless, places such as Blackstar (http:

//www.blackstar.co.uk) and Movie Mail (http://www.moviem.co.uk) should be visited first, even though the actual titles are most likely to be released under the Artificial Eye or Tartan labels.

Gradually, new video distributors based in the countries that the films originate in have started appearing. If you have a clearly defined interest, it is worth searching the Internet for such firms on a regular basis, as they are mushrooming all the time. These outlets usually offer bargain prices. The quality of the videos, however, varies significantly.

Resource centres

The most important contact points are the respective centres for Eastern European and Russian or Soviet studies, many of which also maintain collections of videos from the region. The most active centres in the USA are those at Indiana University at Bloomington, University of Michigan, University of Illinois at Urbana-Champaign, University of Texas at Austin, University of Pittsburgh, University of Washington and Columbia University. The centres (and the respective Slavic departments) often carry a collection of about 100 to 200 films on videotape that they would be willing to lend. In the UK, such centres are found at the School of Slavonic and East European Studies in London (http://www.ssees.ac.uk), and at the universities of Glasgow, Leeds, Durham and Birmingham. These collections, however, most often consist of Russian and Soviet films, while the films from all other countries of the former Eastern Bloc combined make up about 20 to 30 per cent of the holdings. In addition, you are likely to encounter some excessively restrictive borrowing rules.

For those teaching East Central European cinema, the most important contacts are with the respective cultural attachés and the cultural centres which operate out of capital cities or large metropolitan areas (such as London and Washington, DC). The attachés usually have access to a collection of videos that they would be more than happy to make available to you. The cultural centres often have a specialist in charge of putting together promotional film events. This is the ideal person to consult on any event you may want to organise or the films that you would like to make available to students during your teaching.

Contacting the organisation of a particular ethnic community also makes sense, as they may be able to assist you with providing videotapes and other film-related materials. They may also put you in touch with a specialised bookstore that carries videos from the country. These groups often schedule film-related events themselves. For example, there is an annual Polish film festival, taking place in Chicago and Ann Arbor, which showcases the recent cinematic output of the country.

If there is a film festival in town, it makes sense to maintain contact with the programmers. Even though they may not be specialised (or particularly interested) in these cinemas, they usually have access to viewing tapes and other videos from the countries in the region and may be able to help you obtain copies of films that do not come into distribution via the usual channels.

If you are planning to screen films in 35mm or 16mm format, you could consult the programmers at your local art-house film theatre (usually located within or near the university campus) who deal with distributors all the time and have their respective catalogues handy. They can tell you whom you need to be in touch with to book a copy of the film you would like to show. In the UK, you can also seek help from the British Film Institute (BFI) (http://www.bfi.org.uk) or from the British Universities Film and Video Council (BUFVC) (http://www.bufvc.ac.uk).

Websites

Throughout this chapter, a number of web references are indicated that may be useful in tracking down further information in East European Cinema. When working on your syllabus or reading list, it would be appropriate if you listed some of the resources that you found useful for the students. The students will use the Web in researching for their work and as their instructor, you can help to direct this process by indicating which resources you believe are most helpful. It is a good idea to ask the students to report in class on websites that may not be on your list that they think are particularly good. You can also ask your resource librarian to teach a class about the available electronic resources in film. If you make provisions for such a session you will give the students a good chance to improve their on-line research skills.[2]

Planning for the Course

Courses in East Central European film are usually taken by two general types of students: either by those majoring in area studies who besides society, politics, culture and literature would also like to learn about cinema, or by those who are interested in film-making and would like to know more about it beyond Hollywood. Often students of this second type are so impressed with the supreme crafting of the films from the region they have accidentally stumbled upon that they would like to see more. If the primary audience for the course is made up of film students, I strongly recommend the regional approach. The national cinema approach may be more suitable for those who are specifically interested in studying the language and the culture of a given country.

Depending on the audience, the course has two goals: first, to make students acquainted with the best in East European film-making, and second to allow them a better comprehension of the specifics of the region and of the artistic and cultural context in which these films are made.

When planning, it is particularly important to keep in mind that the primary texts for this course are the films you will decide to work with. I often come across academics (usually from a language and literature background) who are planning to teach film and are preoccupied with what readings to assign to students. While the issue of readings is, of course, very important, it remains a secondary concern within a film course. First of all, you need to choose about ten films that you will show to the students for the duration of the term (semester), and make sure that copies of these are available not only for your organised screenings but also for students' personal viewing. Readings and other study materials should be decided on after the primary texts have been selected, and these primary texts are the films that will be shown. Similarly, when discussions are held, it is the cinematic text that is to be discussed first and foremost. Critical responses to the film, directors' statements and discussions of style that are included in the selection of readings (either a course packet put together for the specific course, or a book adopted as main course text), while very important, are secondary material.

Depending on the administrative regulations, the screenings may need to take place in a different setting. The best way is to have scheduled screenings once a week, attended both by the students and the instructor, and ideally taking place on the day preceding the class meeting. Many universities have put in place auditoriums that allow for such cinema-like experiences. You need to plan well in advance, however, and book the room, as usually these are in high demand across campus. Some universities request that the screening of the films take place as part of the class meeting. In such cases, you may need to plan for a longer class time, to allow enough time to screen the film, and have a discussion as well as a lecture on the issues that you would like to bring to the students' attention. Yet another option is to make videos of the films available for a short loan and request that students use the video facilities at the library to see each film before the date that discussion is scheduled for.

Teaching National Cinemas

Whereas the national cinema approach has the advantage of giving more insight into a particular tradition, it usually fails to draw a more general picture of the cinema of the region. In a semester of 11 to 13 weeks, then, the first one or two weeks can be devoted to general background exploration, and the rest of the time assigned to the individual countries (for example three weeks each for Poland, the Czech Republic and Hungary, and two for Slovakia). For a variety of reasons (most often pre-determined by the specialisation of the instructor in one national tradition), the majority of film courses are still structured around individual national cinemas. Whatever the context, a film course should aim to go beyond the narrow area studies interest, it should not treat film as a simple extension of literature, and it should make provisions for discussing the specific issues of film art and aesthetics.

Poland

Polish cinema can provide more than enough material to justify an exclusive national cinema course. It is difficult to choose among the wide range of Polish masterpieces and to limit oneself to showing only selected works. If I were to teach a Polish film course, I would do my best to schedule screenings of films by Wojciech Has, Jerzy Kawalerowicz, Andrzej Munk, Andrzej Wajda, Jerzy Skolimowski, Kazimierz Kutz, Krzysztof Zanussi, Krzysztof Kieślowski, Agnieszka Holland, Jan Jakub Kolski, as well as select films by some lesser-known directors.

Many Polish films are available in distribution, and on the web one can find numerous sites maintained by enthusiasts. Useful portals are http://www.slavweb.com/eng/cee/poland-e.html and http://www.filmweb.pl/.

This course would be easy to support with corresponding readings as the body of work on Polish cinema in English is steadily growing, and at the moment there are both survey studies of Polish cinema as well as texts devoted to specific aspects. Most important surveys include texts by Frank Bren (1986), Bolesław Michałek & Frank Turaj (1988) and Marek Haltof (2002).

A series of books and articles look into the work of directors or themes. Authors who worked on Wajda include Michałek (1973), Eagle (1982), Falkowska (1996), Mazierska (2000c) and others. A book containing Wajda's writings was translated into English in 1986, and a documentary *A. Wajda, A Portrait* (E. Lachnit, 1989) is available in the West. There is also a Wajda home page: http://www.wajda.pl. In 2001, the director's oeuvre was the subject of a special conference in Lódź, and a selection of the papers presented there is published in English by Wallflower Press, *The Cinema of Andrzej Wajda: The Art of Irony and Defiance*, edited by John Orr and Elzbieta Ostrowska (2003).

The body of studies on Kieślowski is steadily growing. Besides books in various European languages, in English there are books on Kieślowski by Christopher Garbowski (1996), Geoff Andrew (1998), Annette Insdorf (1999), Slavoj Žižek (2001), and an excellent collection of essays edited by Paul Coates (1999), as well as numerous articles (for example Roberts, 2000). Faber have published the script of *The Decalogue* (1991) and a book of interviews with the director (Stok, 1993). *The Cinema of Krzysztof Kieślowski: Variations on Destiny and Chance* by Marek Haltof is forthcoming from Wallflower Press (2004). A good resource can be found at http://www-personal.engin.umich.edu/~zbigniew/Kieslowski/kieslowski.html.

The English language literature on Polanski is extensive and a simple search of a comprehensive library catalogue should yield scores of texts on him; the issue here is if he is to be considered a Polish director. Out of the many books written on Polanski, Vriginia Wright Wexman's (1985) is usually considered to be the most insightful one.

Numerous articles on Polish cinema are published across film and Slavic journals, and in edited books. Besides Paul Coates in the UK, most specialists on Polish film working in the West are of Polish origin, and we often see texts written by established Polish scholars and critics translated into English (for example Helman, Sobolewski, Lubelski). Mazierska has published pieces on a range of directors such as Machulski (1999), Kolski (2000a), Kutz (2000b) and others. In the 1990s, film scholars based in Poland have put out several books on film in English, select chapters of these are also suitable for use.

The Polish films which will be covered by dedicated essays in Wallflower Press' forthcoming *24 Frames* volume on East Central European cinema (edited by Peter Hames, 2004) include *The Dybbuk* (Waszynski, 1937*), Ashes and Diamonds* (Wajda, 1958), *Eroica* (Munk, 1958), *Knife in the Water* (Polanski, 1962*), The Saragossa Manuscript* (Has, 1965), *Man of Marble* (Wajda, 1976) and *The Decalogue* (Kieślowski, 1988).

Czechoslovakia

It will take some time before it is feasible to offer courses on Slovak cinema exclusively. Many of the key works of Slovak cinema – by Dušan Hanák and Juraj Jakubisko, for example – remain unavailable, and the English-language literature on Slovak cinema has still to materialise. In addition, it is difficult to divide the film tradition of a country that operated on a federative basis until a decade ago, and decisions on what belongs where are likely to be problematic. Still, a Slovak-focused course should cover, besides the directors already mentioned, the Slovak work of Elmar Klos and Jan Kadár, Peter Solan and the young Martin Šulík. Jakubisko's work is featured on two web pages: http://www.jakubisko.cz and http://www.jakubiskofilm.com

As far as Czech cinema is concerned, the focus of the course would most likely be on three key areas – the New Wave of the 1960s, animation and post-Communist cinema. The range of remarkable films made in the 1960s include works by Miloš Forman, Jan Němec, Jaromil Jireš, Věra Chytilová, Jiří Menzel, Ivan Passer, Vojtěch Jasný and Evald Schorm. While some of the classics from the 1960s remain unavailable, many are gradually being released. The best study of the Czech cinema is Peter Hames' *The Czechoslovak New Wave*, first published in 1985. Hames also authored a number of insightful shorter pieces for *Kinoeye* and for *Censorship: An International Encyclopedia* (Jones 2001). Herbert Eagle is the author of some of the most competent but little-seen texts on Czech film-makers. Other books on the history of Czech cinema include texts by Liehm and Škvorecký. Materials related to Czech cinema can be found at http://maxpages.com/czechcinema.

It is a good idea to include the amazing work of film-makers working in animated film in each film course, but the availability of films from Polish or Hungarian animators is largely unavailable. The case with Czech films is somewhat better, with several of Karel Zeman's, some of Jiří Trnka's and most of Jan Švankmajer's later works easily accessible. There is an English language book of essays on Švankmajer edied by Peter Hames (1995); the script of his *Faust* has also been translated (1998). Two British-based web pages on the animator can be found at http://www.illumin.co.uk/svank and http://www.svankmajer.com.

Although not nearly as important in comparison to the New Wave's cinematic achievement, the Czech cinema of the 1990s has scored fairly well internationally, with a variety of international awards for directors from the younger generation. Therefore, it should be given appropriate attention in the course.

The director whose work has been explored most is Miloš Forman, perhaps because of his successful later career in the West. It would be appropriate to use parts of his autobiography *Turnaround* (1992), books by Antonín Liehm (1975) and Slater (1987), and chapters by Liehm in *Politics, Art and Commitment in the East European Cinema* (Paul 1983) and Hames in *Five Filmmakers* (Goulding, 1995). Recently, special issues of *Kinoeye* were devoted to the work of Jan Němec and Věra Chytilová and are available online.

The forthcoming volume of Wallflower Press' *24 Frames* series will contain essays on a number of films from Czechoslovakia: *Erotikon* (Machatý, 1929), *Heave Ho!* (Fric, 1934), *The Long Journey* (Radok, 1948), *A Shop on the High Street* (Kadár and Klos, 1965), *Closely Observed Trains* (Menzel, 1966), *Marketa Lazarova* (František Vláčil, 1965–67), *Daisies* (Chytilová, 1966), *Birds, Orphans and Fools* (Jakubisko, 1969), *Alice* (Švankmajer, 1987) and *The Garden* (Šulík, 1995).

Hungary

When considering Hungarian cinema, proper attention should be paid to the best of world film-making directors such as Miklós Jancsó, István Szabó, Zoltán Fábri, as well as to recognised masters such as Károly Makk, Pál Sándor, Péter Bacsó, Márta Mészarós, Judit Elek, Péter Gothár, Béla Tarr and Ibolya Fekete.

The availability of Hungarian films in the West is limited; yet many of the most important cinematic texts are in circulation. The Hungarian film-makers organisation, Magyar Filmunió, have the reputation of being particularly helpful with supplying tapes and materials when they are requested by instructors.

While Hungary's remarkable film tradition has been the subject of competent writing, the need for an up-to-date comprehensive study of Hungarian cinema is strongly felt, as most of the texts on Hungarian film in English are from the 1970s and 1980s. Survey studies include an early text by István Nemeskürty (1968) and a more comprehensive treatment by Bryan

Burns (1996). Though out-of-date, the finest text on Hungarian film still remains Graham Petrie's book *History Must Answer to Man* (1978). *Hungarian Cinema: From Coffee House to Multiplex* by John Cunnigham is forthcoming from Wallflower Press (2004); besides other lesser-known aspects of this cinema, it will highlight the work of directors like Zoltán Fábri, as well as Hungary's rich documentary and animation tradition. Authors that specialise in Hungarian cinema include New York-based Yvette Bíró, as well as groups of scholars working at Cleveland's John Carroll University and at the University of Toronto. Derek Elley, one of the leading critcs and a consultant editor for the *Variety International Cinema Yearbook*, specialises in Hungary and has written extensively on this cinema. Catherine Portuges' book on Márta Mészáros (1993) is one of the few studies devoted to a single director. Jancsó's work has been the subject of books in other languages but there is no study on him in English so far. A special double issue of *Kinoeye* tries to compensate this shortcoming (http://www.kinoeye.org/index_03_03.html). Graham Petrie has published a text dedicated to a single film by the director, *Red Psalm* (1998). Texts discussing Szabó include one by David Paul (in Goulding 1995) and Imre (1999). Articles on a range of other subjects and directors can be found in various film-related publications, and often in the specialised journals in Hungarian studies (*Hungarian Quarterly, Budapest Review of Books*) and in *Kinoeye*. For an overview of the film industry in Hungary, see James (in Kindem 2000) and Gálik (1998). For an informative discussion of documentary film-making in Communist Hungary, see J. Hoberman (1998: 43-67). The on-line version of the journal *Filmkultura* carries some excellent articles in English: http://www.filmkultura.iif.hu.

Wallflower Press' *24 Frames* volume will include essays on *People on the Alps* (Szots, 1942), *The Round-Up* (Jancsó, 1965), *Love* (Makk, 1971), *Diary for my Children* (Mészáros, 1982), *Colonel Redl* (Szabó, 1985), *Satan's Tango* (Tarr, 1994) and *Bolshe Vita* (Fekete, 1996).

Teaching Regional Cinema

Other ways to organise the course revolve around topics rather than national cinemas and directors. The material is structured around several major topics that are all linked with important issues of East Central Europe's historical and social experience.

When teaching cinema in a regional context it is important to identify various geographic, ethno-linguistic, religious and socio-historical characteristics of the shared background that support this argument. Geographically, it is useful to identify the locations of the countries and their main cities, and their positioning in relation to other main points on the continent (for example Prague, Vienna, Warsaw, Berlin, Bratislava, Budapest); it is even better to look at historical maps that show the fluctuating borders, as well as the positioning of countries that no longer exist, such as the Ottoman Empire, and, more importantly, Austria-Hungary, and to clarify historical geographical names that do not have the respective connotation on the political map of the region today (such as Transylvania, Ruthenia, Bohemia, Moravia, Silesia). It is important to have an idea of the countries by territory and population, of the character and location of important historical sites and routes, the major mountain chains and rivers in the region. Issues of the ethno-linguistic tapestry include identifying the main groups of languages spoken here, as well as the main minority groups and their distribution, especially the Jews and the Romanies. This is also the time to discuss rules of spelling and pronunciation of East European names. The denominational make-up is another background topic, within the context of which the importance of the Catholic and Protestant traditions in the region are to be discussed, maybe to also include references to Judaism, Orthodox Christianity and Islam, as well as to evaluate the historical role and influence of religious figures such as Pope John Paul II.

The shared social and political history of the countries in the region needs to be highlighted with a special focus on the twentieth century. While in a national film course the respective background would be limited to the history of the given country, here it would be important to emphasise such moments where the interaction of the big powers and the acts of the various countries have determined developments in the whole region. One needs to explain the constrains of their 'imposed' togetherness throughout the Cold War period, for example the end of Austria-Hungary (1918), the Molotov-Ribbentrop agreement (1939), the Yalta conference (1945), the establishment of Communist regimes in East Central Europe (1945 to 1948), Khrushchev's denunciation of Stalinism (1956), the Hungarian Uprising (1956), the Prague Spring and the Warsaw pact invasion (1968), or the launch of *glasnost* (1986). In the context of cultural history, it is important to stress the fact that East Central European intellectuals have played a role in all major ideological and artistic movements in the twentieth century (for example positivism, psychoanalysis, Constructivism, Futurism, Dadaism, Surrealism, and so on).

The regional approach not only provides insights into the cultures of the region but also allows general trends in the film industry and aesthetics to be traced. The students may then become familiar with major schools of film-making and with specific developments in the film tradition. There is also the opportunity for extensive comparisons with Western cinemas.

The course could be structured around periods in film-making (such as the New Wave, the 1980s, the 1990s). Such structuring, however, would imply clarification of the respective socio-historical background. The course could also be focused on textual analysis or on the application of various critical methods to specific film texts (and there is an abundance of such cinematic texts in this film tradition). Once again, however, the discussion of the specific socio-cultural context cannot be overlooked and the context will very likely become a key part of any venture into textual analysis. Thus, the course would be most successful if structured so that discussion of cinematic texts would keep their specific socio-cultural origins and concerns to the fore.

An instructor could use the structure proposed here but substitute some of the topics with others as he/she considers most appropriate. In addition to the themes discussed here, in my teaching I have experimented with more topics such as the image of the Communist, representations of the West, sexuality, folklore and so on. It is possible to develop units that explore issues of cinematic adaptation of literary works, or specific genres – comedy, science fiction and drama. If the preference is for cinematic language and film form, East European film has a lot to offer with possible explorations of experimental and avant-garde film-making (Surrealism, political film, animation) and masterpieces that have influenced world cinema (by Jancsó, Wajda, Kieślowski, Mészarós).

It is possible to structure the course around individual directors. Besides the best-known directors who should be included if one chooses to follow the 'auteur' approach (and East Central European film provides excellent material for illustrating the 'auteur' theory), one should not overlook film artists such as Has and Kawalerowicz, Kutz and Kolski, Němec and Chytilová, Jakubisko and Hanák, Tarr and Fábri.

Resources by Chapter

Without attempting to be fully comprehensive, it is useful to indicate some resources that I have found particularly useful in relation to some of the themes that are covered in the respective chapters of this book.

Chapter One: East Central European Film Studies

Some of the key studies of East European cinema have pursued a similar approach, unifying the countries mostly on the political principle. Antonín and Mira Liehm's influential study *The Most Important Art* (1977) discusses all these cinemas, as well as the Soviet, East German and Balkan cinemas. The two important books edited by Daniel Goulding (1989; 1985) also cover the region (even though within the volumes the approach is by national cinemas). *The BFI Companion to Eastern European and Russian Cinema* (2000) contains a number of useful topical entries to these cinemas.

Chapter Two: The Industry

Good background reading on the position of intellectuals under communism is Václav Havel's text *The Power of the Powerless* (1978). Parts of Miklós Haraszty's text *The Velvet Prison* (1987) and select articles from Ludvik Vaculik's *A Cup of Coffee with My Interrogator* (1987) are particularly useful on the issues of censorship. The journal *Index on Censorship* has regularly included overviews on the cinema in Eastern Europe, particularly in volumes 14/1 (1981), 20/3 (1991) and 24/6 (1995). Some excellent articles that clarify issues of East European censorship and cinema are included in *Censorship: An International Encyclopedia*, edited by Derek Jones (2001).

Authors who have written extensively on East European animation include David Ehrlich, Marcin Gyzicki, Michael O'Pray and Ronald Holloway (see in particular his 'The Short Film in Eastern Europe: Art and Politics of Cartoons and Puppets' in David Paul's edited volume, 1983). A compilation tape of interesting examples of East European animation is volume 3 (1986) of the series *Masters of World Animation*; another is volume 8, *Animated Journey*, in the 1990 series *Eastern Europe Breaking with the Past*. Lately, *Facets* (www.facets.org) has released a number of animations from the former Eastern Bloc on DVD. Zagreb's animation film festival website is very interesting and can be found at http://www.animafest.hr.

The work of directors who migrated and worked in diaspora seems to be covered better than the work of those who stayed, both in print and on the Internet. Some very useful texts are included in the book devoted to directors working in the West before 1990 (Petrie & Dwyer 1990). Dedicated home pages cover the work of film-makers such as Michael Curtiz (http://members.tripod.com/~candide), Polanski (http://www.rp-productions.com), Borowczyk (http://www.vidmarc.demon.co.uk/mondo-erotico/indexboro.html) and Holland (http://www.perfectnet.com/holland/ahpl.htm). Gustav Machatý's tireless movements between continents are discussed in a book by Škvorecký (1971). Writings on and by Forman are listed in the section on Czech cinema.

Chapter Three: Historical Film I: Narratives of Identity

Hegyi's text on *Central Europe as a Hypothesis and a Way of Life* (2001), mostly discusses the fine arts but develops a convincing view of the peculiar understanding of the relationship between history and individual fate in the region. On Polish heritage cinema, see Mazierska (2001). Supporting texts on *Angi Vera*, a film that is suitable to screen as an illustration of the discussion on Stalinism, include Quart (1980), Burns (1996) and Gallagher's interview with Pál Gábor (1980). Of relevance here would be those chapters in national cinema books that discuss the work of Wajda, Szabó and Munk.

Chapter Four: Historical Film II: Discourse on Morality

Some of the texts that can be used here include chapters two and three of Ilan Avisar's book on Holocaust film (1988), as well as select parts of Annette

Insdorf's (1989; third edition 2003) book on Holocaust cinema. On Andrzej Munk, see Michałek and Turaj (1988: 114–28) and Stolarska (1995). An American documentary, *Fighter* (Amir Bar-Lev, 2000) shows the return of Holocaust survivor and author/screenwriter Arnošt Lustig to the sites of his experiences fifty years earlier.

Chapter Five: State Socialist Modernity: The Urban and the Rural

The Czechoslovak New Wave is most comprehensively covered in the writing of Peter Hames. Important aspects of the experience of Czechoslovak New Wave generation are discussed in interviews included in the documentary *The Velvet Hangover* (2000). All books on Polish cinema include chapters on the 'cinema of moral concern', and there are a number of texts that analyse Kieślowski's work.

Chapter Six: Women's Cinema, Women's Concerns

For general information on women film-makers it is appropriate to use Barbara Quart's text in *Women Directors* (1988: 191–239), and the respective personal and national entries in the specialised film companion on international women's film (Kuhn & Radstone 1990). Texts focusing on individual directors include Portuges' book on Mészáros (1993) and Mazierska's essay on Jakubowska (2001b). The work of Chytilová is covered extensively in a special issue of the on-line journal *Kinoeye* Vol. 2, No. 8, 29 April 2002 (http://www.kinoeye.org/index_02_08.html) which includes original contributions and translated essays by leading Czech film scholars. In 2002, *Kinoeye* also ran a special issue on women in Polish film (http://www.kinoeye.org/index_02_06.html).

Chapter Seven: East Central European Cinema since 1989

Film journals have run occasional special issues on post-Communist film-making, for example, *Cineaste* (Vol. 19, No. 4, 1992) and *Film Criticism* (Winter 1996/97, Vol. 21), and Slavic journals have run overview pieces on these issues (see Portuges 1992). Since 1992 the trade magazines such as *Variety* and *Screen International* have regularly published articles covering the status of the industry. *Kinoeye* remains one of the best resources covering the most recent films from the region. The re-structuring of the film industries is covered in articles discussing the issues in Europe-wide context (see Jäckel 1996, Iordanova 1999a, 2002a). Specific countries are discussed by Portuges (1995) and by Gálik on Hungary (1998), Haltof on Poland (1996) and Hames on the Czech Republic (2000a). Texts covering various aspects of the current cinema of the region appear in the specialised academic journals dealing with the region (including *Slavic Review*, *Polish Review* and *Hungarian Quarterly*).

NOTES

Part I – Overview

1   However it is important to acknowledge that East Central European film is closely dependent on literature. Leading film-makers from the region have repeatedly stated that key works of literature (from Dostoevsky to Kafka) are more important for them than the works of other film-makers. It is not possible to understand the work of a key figure of this cinema like Jiří Menzel, for example, without delving into the provincial world of someone like Bohumil Hrabal. The inspiration that East Central European film takes from literary traditions is of crucial importance; the feeling of abstract detachment that this cinema often engenders stems from the fact that its primary impulses come from words, not from images (Boris Jocić, personal correspondence, 2003).

Chapter 1

1   The periodisation in each country differs slightly depending on the main historical dates of the country's specific experience. It is understandable that the year 1956 is of particular importance for Hungary (a failed attempt to overthrow the Communist government), the year 1968 for Czechoslovakia (the Prague Spring and Warsaw Pact invasion) and the year 1981 for Poland (the imposition of martial law).
2   The cinematic heritage is preserved in the respective national archives. For information on archival availability of older films see references in Paolo Cherchi Usai (1993). The festival of silent cinema that takes place in Italy every October (formerly at Pordenone, now Sacile) has also conducted research work, specifically on Hungarian silent cinema.
3   Particularly noteworthy examples are the silent films by the Hungarian-born Mihály Kertész (better-known as leading American director Michael Curtiz), or the erotic

classics made by the Czech director Gustav Machatý (*Eroticon*, 1929; *Extase/Ecstasy*, 1932), and the Polish-Yiddish cinema of Joseph Green.

4   This project was carried out by intellectuals, many of whom were either in exile or were internal dissidents. Some important names to be mentioned here are the Czech exiled writer Milan Kundera (*The Joke, The Unbearable Lightness of Being, Life is Elsewhere*) and playwright (and later president) Václav Havel (*The Power of Powerless*); the Hungarian dissidents György Konrad (*Anti-Politics*) and Miklós Haraszty (*The Velvet Prison*); Polish poet Czesław Miłosz (*The Captive Mind*) and dissidents Jacek Kuroń, Adam Michnik or exiled intellectuals such as philosopher Leszek Kołakowski and literary scholar Stanisław Barańczak. These are only a few names, of course, as many more contributed to the project of 'the idea of Central Europe' discussed in more detail in the writings of Timothy Garton Ash (1983) and Jacques Rupnik (1988). In the 1980s Garton Ash and Rupnik also contributed with their writing to the crystallisation of the idea of Central Europe as a unique cultural space.

5   Some extra dimensions of this investigation not covered here (not least because they have been discussed in *Cinema of Flames*, 2001) were brought to my attention by colleagues specialising in these cinemas:. the terms 'Central Europe', 'East Central Europe', 'East-Central Europe' and 'East and Central Europe' have all been used to apply to the region in the post-Cold War period. Yet, there still seems to be a lack of consensus and they are applied by different authors in a variety of ways. In addition to Poland, Hungary and the former Czechoslovakia, at times they have also included Bulgaria and Romania, Belarus, Ukraine and Moldova, the former Yugoslavia and the Baltic countries. While this is not the place to examine these contradictions in detail, it is important to bear in mind the conflicting usages. In particular, it is worth considering if the methodologies applied here to a 'region' (searcing for similarities rather than differences) can also be applied to Western Europe, in particular the 'big' countries, or if they are reserved only for 'small' countries or those 'on the periphery' (of the West)? The term 'East Central Europe' has, for instance, been used quite explicitly to replace the Cold War term 'Eastern Europe', but can still be used to marginalise the area and its cultures. Thus, the claim for trans-national/regional commonalities may occasionally come across as too strong, because such commonalities really are those of 'etatist', and in this sense modernist, societies, and the practical co-operation among the socialist Bloc, but not of actively pursued cultural kinship.

6   I am indebted to Natasa Ďurovičová for bringing these aspects to my attention.

7   The cinemas of Central Asia make an impact at international film festivals occasionally so Soviet specialists write about them. No entries on the Ukraine, Belarus or the other former Soviet republics are included in *The BFI Companion to Eastern European and Russian Cinema* (2000), for example, nor are there entries on major Soviet cineastes such as Ukrainian cameraman/director Yuri Ilienko or Latvian actor Donatas Banionis. In a text devoted to recent debates surrounding national cinemas, Susan Hayward (editor of Routledge's national cinemas series) recounted an episode that confirmed this overall attitude:. 'I am reminded here of the sigh of relief from the author, who originally was to write the Soviet national cinema book, when the Soviet Union dissolved – "now," he declared, "I need only write the *Russian* National Cinema book"' (2000: 91).

8   In the former Yugoslavia, where before we talked of one, albeit diverse, national cinema, now we distinguish Croatian, Slovene, Bosnian, Macedonian, Serbian and Montenegrin ones, and are confronted with difficult decisions about who and what belongs where (see the respective entries in *The BFI Companion to Eastern European and Russian Cinema*).

9   Some examples: in the series of Companions published by the British Film Institute only selected aspects of East German Cinema are covered in the volume on German

Film (Elsaesser 2000), and East German cinema has no presence at all in the volume on Eastern Europe (Taylor *et al.* 2000); *DEFA: East German Cinema, 1946–1992* (Allan & Sandford 1999) is written exclusively by Germanists, a lecture given during the 2002 Berlin Film Festival on East Europe's cinema of the 1960s by film historian Hans-Joachim Schlegel fully excluded East Germany (even though the period had been one of the most intense cinematic exchanges between the former East Germany and the other Eastern Bloc countries). The situation with 'placing' East German cinema was quite different in earlier writings, where East German cinema was routinely considered as an inextricable part of East European cinema and was regularly included in monographs and collections of writings by film scholars specialising in the region (for example, Liehm & Liehm 1977; Goulding 1989). In the period after 1989 significant work on East German cinema was carried out by scholars at the University of Massachusetts at Amherst (Barton Byg, Beth Moore), and also by authors such as Katie Trumpener and Daniela Berghahn.

10 The Jewish film tradition in Poland is discussed in *When Joseph Met Molly: A Reader on Yiddish Film* (Paskin 1999) and in Marek Haltof's *Polish National Cinema* (2002).

11 However, this is the place to mention that scholars have somewhat different views on the issue of how urgent or needed is such a reevaluation of Cold War frameworks. In personal correspondence (2003), for example, Ďurovičová writes: 'The cliché of Eastern Europe – like all historical memory surrounding us – is receding so quickly that there really is no need to keep resuscitating it just to bat it down. These cinemas are neglected not because of bad political sensibilities but because most anything is anyway, which has more to do with Hollywood than with political prejudice'. At the same time, Imre (proposal for *East European Cinemas in New Perspectives: A Reader*, March 2003, 1) stresses that there is an 'urgent need to reevaluate East European cinemas from global, comparative theoretical and critical perspectives'. She also notes that 'the authoritative body of existing work on East European films was written within the area-studies parameters of the Cold War paradigm: it locked the cinematic production of the former Soviet empire into its national and regional specificity, perpetuating a narrow Eurocentric, modernist approach within an auteurist or national-cinema model, often evaluating films based on their overt dissident politics. During the first few years of the post-communist transition, cultural-studies approaches proliferated, but they primarily produced social scientific investigations of the media. There have only been scattered attempts to reposition East European cinemas as parts of world cinema in an age of globalisation. Since the initial celebration of the fall of the Wall faded in the late 1990s, emergent geopolitical concerns have pushed East European cinemas out of the critical spotlight altogether, relegating the forgotten "Second World" to a twilight zone between the "First" and the "Third"'.

12 I am grateful to Boris Jocić for bringing these particular aspects to my attention.

Chapter 2

1 The leading school in this respect was Moscow's Academy of Film Art VGIK (literally Vsesoyuznyi Gosudarstvennyi Institut Kinematografii/All-union State Cinema Institute), which, along with Moscow's Patrice Lumumba People's Friendship University and other higher education instituons across the USSR count among its alumni many of the leading African cineastes (such as Abderrahmane Sissako and others coming from countries like Angola, Congo, Mauritania and elsewhere). The international contingent of the highly respected Prague-based FAMU was equally important and included students from Latin America and Asia. Indeed, when considering African cinema, the educational background of many of the leading film-makers needs to be taken into consideration when exploring the artistic influences on their work.

2   Busy film studios functioned in all the Balkan countries as well. These included Boyana in Bulgaria, Buftea in Romania, Shqiperia e re (New Albania) in Albania. The largest studio in the Balkans, Jadran, was initially established near the Croatian capital, Zagreb, in 1946 and expanded in 1955. Other studios in Yugoslavia included Avala in Belgrade, as well as studios run by companies located in the capitals of the constituent republics, Sarajevo (Sutjeska), Skopje (Vardar) and Ljubljana (Triglav).

3   For more details on the Hungarian film industry see Gálik (1998) and the Beverly James chapter in Kindem (2000).

4   Béla Balázs (1884–1949) was a prominent Hungarian film theoretician associated with the group of critics who wrote on German Expressionism. One of the first intellectuals to regard cinema as an independent art form, Balázs lived in Germany and later in the Soviet Union, teaching at the Moscow Academy of Film Art, VGIK, throughout the 1930s. After World War Two he returned to Hungary and launched what was to become the Hungarian Film Institute. 'Ironically, given his earlier communist allegiances, he was viewed by the communists as a "bourgeois" theorist and author, which is why they began to marginalise him shortly before his death' (Taylor *et al.* 2000: 26). For more on Balázs's theoretical legacy see Ian Aitken's *European Film Theory and Cinema: A Critical Introduction* (2001).

5   DEFA feature film studios were based at Babelsberg, former site of Ufa, both known for the golden age of German Expressionist films made during the period of the Weimar Republic and, of course, for many of the films commissioned and released by the Nazi regime (see Allan & Sandford 1999; Berghahn, 1999 & 2000).

6   There were numerous changes in the ownership/shareholder structure of Barrandov, and the 'coups' over control of the studio included moves by a range of actors, from energetic individual entrepreneurs to domestic and international corporations. The story is so eventful and filled with so many colourful twists and turns that it is worthy of a film itself. At the time of writing, Barrandov's main shareholder is a Czech steel company that is not particularly interested in the film industry and has been seeking to sell the studio since 1997. It is likely that Barrandov will change hands once again sometime in the near future. Throughout 2001 and 2002, several domestic and foreign contenders were in the running for the sale. As recently as February 2003, however, Moravia Steel announced that they would keep ownership of the studio for the time being.

7   So far Barrandov has been most successful in attracting runaway productions, but other studios in the region have also had a (smaller) share in this lucrative business. A number of recent Western films were shot in Budapest and a growing number of productions opt to use facilities in Romania.

8   The economic and socio-cultural causes that led to the forced anti-monopoly break-up of the vertically integrated system of Classical Hollywood have been explored in detail in a range of studies. See, for example, Balio 1985, Bordwell *et al.* 1985, Gomery 1986 and 1992.

9   A case in point, for example, is Polish film scholar Anita Skwara who, writing in *Popular European Cinema*, spoke of 'the absence of popular cinema in Poland' (1992: 221) and claimed that nothing like popular cinema had existed there in the previous four decades

10 Festivals beyond East Central Europe included Yugoslavia's national showcase in Pula and the international Belgrade FEST, the Bulgarian national film festival Golden Rose and the annual international Red Cross Film Festival (both in Varna on the Black Sea coast), and the Romanian national festival in Costineşti.

11 The importance of festivals seems finally to be gaining recognition, and they increasingly come at the centre of attention of those studying the dynamics of the international film industry. Two recent texts may be of interest for readers who would like to learn more of

Notes

the mechanics of the festival circuit: Kenneth Turan's book *Sundance to Sarajevo: Film Festivals and the World They Made* (University of California Press, 2002) and Julian Stringer's text in *Cinema and the City* (2001).

12 Other festivals that merit mention include the Sarajevo Film Festival that came to existence during the last year of the Bosnian war and has since become a high profile venue. The Thessaloniki International Film Festival in Greece has been in existence since the early 1950s, and since the 1990s it has regularly included a Balkan Survey sidebar that showcases the best work from the region.

13 Beyond East Central Europe, the Yugoslav Zagreb school of animation is well known for its 'reduced animation' style with animators like Vatroslav Mimica, Dušan Vukotić, Nedeljko Dragić and Borivoj Dovniković-Bordo; their work is discussed in Ron Holloway's 1972 book *Z is for Zagreb*. The best-known animator from Romania was Ion Popescu-Gopo, and from Bulgaria Todor Dinov, creator of award-winning cartoons such as *Margaritkata/The Daisy* (1963) and *Prometei/Prometheus* (1969). Donio Donev created the popular series *Trimata Glupats/The Three Fools* in the 1980s, a satire of traditional mores. Other important figures from Bulgaria include Stoyan Dukov, Roumen Petkov and Velislav Kazakov.

14 The documentary output of East European film-makers is little known in the West. A certain effort is made to compensate for the lack of scholarship on these issues, and some entries on East European documentary directors are included in the forthcoming *Encyclopedia of Documentary Film*, edited by Ian Aitken (Routledge).

15 The protagonist of Kieślowski's early feature, *Camera Buff* (1979), embarks on what will become an idiosyncratic career of subversive documentary film-making within the context of one such amateur video club.

16 Awarding the Palme d'Or at Cannes to the over-rated Polish film *Człowiek z żelaza/Man of Iron* (1981), for example, revealed overtly ideological considerations. Only on some occasions was the work of East Central European directors appreciated independently from politics. In the UK, critics such as David Robinson and Derek Malcolm championed films from the area (as did the British Federation of Film Societies magazine *Film* in its festival reports).

17 The new *Censorship: An International Encyclopedia*, edited by Derek Jones (2001) includes some very good articles on issues of censorship across the region, containing concrete accounts and explanation of censorship practices and instances. Peter Hames, for example, gives an excellent and concise listing of the reasons for banning films in Czechoslovakia after 1968: 'The criteria for the bans could be summarised as: suspect subject matter, suspect formal elements, and links to individuals who were proscribed, including, of course, those who had gone into exile' (Vol. I: 637).

18 One could also argue that many films in the West are effectively 'shelved' due to the functioning of market forces since they never find a distributor. Currently, about 30 per cent of the films that are made in the UK never make it into distribution. No official data are available for Poland, Hungary, the Czech and Slovak republics, yet one could safely claim that with the advent of market economy in the region the situation with non-released films in the region has become similar to that in the West. Scholars familiar with the region claim that by the early 2000s the number of films that have not been properly distributed in their own country due to the limited prospects for profits has already surpassed the number of films that were not released due to Communist censorship (John Cunningham, a specialist on Hungarian film, speaking at the Trading Cultures conference, Sheffield, UK, July 2002; see his fuller survey, *Hungarian Cinema: From Coffee House to Multiplex*, Wallflower Press, 2003)

19 In the documentary *Sametová kocovina/The Velvet Hangover* (Robert Buchar and David

181

Lawrence, USA, 2000) director Jiří Menzel makes a valid comment on the issue of conformism: 'If you want to make a good film and there is no other way, then you have the right to join the Communist Party, if that film is worth it. To join the Party and make films just for money is low. It's not worth it. But I know that if Vojtěch Jasný wasn't in the Communist Party, he wouldn't have made the nice films he did. It is the same thing as blaming someone who emigrated. If Forman had not emigrated, he never would have made all those films he did in America. Excuse me for putting it in the same bag. But conditions are never ideal. In these days there was this condition, to be a member of the Communist Party. And maybe I have more respect to those who swallowed it and worked then for those who did not overcome their pride, didn't join the Communist Party, and didn't make the good films they could.'

20 Polish veteran Aleksander Ford was a man of nepotistic reputation, who had been head of Film Polski and leader of one of the film units, and yet his 1958 film *Ósmy dzień tygodnia/The Eighth Day of the Week.* was only released in 1983. The ban on the film (as well as growing anti-Semitism) effectively led to the director's emigration in the early 1960s. After emigrating, Ford worked in various countries, making films in West Germany, Denmark and Israel, but never attained the fame he had enjoyed as a leading director in Poland.

21 It may be rather more complicated to carry out such an investigation in film than in literature because in addition to acknowledging and investigating the movement of specific talents we also need to take into consideration the greater dependency of film on industrial factors. While writing is a solitary activity, film-making is primarily collective and depends on finance, crew and technology that need to be in place for the creative process to take place. Alongside the work of émigré directors, it is necessary to mention the work of numerous other film professionals who also emigrated and transferred the skills and stylistic visions of East Central European cinema to the West. Some of those who have left a stylistic mark on Western film-making include Miroslav Ondříček, the cameraman responsible for some of the best works of the Czechoslovak New Wave, who worked on Lindsay Anderson's *If...* (1968) and *O, Lucky Man!* (1973), Hungarian-educated émigré Vilmos Zsigmond, cinematographer of classics like *McCabe and Mrs. Miller* (Robert Altman, 1971) and *Deliverance* (John Boorman, 1972), or veteran Polish cinematographer Slawomir Idziak, best-known for his work with Zanussi and Kieślowski, who filmed projects such as *Gattaca* (Andrew Niccol, 1997) and John Sayles' *Men with Guns* (1997), and who applied his daring innovations in using yellow lenses in the spectacular *Black Hawk Down* (Ridley Scott, 2001). Since the 1970s and 1980s numerous émigré actors from Eastern Europe have appeared in Hollywood, in American independent film, in European cinema, as well as in domestic productions. English-language cinema, for example, found its quintessential East European protagonist in the East German émigré actor Armin Müller-Stahl, who patented the role of an East European immigrant in films like Costa-Gavras' *Music Box* (1989), Jim Jarmusch's *Night on Earth* (1991), Barry Levinson's *Avalon* (1991) and Scott Hicks' *Shine* (1996).

22 One of the most prolific directors in the history of cinema, Michael Curtiz (1888–1962), was born to a Jewish family in Budapest, where he studied acting and directed stage productions. Starting his career in 1912 (with *Az Utolsó bohém/The Last Bohemian*), he worked intensely and made over thirty silent films in seven years, thus greatly influencing the development of the film industry in what was still Austria-Hungary. The 1919 nationalisation of the film industry by Béla Kun's short-lived Communist government prompted Curtiz's migration – first to Vienna, and eventually, in 1926, to the USA. In America, he established himself as a key Hollywood director and worked for various major studios, making over 100 feature films. Today Curtiz is considered one

of the greatest American directors, best remembered for *Angels with Dirty Faces* (1938), *Casablanca* (1942) and *Mildred Pierce* (1945).

23 Some first migrated a shorter distance, to Germany or Britain, and after several years working in Western European film capitals made a second migratory step to America, like the silent movie star Pola Negri (1884–1987), born as Barbara Apollonia Chalupiec in Poland, or the king of horror films Béla Lugosi (1882–1956), who was born as an ethnic Hungarian, Béla Ferenc Dezsö Blaskó, in a place which was part of Austria-Hungary then, and today is in Romania. But there were migrations that remained confined to Europe, as seen in the case of high-profile British producer Alexander Korda (born 1894 in Hungary) for instance. Others moved incessantly back and forth, like Czech Gustav Machatý (1898–1963), who worked in America's West Coast and also in Italy, Austria and Germany, or Hungarian Géza von Radványi (1907–86) who made films in Hungary, France and Germany. Many of the migrating film-makers spent significant periods in France's, thus the 'Paris-stop-over' which Thomas Elsaesser (1999: 104) has observed in the case of many migrating German directors is also characteristic for the migratory routes of East Central Europeans.

24 The rigidity of the politicised framework used to evaluate the work of East Central European émigré directors is very similar to the rigidity of the framework that has traditionally been applied to German émigré directors from the Nazi period. This has been criticised by Thomas Elsaesser who, looking at film scholarship and journalistic writing, spoke of the tendency to straighten the experiences of German émigré cineastes by simplifying and reducing their migratory experiences to the 'ready-made' template of a 'narrative emplotment' that sees them all as 'political refugees, first fleeing Europe because of Fascism, then frustrated by uncouth and uncultured movie moguls, and finally persecuted and witch-hunted by paranoid anti-Communist US senators' (1999: 97).

25 A case in point is Czech Miloš Forman. While formally a supporter of the dissident intellectuals in Czechoslovakia, in his American work the director opted to concentrate on new interesting projects rather than remain focused on East European politics. Since the time he established himself as a leading American director in the mid-1970s and became Chair of the film department at Columbia University, Forman has not been particularly concerned with subverting communism in Czechoslovakia. By choosing to film his award-winning *Amadeus* at Barrandov in 1984 (at the time still behind the Iron Curtain) Forman came across more as a pragmatic American who cared about cutting costs and achieving the authentic feel of Mitteleuropa rather than as an adverse dissident émigré who would take every opportunity to renounce the political gloom of early-1980s Czechoslovakia.

26 Such investigation would include, for example, studying a variety of less traditional creative trajectories driven by conscious ideological considerations. One of these is revealed in the form of Bulgarian-born German leftist Zlatan Dudow (1903–63), whose name is synonymous with socially committed film-making. Dudow had emigrated in 1923 after Bulgaria's pro-fascist coup, had studied theatre in Berlin and started his film career as a crew member for productions directed by Fritz Lang and G. W. Pabst. Working closely with co-scriptwriter Bertolt Brecht, in 1932 Dudow directed one of the classic works of socialist anti-fascist cinema, *Kühle Wampe oder: Wem gehört die Welt?/To Whom Does the World Belong?* (1932). After a prolonged exile in Switzerland during the Nazi period, Dudow returned to the Soviet-controlled part of Berlin and until the end of his life worked at the DEFA studio as a leading East German cineaste.

27 Pole Andrzej Wajda, for example, worked in liberal Yugoslavia (*Sibirska Ledi Magbet/A Siberian Lady Macbeth*, 1961), as did Romanian Lucian Pintilie (*Paviljon broj VI/Ward*

Six, 1978). Bulgarian Rangel Vulchanov escaped political gloom at home to make socially critical films within the context of the Prague Spring. Ironically, his works were released only in 1970, after the Soviet invasion, when the best Czech films were shelved (*Tvář pod maskou/Face Behind the Mask*, 1970 and *Ezop/Aesop*, 1970). Actors were crossing borders more than anyone else: in the 1960s, DEFA star Manfred Krug appeared in a Slovak Holocaust feature and a Bulgarian love story, while handsome Serbian Gojko Mitić established himself as DEFA's key character actor, specialising in roles of native Indians in a range of Karl May adaptations. In the 1980s, Pole Jan Nowicki had a permanent presence in Márta Mészáros' features.

28 In this, film directors differed substantially from vocal intellectuals engaged in writing, like Czechs Milan Kundera and Josef Škvorecký, Pole Czesław Miłosz, Leszek Kołakowski and Stanisław Barańczak, or Hungarians Agnes Heller and Ferenc Feher. A rare exception among film-makers is Polish director Jerzy Skolimowski, who remained true to leftist critical commitments. Born in 1938 in Poland, he had been best known for his versatile talents (from poetry to boxing), for collaborating with Andrzej Wajda and Roman Polanski, and for directing the critical *Rysopis/Identification Marks: None* (1964), *Walkover* (1965) and *Bariera/Barrier* (1966). An early version of his key film, *Hands Up!* (1967), a treatise on historical memory and conformity, was banned, which prompted the director's emigration to the West. Skolimowski has since worked internationally and has retained his critical interest in exploring the mechanics of dictatorship and the demoralising effects of power, even if these would play out in the confined settings of a remote family home (in *The Shout*, 1978, starring Alan Bates) or on a ship (in *The Lightship*, 1985, starring Robert Duvall).

29 Not only were not all of the East Central European émigrés fixated on politics, some did not even try to capitalise on the fact they were exiled from a totalitarian regime. Three major directors of Polish origin who enjoyed a substantial cult following for work that has not been political for the most part are Roman Polanski, Walerian Borowczyk and Andrzej Żuławski. It may be their reluctance to engage with Cold War rhetorics that has kept them away from the spotlight – not as directors (because each one of them enjoys an extensive and dedicated fan base), but as *East European* ones. As a rule they were primarily concerned with more existential and less socially-determined sides of human experience: the shadowy depths of the human soul, the macabre dimensions of sexuality and desire, and the metaphysical dynamics of good and evil. Given the type of issues they dealt with – psychological deviation, madness, sexuality, transcendence – they remained outside of the mainstream also in the West, occupying the revered space of subversive cinema away from politics. The best-known representative of this cluster of cult directors remains Polanski whose *Repulsion* (1965), *Rosemary's Baby* (1968), and the lesser-seen *Le Locataire/The Tenant* (1976) have become textbook examples of psychological horror. Borowczyk (also known as a leading animator) is best-known as the master of radically subversive, blasphemous and sexually explicit films like *Contes immoraux/Immoral Tales* (1974) and *La Bête/The Beast* (1975), even though his early *Goto, l'île d'amour/Goto, Island of Love* (1968) was predominantly concerned with issues of power and totalitarianism. Extremely popular among an international cult following, Paris-based Żuławski came to prominence in France with the notorious *Possession* (1981), a film that challenged the limits of human sexuality and is regarded as a precursor to the work of equally controversial film-maker David Cronenberg.

30 This is in contrast to other exilic groups discussed by authors that have looked into a range of cinema examples from the Third World (see Pines & Willemen 1989; Naficy 2001; Wayne 2001). Very little of the characterisation and conceptualisation of exilic and diasporic cinema developed by Hamid Naficy in his 2001 study *Accented Cinema*

– building on concepts like 'interstitial' and 'collective' modes of production that mark diasporic film-making – can be applied to the East Central European experience.

Chapter 3

1   Adapted novels by Henryk Sienkiewicz include *Krzyżacy/Knights of the Teutonic Order* (Aleksander Ford, 1960), *Pan Wołodyjowski/Colonel Wołodyjowski* (Jerzy Hoffman, 1969), *Potop/The Deluge* (Hoffman, 1974), *With Fire and Sword* (Hoffman, 1999) and *Quo Vadis* (Jerzy Kawalerowicz, 2001). By Stefan Żeromski, *Popioły/Ashes* (Wajda, 1966) and *Przedwiośnie/The Spring to Come* (Filip Bajon, 2001). By Adam Mickiewicz, the epic poem *Pan Tadeusz* (Wajda, 1999). By Władysław Reymont, *Chłopi/The Peasants* (Jan Rybkowski, 1973) and *Ziemia obiecana/Promised Land* (Wajda, 1974). By Bolesław Prus, *Faraon/Pharaoh* (Jerzy Kawalerowicz, 1966) and *Lalka/The Doll* (Wojciech Has, 1969).

2   These films, fostering the national consciousness, have been used alongside other key texts within the school curriculum. While acknowledging this function of historical film-making in Poland, it is important to note that historically the country has traditionally conceptualised itself as a vulnerable nation, given that several times its presence has been fully erased from Europe's map.

3   The average budget for a European film at this time was set at around $5 million; the average budget for an East European film was about $1 million. It should be noted, however, that another historical super-production, Nikita Mikhalkov's failed blockbuster *Sibirskiy tsiryulnik/The Barber of Siberia* (Russia/France, 1998), was the most expensive European film at the time, with a budget estimated by various sources at almost $50 million.

4   It is necessary to remember that this commentary is somewhat misleading for it implies that modern-day Polish heritage blockbusters have totally spurned contemporary digital post-production techniques, which is not the case. *With Fire and Sword*, for example, uses digital effects to create computer-generated castles.

5   Wajda completed recently yet another historical film, *Zemsta/Revenge* (2002), based on a play by Aleksander Fredro.

6   Even though *With Fire and Sword* was the first part in Sienkiewicz's trilogy (1883, 1886, 1888), the story of clashes with Ukrainian Cossacks could not have been adapted for the screen during the years of communism as such a film would be read as anti-Soviet. The third part, *Pan Wołodyjowski* (1969), was thus made first, and featured the resistance against invading Ottomans. *The Deluge* (1974), set on the backdrop of a Swedish invasion, was second

7   A print of the film was recently restored and released in the US by the Pacific Film Archives (Berkeley, CA). The restoration had been financed by the late Jerry Garcia, leading member of The Grateful Dead, who was said to have loved *The Saragossa Manuscript*. Information on this aspect of the film's reception history is available at <http://www cowboybi com/saragossa/main htm>.

8   It should be noted, however, that the films of Jodorowsky that can be considered of relevance were made several years later (for example *El Topo*, 1970; *La Montaña sagrada/ Holy Mountain*, 1973), as were Pasolini's adaptations of literary epics (*Il Decameron/The Decameron*, 1970; *I racconti di Canterbury/The Canterbury Tales*, 1971; *Il fiore delle mille e una notte/Arabian Nights*, 1974).

9   The aesthetic influences on this lavish production are derived more from Eisenstein films such as *Oktiabr/October* (1927) and *Ivan Grozniy/Ivan the Terrible, part I and II* (1945/ 1946) than from any of the numerous European and American super-productions of the 'ancient Egypt' franchise.

10 These two films are part of what Jakubisko calls 'a trilogy of skepsis'. The third part, *Dovidenia v pekle priatelia/See You in Hell, My Friends!* (1970), was not officially completed until 1990, although its Italian co-producer assembled and distributed an unauthorised version earlier.

11 Perhaps the authorities also saw Jakubisko's intention this way, since the two films were banned in Czechoslovakia.

12 Even though the region's history since 1945 abounds with absurd situations that make it a particularly suitable material for surrealist exploration, the postwar period has not been a subject of great interest for surrealists. One important exception is Czech animator Jan Švankmajer's *Death of Stalinism in Bohemia* (1990), a remarkably witty surrealist account of the period 1949–89.

13 Examples include László Lugossy's 1848-set *Szirmok, virágok, koszorúk/Flowers of Reverie* (1984), starring György Cserhalmi, a remarkable treatise on individual freedom colliding with historical coercion, or Jerzy Kawalerowicz's *Śmierć prezydenta/Death of a President* (Poland, 1978), an account of the assassination of the first Polish president, Gabriel Narutowicz, in 1922.

14 Wajda's exploration of the interaction (and occasional confrontation) of the individual and history is not limited to Polish subjects. One of his most interesting films was the French-made *Danton* (1982), starring Gérard Depardieu as the deeply contradictory hero of the French Revolution, now facing the trial of history over decisions on justice and terror (there is a chapter on *Danton* in Falkowska 1996).

15 Born in 1921 in Kraków, Munk trained as a cameraman and graduated from the Film Academy in Łódź in 1950. He started in documentaries and gradually switched to fiction in the second half of the 1950s, becoming one of the most prolific film-makers working in Poland. He died about a month before turning forty, in a car accident, in 1961.

16 It appears that screenwriter Jerzy Stefan Stawiński, who was responsible for most of Munk's scripts, made an important contribution to these narrative innovations, particularly with his acute sense for the relativism of history. It is no wonder that Wajda's *Kanał*, also based on Stawiński, bears many of the pessimistic and ironic elements that are characteristic of Munk's approach.

17 The clever narrative point of the film is revealed only towards the end: we realise that Piszczyk tells his life story to the director of the prison where he is serving time for his inopportune misdemeanours. Piszczyk insists that he has greatly enjoyed the experience of incarceration: for him jail has become synonymous with the safe space where he is sheltered from his 'bad luck' and does not need to constantly adjust. He is begging the director to keep him in jail rather than throw him out him out into the hostile world where he will, once again, be exposed to adverse forces that will coerce him to comply and take sides, and will ultimately destroy him.

18 Some critics believe that there was some sort of dialogue taking place between Wajda and Munk on screen, with each of them releasing around one film a year in the late 1950s dealing with contemporary themes of recent history (the Second World War), featuring serious moral considerations as their central focus. This dialogue comes to light if one compares Munk's *Błękitny krzyż/Men of the Blue Cross* and Wajda's *Generation* (both 1955), Munk's *Man on the Track* and Wajda's *Kanał* (both 1957), as well as Munk's *Eroica* and Wajda's *Ashes and Diamonds* (both 1958). At the time of his death, Munk was working on the Holocaust-themed *Passenger* (the film was only released in 1963), another feature that can be seen to enter into a dialogue, this time with Wajda's *Samson* (1961), on issues of anti-Semitism. It is important to note, however, that the view of the 'dialogue' between these two auteurs may be somewhat speculative, given that they worked in the context of a lively film culture where a number of other directors of the

same generation (the so-called 'Columbuses') also made films on the same range of topics and of equal significance and originality. Most of the directors belonging to this loose group were born in the 1920s and had graduated from the film school in Łódź after the war. Besides Wajda and Munk, the group comprised of Wojciech Has, Kazimierz Kutz, Janusz Morgenstern, Jerzy Kawalerowicz and others.

19 The consequences of difficult personal choices (best seen in instances of wrong decisions) have remained the focus of Szabó's attention throughout his career. Most importantly, he returns to these issues once again in his film *Taking Sides* (UK/France/Germany/Austria, 2001), exploring the story of conductor Wilhelm Furtwängler who sided with the Nazis.

Chapter 4

1 Jancsó's ritualistic stylisation of violence is one of the most important features of these films: they contain haunting scenes of physical and moral cruelty. In discussing Jancsó's handling of violence, Graham Petrie talks of a refusal to dwell on the intimate details of pain and cold alienation rather than involvement with the supposed victim. He underlines, however, that: 'It is strange that so many people attack Jancsó for presenting violence and cruelty as being cold, inhumane and horrible; this is surely a far more responsible and honest position than to suggest that violence is liberating, glamorous or exciting, as so many other directors tend to do' (1978: 25).

2 With time, Jancsó's elaborate choreography becomes so pervasive by the end of the 1960s that many critics believe it constitutes something of an end in itself. According to Petrie (1978), Jancsó's way of working involved numerous rehearsals and spending most time on the staging of a particular episode. The rehearsals included both the positioning and the movements of actors and extras and the elaborate camera choreography (often enhanced by extensive tracks and a crane platform). After such careful preparation, the scene would be shot at the end of the day only once or twice; editing would be minimal as it was practically taking place at the stage of shooting.

3 Other 'formalist' films by Miklós Jancsó that can be considered in this context include *Csend és kiáltás/Silence and Cry* (1968), *Fényes szelek/Confrontation* (1968) and *Még kér a nép/Red Psalm* (1971). This list could be expanded to include the later *Magyar rapszódia/ Hungarian Rhapsody* (1979). It should be noted, however, that since the mid-1980s, Jancsó rejected some of his most characteristic tropes and focused more on individual characters in contemporary urban settings.

4 Critics have spoken of Jancsó's influence over the work of Béla Tarr, and the effects can be seen in Tarr's harrowing plots where desolate alienated characters keep going back and forth and nothing seems to 'happen'. However, while it is possible to make a case for linking Tarr to Jancsó, Tarr's approach to plotline and confined *mise-en-scène* – poorly-lit pub interiors, public spaces dominated by overwhelming discomfort, desolate sidewalks – is more influenced by the work of Fábri (as seen, for example, in films from the 1970s such as *One Day More, One Day Less* (1973) or *The Fifth Seal* (1976))

5 The explicit religious references in Fábri's film (for example the use of blinding light coming from the Christ-like martyr figure of the resistance fighter) are not unique to his work. Referencing of religion, be it in the critical-atheist mode encouraged by the Communist Party or in an existential-philosophical mode, was widely spread in the region's cinema (and particularly in Polish film, reflecting a culture with an omnipresent Catholic Church). Discussing the treatment of faith in this cinematic tradition, however, one would first and foremost look at the work of directors such as Kawalerowicz, Kutz and Kieślowski, Evald Schorm and Vladimír Michálek. The official take on religious faith in state socialist societies is summarised in a line delivered by a Communist party

bureaucrat in Karel Kachyňa's *Ucho/The Ear* (1970) who says: 'Catholic or Muslim, it is all the same to me. All that counts is whether they accept the socialist goals!'

6   A whole range of relevant films that cannot be discussed in detail here includes those many remarkable Western-produced Holocaust features and documentaries investigating episodes that took place in East Central Europe. These films, however, should necessarily be taken into account when teaching on Holocaust cinema. These include films such as Alain Resnais' *Night and Fog* (1955), Claude Lanzman's *Shoah* (in particular, the shattering interview in the second part with barber Abraham Bomba, originally from the Polish town of Częstochowa), or the well-known *The Łódź Ghetto* (Alan Adelson and Kate Taverna, USA, 1989). Agnieszka Holland's German-produced Holocaust films also belong to this category: the claustrophobic 1985 *Bittere Ernte/Angry Harvest* (where a female Jewish escapee from a transport, played by Elizabeth Trissenaar, is taken in and kept in hiding by a bullish Gentile farmer played by Armin Müller-Stahl) and the witty 1990 *Hitlerjunge Salomon/Europa, Europa* (the thrilling story of a brave Jewish teenager who ends up hiding among high-placed Germans at an elite Nazi school, a film openly mocking the theory of the superiority of Aryan race).

7   Before the Second World War, film-makers made a number of features that focused on Jewry in the region, and Poland had a well-established Yiddish-language film production in the early 1930s. Some of these remarkable films are available in distribution today (for example *Yidl mitn Fidl/Yidl with a Fiddle*, 1935 and *Dybuk/The Dybbuk*, 1927). Later, a range of films attempted to offer an authentic ethnographic representation of Jewish life. One of the most important works is Jerzy Kawalerowicz's *Austeria/The Inn* (1983), featuring Jewish life early in the century. Anti-Semitism in a Hungarian village is the topic of Judit Elek's *Raftsmen* (1989). Karel Kachyňa's *Hanele* (1999) is another exploration of Jewish life from the period between the Wars, a film in which the young female protagonist experiences diverse encounters, both with Zionists who are thinking of moving to Palestine and with Jews who have renounced Judaism. Even though a French production, it is necessary to also mention Yolande Zauberman's *Moi Ivan, toi Abraham/Ivan and Abraham* (France/Belarus, 1993), which depicts a complex web of inter-ethnic relations involving Poles, Jews and Gypsies.

8   Films that focus on the humanistic considerations of the helpers are Konrad Wolf's poetic *Stars/Sterne /Zvezdi* (East Germany/Bulgaria, 1959), Jiří Weiss romantic *Romeo, Julia a tma/Sweet Light in a Dark Room* (1960, a.k.a. *Romeo, Juliet, and Darkness*) and Wajda's theatrical *Wielki tydzień/Holy Week* (1995). A range of films, however, deglamorise the helpers' motives. These include Klos and Kadár's *A Shop on the High Street*, Holland's German-made *Angry Harvest* and Jan Hřebejk's *Musíme si pomáhat/Divided We Fall* (2000). A very fine psychological portrayal of the relations between Jews and Gentiles within the same family is Imre Gyöngyössy and Barna Kabay's *Jób lázadása/The Revolt of Job* (1983). The story is set during the rushed deportation of Hungarian Jews near the end of the Second World War and tells of the uneasy parting of an orphan gentile boy with his adoptive Jewish family.

9   Important films in this range include the family sagas by Alfréd Radok (*Daleká cesta/ Distant Journey,* a k a. *The Long Journey,* 1949) and István Szabó (*Sunshine,* 1999), as well as Roman Polanski's *Le Pianiste/The Pianist* (2002).

10 Terezín is the setting of action in Radok's *Distant Journey,* Zbynek Brynych's *Transport z raje/Transport from Paradise* (1963), and, most recently, Karel Kachyňa's *Poslední motyl/ The Last Butterfly* (France/Czechoslovakia/UK, 1990).

11 These include (but are not limited to) Aleksander Ford's *Ulica Graniczna/Border Street* (1948), Wajda's *Samson* (1961) and Polanski's *The Pianist* (2002). Wajda's *Korczak* (1990), the portrayal of educator Janusz Korczak who runs an orphanage in the ghetto, provides

a remarkable example of moral self-sacrifice. The film strongly influenced the visual style of *Schindler's List* (USA, 1993) largely due to the fact that *Korczak*'s set designer Allan Starski was subsequently recruited to work on Spielberg's film. The film by Danish director Søren Kragh-Jacobsen *Øen i fuglegaden/The Island on Bird Street* (1997) is a story of heroic survival also set in the Warsaw Ghetto.

12 The most important titles include: the Polish *Ostatni etap/The Last Stage* (Wanda Jakubowska, 1948), the story of several women organising a resistance group in the camp; the Slovak *Boxer a smrt/The Boxer and Death* (Peter Solan, 1963), the story of a boxer, played by East Germany's Manfred Krug, who is forced to act as a sparring partner for the camp commander; and the East German *Nackt unter Wölfen/Naked Among Wolves* (Frank Beyer, 1962), the story of an effort to hide a little Jewish boy, based on the novel by Bruno Apitz.

13 A Holocaust survivor, award-winning Arnošt Lustig authored a number of short stories that became the literary source for some of the best-known Czech films about the Holocaust – *Transport from Paradise* and *Diamonds of the Night*, and two films directed by Antonín Moskalyk, *Dita Saxová* (1967) and *Modlitba pro Katerinu Horovitzovou/A Prayer for Katerina Horovoitzova*, 1969). Wajda's *Krajobraz po bitwie/Landscape After the Battle* (1970), based on Tadeusz Borowski's classic collection *This Way for the Gas, Ladies and Gentlemen*, traces the tragic fate of a poet who has survived the camp but is so traumatised that he has difficulties adjusting to life after the imprisonment. Francesco Rosi's film *La Tregua/The Truce* (1996), based on Primo Levi's book, bears stylistic parallels with *Landscape After the Battle*.

14 It is important to note that Sidney Lumet's *The Pawnbroker* (1964), another key Holocaust film made at the time of *Diamonds of the Night*, also relied on contrasting the darkness of present-day events with the traumatic shine of the flashbacks, as well as on the contrast between sound and deafening silence.

15 *Hands Up!* is one of the rare films in which a film-maker from the Eastern Bloc has undertaken to comment on political issues stretching beyond the immediate concerns of the region. Originally, the film had been conceived as an avant-garde examination of the way young Poles of the post-war generation come to terms with the memory of Holocaust and confront the hypocrisy of the Stalinist present. Shelved in 1967, *Hands Up!* premiered only in 1985, after the end of martial law, in a version that was extensively re-cut by the director, to include a new introductory section as well as multiple collage-type incursions into themes ranging from Solidarity's struggle to the destruction of Beirut, after years of devastating civil war. Thus, the film effectively addressed general issues of social disorder and political violence, making it clear that ultimately the specifically Polish worries should be seen in the context of wider humanitarian concerns. In this, Skolimowski is a rare example of a director who rejected the Eurocentric stance of most of his peers and fellow East Europeans.

16 A film that escapes categorisation is Zbynek Brynych's *...a páty jezdec je Strach/The Fifth Horseman is Fear* (1964). It focuses on the psychological decline of a protagonist who has sided with the Nazis. Another category that needs to be mentioned here includes those films that look at the uneasy relations between groups of Gentiles belonging to different warring sides; such as Wajda's German-produced *A Love in Germany* about the doomed love of a German woman (Hanna Schygulla) with a Polish prisoner of war (Daniel Olbrychski). Frank Beyer's DEFA production *Der Aufenthalt/The Turning Point* (1983), based on Hermann Kant's novel, was made in the same year as *A Love in Germany*. Set on Polish territory at the end of the Second World War, it tells the story of an arrested German soldier who is wrongly charged for crimes he has not committed. Representing a German protagonist as a victim, the film was particularly challenging; Polish objections

led to the withdrawal of the film from the Berlin International Film Festival in 1983

17   The specific historical incident referred to is known as *Razija* and took place in January 1942, when thousands of Jews and Serbs from the city of Novi Sad were shot and thrown in the icy Danube. The city, which is the capital of Yugoslavia's Vojvodina (an area inhabited by a large Hungarian minority), was occupied by Hungarian forces allied with the Nazis. As Petrie has appropriately remarked, by making this film the director was taking a radical step: it was 'an extremely courageous subject to tackle, in view of the embarrassed silence that, till then, had shrouded Hungary's role in the Second World War (1978: 185). In its pace and emotions, *Cold Days* bears direct parallels with the Yugoslav Black Wave war classic *Tri/Three*, made the same year (1965) by director Aleksandar Petrović

18   In 2001, Andrzej Brzozowski, who worked as Munk's assistant on *Passenger*, released a documentary (*Ostatnie zdięcia/The Last Picture*) in which he offers a detailed commentary on what Munk's intentions of the film were. *Passenger* is based on a book and a radio play by Zofia Posmysz, which Munk first filmed for television in 1960. A comparison between this early version and the film adaptation can be found in Stolarska 1995. One of the main differences seems to be that the television drama did not contain any visualisation of Auschwitz, the camp was only verbally discussed. In the film the focus shifted to the Auschwitz experience.

19   We never learn if Marta is actually Jewish; from the way she is depicted it appears more likely that she is a political prisoner.

20   *Train de vie/Train of Life* (1998), a Holocaust comedy by Romanian director Radu Mihaileanu, played in cinemas around the time of *Life is Beautiful* but only had a limited release. The few people who have seen it frequently compare it with Begnini's humour. This is the story of a group of Romanian Jews from a remote *shtetl* who conspire to secretly build a train, dress up as Germans and try to 'deport' themselves to Palestine. In one of the film's most memorable episodes, the train is apprehended by Germans yet it soon turns out that these 'Nazis' are just as fake as the Jewish 'Germans' on the train: they are actually a group of Romanies in disguise who have conspired to confiscate a train (and use it to 'deport' themselves to India). They soon recognise each other, however, and embrace, ending up around a bonfire where they all drink and dance to a frolic mixture of Kletzmer and Gypsy music.

21   Among the many awards for the films discussed in this section, it is worth mentioning the Academy Awards for Best Foreign Language Film for *A Shop on the High Street* (in 1965) and *Closely Observed Trains* (in 1968), as well as a nomination in the same category for *Jakob the Liar*. *Jakob* was the first film which East Germany sent to the festival in West Berlin where it won Vlastimil Brodský the Best Actor award.

22   It may not be by chance that one of Peter Sellers' most memorable and funniest roles – the simpleton gardener Chance who becomes embroiled in a series of mistakes with top political circles in Hal Ashby's *Being There* (1979) – not only relied on the same premise, that of a small man who is accidentally involved on a much higher level, but was based on the work of Polish émigré writer Jerzy Kosinski.

23   One of the 'forgotten' films of this type is Zoltán Fábri's satire *Hannibál tanár úr/Professor Hannibal* (1957), a treatise on the politicised and volatile shifts in public approval and disapproval, and the manipulation of historical interpretation. It tells the story of an innocuous schoolmaster who has recently published a historical study which accidentally resonates with the present day politics of Il Duke and his Hungarian epigones. At first, the schoolmaster is elevated to a nearly heroic status, to soon thereafter suffer a downfall and find himself in trouble of Kafkaesque proportions. Set at the time of rising fascism, in a period fifty years earlier, the film can also be read as an allegory of present-day events in

contemporaneous Hungary.

24   Hašek's *Švejk* has regularly inspired film-makers. It was been adapted for the cinema as early as 1926 (as a silent comedy by veteran director Karel Lamač). There are more Czech adaptations: a 1931 one by Martin Fric, for instance, and an animated 1955 version by Jiří Trnka, as well as a range of international adaptations (from the UK, Germany, and even Romania).

25   The tradition of subtly humorous depictions of small-town war experience was continued in the recent Czech tragicomedy *Divided We Fall*, which looked at the interaction between a Czech couple who are friendly with a Sudeten German working for the Nazis while simultaneously hiding a Jewish camp escapee. As in these earlier films, the couple is more concerned about their inability to have children; yet at the end they both have a child and are celebrated as smart and courageous resistance heroes

26   According to some interviews, it was the basic premise of *Jakob the Liar* (telling lies for a higher moral good) that inspired Roberto Begnini's *Life is Beautiful*. It is also the narrative premise of Emir Kusturica's *Underground* (1995). *Jakob* was remade in the US in 1999. Even though the remake features Hollywood's leading funny-man Robin Williams, this adaptation is too sentimental and does not manage to maintain the focus of the subtle humour that characterises the original.

27   *The Joke* is based on Milan Kundera's novel of the same name. Another important Czech film which focuses on the moral degradation of protagonists forced to comply with totalitarianism is *Každý den odvahu/Everyday Courage* (1964) by Evald Schorm, one of the leading figures of the Czechoslovak New Wave. Skolimowski's *Hands Up!* was made around the same time; it is a film that also offers a fine critical view on the totalitarian intrusion in young people's lives.

28   The use of such pseudo-documentary collages presented in the context of mock sociological discourse where fragments of 'documentaries' help to blend fact and fiction is an important feature in the East Central European cinematic tradition. The use of fake documentary footage can be traced to earlier periods of Polish cinema. It is an approach that has also been used by Kieślowski and other directors of his generation.

29   Wojciech Marczewski's *Dreszcze/Shivers* (1981) is another important film in the anti-Stalinist cycle. It is a fine psychological study of a boy who is being 'remodelled' while his father is away in a camp (the premise of the story being very similar to Emir Kusturica's later Cannes-winner *Otac na službenom putu/When Father Was Away on Business*, 1985). Waldemar Krzystek's *W zawieszeniu/Suspended* (1987) tells another depressing story from this period, in which the protagonist who has escaped custody is forced into a new confinement – he has to hide for years in the basement of his female partner's home. The leads are played by Jerzy Radziwiłowicz and Krystyna Janda (both of *Man of Marble* fame) who had already made this type of character their own by 1987.

30   Some important Hungarian films that look at this period and need to be mentioned here include Zoltán Fábri's *Requiem* (1981), Pál Gábor's *Kettévált mennyezet/Wasted Lives* (1982), Pál Sándor's *Szerencsés Dániel/Daniel Takes a Train* (1983), and Péter Gárdos' *Szamárköhögés/Whooping Cough* (1986).

31   Bacsó ridiculed the Communist system for its anti-intellectual and anti-individualist premises in his uncompromising mockery of Stalinist Hungary *Oh, Bloody Life!* (1983). The film followed a group of 'politically untrustworthy' subjects deported from Budapest by the regime in the spring of 1951.

32   A quarter of a century later Bacsó revisited the simple-minded Pelikán (again played by the same actor, Ferenc Kállai), and offered a sarcastic exploration of the social mores in post-Communist times in *The Witness Again*. Here Bacsó exposed the profiteer culture that had replaced state socialist corruption.

33 A prime example of this approach is Márta Mészarós' autobiographical 'Diary' trilogy: *Napló gyermekeimnek/Diary for My Children* (1982), *Napló szerelmeimnek/Diary for My Loved Ones* (1987) and *Napló apámnak, anyámnak/Diary for My Father and Mother* (1990), discussed in chapter six.

34 The flashbacks also reveal a plethora of relatives and neighbours reporting on each other, often leading to arbitrary repression. Even though a secondary plot line, these elements of the story allow the director to question ambiguous actions that, while shown to be dictated by a feeling of social responsibility, were actually the result of purely personal motives like envy or jealousy.

Chapter 5

1 In comparison, the skies of England may be covered with a thick layer of clouds, and the landscape may bear a specific greyish taint. The alienating industrial landscape of films such as *This Sporting Life* (1963) or the dreary rows of uniform terraced houses of films like *Get Carter* (1971) are realist depictions that neither fit with the prevalent image of the country they represent nor make a substantial part of it. England is much more often associated with the perennially green lawns of bountiful gardens of heritage cinema and with colourful flower baskets in glorious sunshine.

2 The 'greyness' metaphor could be further expanded to include the many ways in which the region has been considered 'grey' during socialism (and also after?), where 'greyness' has been seen as an ideological manifestation of something that is easy to ignore in-between the 'white' First World and the 'black' Third World (Anikó Imre, personal correspondence, 2003).

3 One of the exceptions was Miklós Jancsó's allegorical film, *Fényes szelek/The Confrontation* (1968), which was explicitly concerned with the politics of the student movement. Made slightly earlier (in 1966) and not released until much later, Jerzy Skolimowski's *Hands Up!* also explores the issue of the generation gap and political commitments of the younger generation. In contrast to East Central Europe, some overtly political films were made in Yugoslavia (by directors such as Želimir Žilnik and Dušan Makavejev). This was probably due to the idiosyncratic but more relaxed political regime that Tito had established there.

4 The film uses narrative techniques replicating the flashback reconstruction seen in Orson Welles' *Citizen Kane* (1941) and provides three overlapping and yet diverging accounts of the same event, as seen in Kenji Mizoguchi's *Ugetsu monogatari/Ugetsu* (1953). This film of Munk's is believed to have influenced the tripartite narrative structure of Kieślowski's *Blind Chance*.

5 A graduate of the film academy in Łódź, Polanski had appeared as an actor in several films, made two absurdist shorts and directed a well-received feature, *Nóż w wodzie/Knife in the Water*, that explored the power dynamics within a heterosexual couple. With the exception of *Cul-de-sac* (UK, 1966), an allegory of totalitarianism that again looked into a similar closed circle of power dynamics, since his emigration in the mid-1960s Polanski has not made films that comment on the political situation in his home country. He has opted to work on films that concentrate on psychological deviation and sexuality. In the annals of cinema he remains a Western master of superbly crafted psychological suspense, and is extensively studied and written about. He more or less belongs to what can be described as the mainstream of cult film-making – most of his films are readily available, often scheduled at festivals and broadcast on television across the globe. Polanski can be described as some sort of an 'approved', 'permitted' cult director.

6 Some of these films could be seen as subversive by the regime, especially if they happened

to depict couples whose problems were ultimately accountable to the inherent problems of the 'system', such as material shortages or hidden unemployment. However, the attitudes of censorship differed by country and even within a single country censorship practices varied from one Communist Party congress to another, closely reflecting the Party line. While in Hungary or Poland many of the contemporary films that have been discussed did not come across as particularly problematic, and while Yugoslavia's 'black wave' directors were able to put out extremely bold political statements, in the more indoctrinated East Germany relatively innocuous works were being shelved (particularly after the infamous socialist Party plenum that took place in 1965). One of these films, for example, was Jürgen Böttcher's *Jahrgang 45/Born in '45* (1965), telling the story of a marriage breakdown caused by the husband's unemployment. Other East German shelved films include Konrad Wolf's *Der geteilte Himmel/Divided Heaven* (GDR, 1964, based on the 1961 novel by Christa Wolf), Herrmann Zschoche's *Karla* (GDR, 1965) and Kurt Maetzig's *Das Kaninchen bin ich/I am the Rabbit* (GDR, 1965). They all were seen as subversive because they addressed issues of adaptability, adjustment, conformity, corruption, readiness to engage in moral compromise and lack of commitment to the socialist cause (see Berghahn 1999; 2000).

7   Some of their films have already been discussed, particularly in chapter four which looked at films by Jireš, Němec and Menzel; others are further examined in chapter six.

8   Usually triggering a range of familiar Western references among viewers, from the surrealist paintings of René Magritte to the psychedelics of Terry Gilliam, all the films enjoy a specific cult status. Due to limited availability, however, their international fan base is not as populous as it would be had they been made in the West.

9   One such discovery was Jan Vostrčil (first appearing as the sweaty band leader in *If There Were No Music*), who not only was a fixture in all of Forman's films from the Czech period but also makes an unforgettable presence in a number of other Czech films from that time (by directors such as Ivan Passer, František Vláčil, Drahomíra Vihanová and others).

10 It is particularly interesting to compare Forman's later films with the Czech ones in order to observe the amazing continuity in his filming techniques. Looking into the camerawork of a film such as *The People vs. Larry Flynt* (1996), for example, gives an ample opportunity to rediscover the specific mise-en-scène and filming techniques of Forman's early films, such as *Black Peter* or *The Firemen's Ball*.

11 Since then, Forman has been quite evasive in discussing his motives for emigration. While mainstream film criticism persistently presented him as a typical post-1968 exile, the director himself has made sure not to engage in any overt statements identifying politics as the main reason of his migration to the West. In fact, while he clearly states he was a supporter of the Prague Spring and disapproved of the Soviet invasion of Czechoslovakia in 1968, in his autobiography *Turnaround* (1994) he indicates that by 1968 he had already signed agreements with producers that would have taken him to work in the West anyway. Once in America, Forman quickly put behind him the task of battling Czech censorship and restrictions on creative freedom, particularly since he had to establish his talent in the US. It was an uphill struggle at first, and his superb Cassavetes-like analysis of the counter-culture generation, *Taking Off* (1971), remained little noticed. But this was to change with the phenomenal success of *One Flew Over the Cuckoo's Nest* (1975, adapted from Ken Kesey), a film concerned with specifically American topics and featuring Jack Nicholson in an unforgettable performance. Most of Forman's US films – such as the film version of the anti-Vietnam war musical *Hair* (1979), his adaptation of E. L. Doctorow's *Ragtime* (1981), and the biopics of such quintessential American characters as porno tycoon and free speech crusader Larry Flynt (*The People*

vs. Larry Flynt, 1996) and idiosyncratic comedian Andy Hoffman (*Man on the Moon*, 1999) – were preoccupied with American themes. The only subject that took Forman closer to home was the adaptation of Peter Shaffer's play *Amadeus* (1984), a masterful treatment of Mozart's life and another major success.

12 Some of Menzel's films were shelved during the period of 'Normalisation'. He did not emigrate and was later permitted to work. In the early 1980s, he released the bittersweet comedies *Postřižiny/Cutting It Short* (1980) and *Slavnosti sněženek/The Snowdrop Festival* (1983), both based on the work of Bohumil Hrabal.

13 Forman had already made contacts and had started working on projects in America before August 1968. A number of other Czechoslovak New Wave directors – Ivan Passer, Vojtěch Jasný, Jan Kadár – also emigrated, but never came close to the position occupied by Forman. Even though their professionalism was acknowledged and they were successfully employed and respected, they remain best-known for films they had made before emigrating. Jan Němec, the man behind masterpieces such as *Diamonds of the Night* and *The Party and the Guests*, for example, had a very patchy career and managed to make only a few rarely seen features, mostly for television. Having returned to the Czech Republic in the 1990s, Němec discussed his émigré experiences in his impressionistic intimately autobiographical film *Noční hovory s matkou/Late Night Talks with Mother* (2000).

14 There is no space here to pay proper attention to another range of films that are still being made in the region but they should at least be mentioned: the fairy-tales featuring village life and often using magical realist elements. As a rule, they displayed meticulous attention to heritage and folkloric detail.

15 I am indebted to Boris Jocić for bringing several of these aspects to my attention.

16 Judit Elek's documentary *Istenmezején 1972–73-ban/A Hungarian Village 1972–73* (1973), which chronicles the lives of young village women, would be a good example of the 'escape to the city' category.

17 The best example here would be Martin Šulík's endearing *Záhrada/The Garden* (1995). Probably the most acclaimed Slovak film of recent years, it is about a young misfit who returns to the village to restore the old family house and live in it. An attractive side of village life is shown in the work of Polish director Jan Jakub Kolski, most of whose magic realist films from the 1990s are also set in villages.

18 Films that offer ethnographic representation of Jewish life are mentioned in note 7 of chapter four.

19 Along similar lines, another film, this time from Poland, has made these clashes palpable: Dorota Kędzierzawska's debut feature *Diabły, diabły/Devils, Devils* (1991) tells another timeless story of a group of travellers who are ostracised by the inhabitants of a Polish village but where, nevertheless, a tender attraction develops between a Polish girl and a Romani boy. Both *Devils, Devils* and *Rose-Tinted Dreams* are discussed in review articles in the special issue of *Framework* on images of Roma in international cinema (Iordanova 2003).

20 For a listing of more Roma-themed films see my entry on Gypsies in East European cinema in *The BFI Companion to Eastern European and Russian Cinema*, 91–2. The Hungarian tradition of Roma films, for example, includes Sándor Sára's *Cigányok/Gypsies* (1962), Pál Schiffer's *Cséplö Gyuri/Gyuri* (1978) and Lívia Gyarmathy's *Koportos* (1979). Apparently an important Romani-themed film that focuses on the relations within a Romani community, though one I have not seen, is Imre Gyöngyössy's *Meztelen vagy/ Legend about the Death and Resurrection of Two Youg Men* (1971), co-written by Barna Kabay. Graham Petrie describes the plot as the story of a young Gypsy painter who, along with another educated friend, returns to his native settlement. Anxious to help his fellow-

Romanies out of their traditional squalour and ignorance, he is resented as an outsider and his attempts to change things meet with open hostility. When he intervenes to stop them cheapening and prostituting their traditions for the sake of a group of prying tourists, he is judged to be a traitor and suffers the penalty of having his tongue cut out, while his companion, who has been working on a building site, is drowned by his Gypsy co-workers in concrete. (1978: 202–3). Many films may not focus exclusively on the Roma, but have a significant Roma subplot. Some of the most important titles from other Eastern Bloc countries include Aleksandar Petrović's *Skupljači perja/I Even Met Happy Gypsies* (Yugoslavia, 1967), Emil Loteanu's *Tabor ukhodit v nebo/Gypsies Are Found Near Heaven* (USSR, 1975), Goran Paskaljević's *Anđeo čuvar/Guardian Angel* (Yugoslavia, 1987), Emir Kusturica *Dom za vešanje/Time of the Gypsies* (Yugoslavia, 1989) and *Crna mačka, beli macor/White Cat, Black Cat* (Yugoslavia/France, 1998), Stole Popov's *Gypsy Magic* (Macedonia, 1997) and Georgi Dyulgerov's *Chernata Lyastovitza/The Black Swallow* (Bulgaria/France, 1997).

21 From Hungary, the work of Zsolt Kézdi-Kovács (*Ha megjön Jósef/When Joseph Returns*, 1975; *A kedves szomszéd/The Nice Neighbour*, 1979) and András Jeles (*A Kis Valentinó/ Little Valentino*, 1979) should be mentioned. Important East German films of this ilk include Heiner Carow's *Die Legende von Paul und Paula/The Legend of Paul and Paula* (1974) and *Solo Sunny* (Wolfgang Kohlhaase and Konrad Wolf, 1979). Some of the 'women's films' that belong to the cinema of moral concern are discussed in chapter seven.

22 A powerful film that dealt with the events leading to the imposition of martial law in Poland was Kazimierz Kutz's *Śmierć jak kromka chleba/Death as a Slice of Bread* (1994), even though its stress is on religion. Skolimowski is probably the only Polish émigré who, in the early 1980s, immediately and vocally responded to Jaruzelski's dictatorship, as seen in his British-made *Moonlighting* (1982, with Jeremy Irons) and *Success is the Best Revenge* (1984, with Michael York), both films tackling the way Poles in diaspora reacted to the imposition of martial law at home.

23 Even though Agnieszka Holland's *Gorączka/Fever* (1981) told a story from 1905, this widely acclaimed film articulately revealed the political sympathies of the cinema of moral concern as it was one of the first to depict the Communist revolutionaries as moral cripples.

24 Today the best-known films on loss and traumatic mourning may be those by Aleksandr Sokurov (*Krug vtoroy/Second Circle*, 1990; *Mat' i syn/Mother and Son*, 1997). Yet Zanussi's *Constans/The Constant Factor* (1980) is an equally fine exploration.

25 Even though our focus is on the early work of Kieślowski (as the director who achieved most international prominence), we should at least mention some other important works of the moral concern tendency in Poland, such as Agnieszka Holland's *Aktorzy prowincjonalni/Provincial Actors* (1980) and *Kobieta samotna/A Woman Alone* (1981), Feliks Falk's *Wodzirej/Top Dog* (1978) and *Bohater roku/Hero of the Year* (1987), and Janusz Kijowski's *Kung-Fu* (1980).

26 Communal apartments and apartment blocks provided the setting for many East Central European films from the period. For example, Věra Chytilová's *Panelstory/Prefab Story* (1979), or Béla Tarr's *Panelkapcsolat/Prefab People* (1982) and *Öszi almanach/Almanac of Fall* (1984). For a good discussion of the semantic usage of communal urban complexes in classical Soviet (Vertov) and Polish cinema (Wajda, Kieślowski) see Miljacki 2002.

27 It is somewhat ironic that Kieślowski's mentor, Krzysztof Zanussi, whose outspoken public commitment to the Catholic Church has been well publicised, made movies that are closer to social realism and (even in the instances where faith is his direct theme) rarely achieve the strong transcendental resonance of Kieślowski's work.

Part III – Overview

1   Important examples would include *Martyrs of Love, Valerie and Her Week of Wonders* and Jakubisko's *Tisícroná vná vela/The Millenial Bee* (1983), as well as the work of Švankmajer. From Hungary, the exploration would need to include Zoltán Huszárik's *Szindbád/ Sinbad* (1971), based on the work of the proto-surrealist Gyula Krúdy and starring the leading actor of Hungarian cinema, Zoltán Latinovits, as well as the idiosyncratic yet very interesting *Angyali üdvözlet/Annunication* (1984) by András Jeles. The investigation would need to expand to include the films of the Polish director Jan Jakub Kolski, who works in the tradition of magical realism.

2   Czech film specialist Peter Hames, for example, talks with admiration of one such beautiful film, František Vláčil's *Marketa Lazarová* (1967), and discusses it as the best Czech film ever made (Hames 2000b). DEFA and Barrandov produced many fairytale films, now almost forgotten. The DEFA Karl May adaptations with Gojko Mitić and the films based on heroic legends (such as Jerzy Passendorfer's popular Polish adventure *Jánosik/Yanoshik,* 1974) also belong to this range.

3   For example, biopics of composers such as Liszt, Bartók, Chopin, Dvořák, or Zoltán Huszárik's hauntingly beautiful biopic of Hungarian naivist painter *Csontváry* (1980).

4   Only Tarkovsky's sci-fi films are known in the West today, but there were many more made across the region that remain forgotten and need exploration. Classics of this genre include Juliusz Machulski's *Seksmisja/Sexmission* (1984), a film that has a cult following expanding far beyond Poland, as well as the remarkable work of Pole Piotr Szulkin.

5   An example of extremely popular action-adventure comedies are the early films of Juliusz Machulski – *Va Banque* and its sequel *Va Banque, czyli riposta/Va Banque II* (1985), featuring a series of tense and hilarious situations from the life of bank robbers.

6   Television was the main producer of this type of film. Some of the television series that were greatly popular included the war-time adventure *Four Tank Soldiers and the Dog* and *More Than Life at Stake* as well as the highly successful Soviet *Semnadtsat mgnovenij vesny/Seventeen Moments of Spring* (Tatyana Lioznova, 1973). The Czech adventure series *Thirty Cases of Major Zeman* (1975) and the long-running East German series *Polizeiruf 110* (still in existence and with more than 200 instalments so far) also belong to the genre.

7   Taken out of national and historic context today most of these films come across as tediously boring. What is funny and what is not (and why) is an issue worth investigating.

Chapter 6

1   Mészáros was married to prominent director Miklós Jancsó during the 1960s, his most important creative period. In interviews with Catherine Portuges (whose book on the director is one of the rare studies dedicated to a single Hungarian film-maker), Mészáros extensively discussed matters of personal creativity and relationships with men. Mészáros' relationship with Jancsó and later on with Polish actor Jan Nowicki (who appears in most of her 1980s films) are particularly interesting to tackle in that they seem to represent situations where balance between two artistic personalities has been achieved. Despite her marriage to Jancsó, for example, Mészáros never imitated the unmistakable visual idioms of his films. She does, however, admit to needing Nowicki's advice on issues of style and aesthetics.

2   Other films by Chytilová, revealing an uneven career, include *Ovoce stromu rajskych jíme/The Fruit of Paradise* (1969), *Hra o jablko/The Apple Game* (1976), *Panelstory/Prefab*

Story (1979), *Kalamita/Calamity* (1981), *Faunovo příliš pozdní odpoledne/The Very Late Afternoon of a Faun* (1983), *Vyhnání z ráje/Expulsion from Paradise* (2001) and others.

3　Nicknamed the 'Margaret Thatcher of Czech cinema', Chytilová has attracted controversy with her provocative film *Traps* (1998), which split critical opinion, mostly on the issue on how far feminism can go in its vicious reaction to male dominance. The film tells the story of a female veterinarian who is raped by two acquaintances and who then seeks revenge by castrating her rapists and arranging a situation in which one of them eats, without realising, his own testicles. *Traps* was described as a cruel feminist black comedy, that was 'celebrated by a handful of hardcore feminists' (Connolly 2000). Male critics had serious problems endorsing the film. Horton declared it 'notorious' for its 'depressingly reactionary' message, which, he thought, was delivered with 'smutty toilet humour ' (1999a: 2). Herbert Eagle, talking in 1999 at the AAASS's annual convention in St. Louis, was less dismissive but admitted that the film was not easy viewing for men.

4　Krumbachová scripted films such as Němec's *The Party and the Guests* (1996) and *Martyrs of Love* (1966), Jireš' *Valerie and Her Week of Wonders* (1970), and Chytilová's *Daisies*, *The Fruit of Paradise* (1969) and *The Very Late Afternoon of a Faun* (1983).

5　Jakubowska's oeuvre is discussed in the *European Journal of Women Studies* by Ewa Mazierska (2001b).

6　Once abroad Holland first worked in Europe, making films with a clear social commitment (like the Holocaust-themed *Angry Harvest* and *Europa, Europa*, and the Solidarity-themed *To Kill a Priest*). In the 1990s, she continued working on European art-house productions, switching to themes of subtle psychology and somewhat more popular appeal (a family drama of a lost child, *Olivier, Olivier*, 1992, and a drama exploring the tempestuous relationship between French poets Rimbaud and Baudelaire, *Total Eclipse*, 1995). In the 1990s, she was noticed by Hollywood and invited to work on projects to which she did not appear to have a specific artistic commitment but which she nonetheless directed competently (*The Secret Garden*, 1993 and *Washington Square*, 1997). Acclaimed for her work, by the end of the decade Holland established herself as one of the few international female directors whose name can guarantee good pre-sales. Having become the established and respected director she is, Holland keeps putting out one film after another, her work becoming more versatile but less recognisable. Most of her films do well at the box office, and she enjoys the robust reputation of a reliable professional who is equally comfortable in low-key dramas and in lavish period productions, and who is every bit as competent as her male counterparts.

7　There is a whole strand of scholarship that explores the use of female images within the range of nationalist symbolism. It is an enormous topic, one which is beyond the scope of this study. East Central European cinema offers an equally rich material for explorations of this nature as any of the other European film traditions (see, for example, Elzbieta Ostrowska's 1998 text on the 'Polish Mother'). Writing on European cinema in general, authors Jill Forbes and Sarah Street correctly noted that, 'Perhaps the most interesting representation of the national question is through the sensibilities, and above all, over the bodies, of women. [...] In *Le Mépris*, the body of Brigitte Bardot became the site of a cultural contest between Europe and America, the locus of both pleasure and conflict. In the New German cinema, and especially perhaps in films such as Rainer Werner Fassbinder's *The Marriage of Maria Braun* (1978) or Helma Sanders-Brahms' *Germany, Pale Mother* (1980) the suffering, sometimes prostituted, woman becomes the symbol of the state of Germany, while in Spanish cinema of the 1980s and 1990s, in the work of the director Almodovar, sexually mobile bodies establish "a new cultural stereotype for a hyperliberated Spain" (Kinder, 3) in films like *Matador* (1986) and *The Law of Desire* (1987). (2000: 41). If East European film was included in the discussion of European cinema, this observation could undoubtedly be expanded to encompass similar examples from the work of Holland and Bugajski (Poland), Makk and Szabó (Hungary), and Menzel and Jakubisko (Czechoslovakia), to name but a few.

8   Anikó Imre in personal correspondence, 2003. She also adds: 'A postcolonial analogy is most useful here: Third World women and feminist critics of postcolonial cultures insist on demystifying a system of representation that turns women into metaphors and allegories of the masculine project of nationalist decolonisation. In this context it is still far from certain if East Central European female film-makers' attitudes towards the brand of imported feminism can be read as a challenge to the white, liberal, late-capitalist, affluent connotations of this particular brand (just like Third World women's resistance to the very term can).'

9   A woman with a child finding a solution by looking for a new partner is not a typical narrative move for these cinematic plots. Such a turn is more likely to be found in American cinema (for example in *This Boy's Life*, Michael Caton-Jones, 1993). Only lately has it been explored in Russian cinema: in the acclaimed *Vor/Thief* (Pavel Chukhrai, 1997), a story told from the point of view of a boy whose mother finds a new partner and tries to build a new life (but fails).

10 Within Soviet cinema the film that fully fits this description – Stalinism as an adverse force that destroys the family – is Tengiz Abuladze's *Monanieba/Repentance* (1986). It is not by accident that this film was received as one of the strongest indictments of totalitarianism.

11 One would expect to find interesting depictions of life in dormitories in Soviet cinema, but surprisingly it has not been such a prominent feature there: Russians seem to be more preoccupied with featuring life in communal apartments (*komunalka*). Vladimir Menshov's *Moskva slezam ne verit/Moscow Does Not Believe in Tears* (1979) shows life in female dorms in a comedic way which is far removed from the sensibility of Mészáros' approach.

12 At the time Holland's *A Woman Alone* was released, a very similar film featuring the difficult life of a single mother was censored in Bulgaria. Hristo Hristov's *Edna zhena na trideset i tri/A Woman at 33* (1981) was taken off the screens after an orchestrated critical campaign in the Party-controlled media, a situation suggesting that this type of social critique was becoming unwelcome.

13 It was the tradition in the Eastern Bloc that terminally ill people were not told of the true nature of their ailment. Cancerous patients were kept in the dark about their real condition while their relatives were informed of the outlook by the doctors. Hiding from one's loved ones that they only have a limited time to live, pretending that everything is allright and they are on the road to recovery, created a number of sad situations between close people, bordering on absurdity. Many East Central European films dealt with this game of hiding the truth from the terminally ill, all featuring dramatic plots structured around a simple premise that would not be there if the film was set in the West (where the patients would be informed of their true condition).

14 Scenes of lesbian attraction are featured in a number of films, particularly those focusing on women in forced confinement, like *The Interrogation* (Ryszard Bugajski, 1982) or *Surveillance* (Wiesław Saniewski, 1985). These remain marginal subplots though. Here same-sex attraction is never tackled with the subtlety found in Makk's film.

15 Makk, who has created some unique portrayals of women, is particularly interested in exploring women of an advanced age. In *Love* his focus is on the close relationship between the elderly protagonist and her daughter-in-law, both women united by the concern of the absent son/husband. This interest is further developed in *Cat's Play*, a film about the relationship of two elderly women who share an apartment but do not

like each other. Like in *Love*, here Makk also uses interiors full of antiques and flashback references to a distant Austro-Hungarian youth twinkling in foggy vignettes. Behind the daily routine of cooking and eating, of letter writing and talking on the phone, a whole range of political and generation gap problems gradually come to the surface. Elderly women have regularly been the centre of attention for other Hungarian directors as well, resulting in remarkable films featuring women of an advanced age, such as Judit Elek's *Sziget a szárazföldön/The Lady from Constantinople* (1969) or István Szabó's *Tüzoltó utca 25/25 Firemen Street* (1973).

16   In addition, by the year 2000 the Hungarian capital Budapest was believed to have become the most active production site for Europe's thriving porn film industry.

17   East Central European cinema, for example, is still to produce a serious film tackling one of the key problems of women in the region: international trafficking, the coercion of scores of young women into sexual slavery. Márta Mészáros did make a film that looked into this problem (*A Szerencse lányai/Daughters of Luck*, 1998), but, like most of her work in the 1990s, it triggered mixed critical reactions. A lesser-seen film on the theme of trafficking was Romanian Nae Caranfil's *Asphalt Tango* (1997), starring Charlotte Rampling as a callous Madam who has come to Romania to recruit hopeful young girls to work for her as 'dancers'. It is symptomatic, however, that the best film on this issue so far, one that tackles the roots of the trafficking problem as well as its appalling consequences, was to be made by a Swede (Lukas Moodysson's 2002 *Lilja 4-Ever*).

18   For a good discussion of an art-house film which represents yet another carnivorously sexual woman (Żuławski's *Shaman*, 1996) see Mazierska 2002.

Chapter 7

1   This is not the picture for the rest of the former Eastern Bloc, however. The crisis still persists in countries like Romania, Albania and Bulgaria.

2   The presence of a domestic film in the box office 'top ten' differed depending on the country. Films such as *Kolya* (1996) in the Czech Republic, *Dollybirds* (1997) in Hungary and *With Fire and Sword* (1999) in Poland set a trend that is there to persist. A Czech film reached the number one spot (in terms of admissions for films of all nationalities playing in the territory) in 1991, 1992, 1994, 1996, 1997, 1999, 2000 and 2001. In all the other years, there was at least one film, and usually more in other slots in the top ten (for example there were four Czech films in the top ten in 1993). On the other hand, Slovakia had a domestic entry in the top ten only in 1993 and 1999.

3   International distribution is at a record low but not so much in regard to distribution in the West where the numbers of exported films remain as low as before (there has not been big decline, but there has not been growth in exchanges either). The real decline is most clearly seen in regard to other parts of the world, where this cinema was previously in regular distribution and has now effectively disappeared (like India, Africa and the Soviet Union, as well as the other countries from the former Eastern Bloc).

4   Here is a suitable place to mention the efforts of producers who, by virtue of their East European origins, have made it possible for films that explored East Central European experiences and concerns to be made and seen internationally: Romanian-born Marin Karmitz in France, Hungarian-born Robert Lantos in Canada, or Polish-born Marek Rozenbaum in Israel, all key movers in film production in their respective countries. Karmitz sponsored Kieślowski's work (as well as the films of the Romanian director Lucian Pintilie), while Lantos supported István Szabó's *Sunshine*, a project that had run into serious financial difficulties. Marek Rozenbaum's production work in Israel has been consistently dedicated to themes linked with East European immigrants; the films he

produces are regularly directed by immigrant film-makers educated in the former Soviet Union and Eastern Europe.

5   For a more detailed analysis of the studio privatisation, see my study in *Javnost/ The Public* (1999) and for details of the Czech film industry, see Hames (2000a). While all studios have been fairly successful in securing a flow of foreign productions, Barrandov has been the undisputed champion specialising in blockbusters – from *Mission Impossible* (1996) to *A Knight's Tale* (2000) and Jackie Chan's vehicle *Shanghai Knights* (2003). Dubbed 'Hollywood on the Vltava,' Prague is well on its way to becoming Europe's number one location for film shoots, a threat that has been confirmed both by scholars (Miller *et al.* 2001: 72) and journalists (Connolly 2002: 8).

6   The issues of post-Communist transformation of the film industries in the region are the subject of my forthcoming monograph, *Film Industries and Cultures in Transition: Europe's New Image Markets*, part of Rowman and Littlefield's *Critical Media Studies* series. Miller *et al*'s concept of the New International Division of Cultural Labour relates to a situation clearly seen in the region today. It is characterised by free movement of screen capital to cheap production locations, containment of labour mobility and denial of labour internationalism, in this case all brokered on the exploitation of skills and facilities developed under state socialism.

7   On the issue of the older generation directors in Poland, see the article of Alicja Helman (2000) in *Canadian Slavonic Papers*.

8   Born into the family of screenwriter and actor Zdeněk Svěrák, Jan studied at FAMU where he made two well-received shorts in the mock-documentary genre. His debut feature, *Obecná skola/Elementary School* (1991), was a tongue-in-cheek bittersweet comedy in the best tradition of the Czechoslovak New Wave. It was distributed internationally and even received an Academy Award nomination. The lighthearted road movie *Jizda/The Ride* (1994) made for a mere $30,000, won at Karlovy Vary, and *Akumulator 1/Accumulator 1* (1994), an anti-technological sci-fi satire budgeted at $2 million, both had significant box office success in the Czech Republic. In 1996, Svěrák directed and co-produced what was to be his biggest hit, *Kolya*. His father, who also starred in the film, wrote the script. The film won numerous international awards, including a Golden Globe and an Academy Award, both for best foreign-language film, in 1997. When receiving his award in 1997, Svěrák promised to work hard to make more 'little brothers' for the Oscar.

9   Examples include French director Artemio Benki and the American animator John Cahill, both working in Prague.

10 Němec made several films after his return. (Some interesting texts discussing his career and an interview extensively covering his experiences in emigration can be found at the site of *Central Europe Review*, Vol. 3, No. 17, 14 May 2001, http://www ce-review org/01/17/kinoeye17_hames html) Jasný made a feature, *Návrat ztraceného ráje/Return to Paradise Lost* (1999). Skolimowski worked on an adaptation of Witold Gombrowicz's complex novel *Ferdydurke/30 Door Key* (1992), Miloš Forman became a shareholder in Cinepont, the company which purchased the Barrandov studios at the initial privatisation stage in 1993, and Roman Polanski shot his *The Pianist* in Warsaw and Berlin. The director of *The Interrogation*, Ryszard Bugajski, who had emigrated to Canada, had managed to make only one feature film, *Clearcut* (1991), about the struggle of Native Indians against corporations on Canada's West Coast, and worked in television for the rest of the time. Bugajski returned to Poland in the 1990s where he completed the feature *Gracze/Players* (1995).

11 Many of the internationally known film-makers maintain residential ties with some location in the West, and are in possession of personal documents that secure them freedom of movement which is not available to their ordinary compatriots. To establish

oneself in the West and to obtain some sort of Western personal ID, either a second citizenship or just a residence card, is often it a matter of practical wisdom. Such arrangements give access to extra funding that is not available to those who stay at home. Although, according to the definition of the pan-European funding body *Eurimages*, a passport of any European country would qualify a director as 'European', factual residency in the West becomes equally and even more important than nationality. A simple domicile in France, for example, makes directors eligible for support via French programs not normally open to them as foreigners. Also in other European countries it is the residence of the director, and not the citizenship, that is important when seeking funding.

12 The work of a new generation of diasporic film-makers who began their careers in the West after the end of the Cold War – like British-Polish director Pawel Pawlikowski (*Last Resort*, 2000) and American cinematographer Janusz Kaminski (who filmed all of Stephen Spielberg's films since *Schindler's List*, 1993) should be mentioned here as well. More recently, Kaminski also directed a Hollywood feature, *Lost Souls* (2000). Polish-American cinematographer Andrzej Bartkowiak was responsible for the photography of action blockbusters like *Speed* (1994), *Dante's Peak* (1997) and *Lethal Weapon 4* (1998); Bartkowiak also directs action-adventure films, most importantly Jet Li's action vehicle, *Romeo Must Die* (2000).

13 György Szomjas' *Roncsfilm/Junk Movie* (Hungary, 1992) is a film that reflects these problems very well.

14 Grodecki first made the documentary *Not Angels, But Angels* (1994), and then the feature *Mandragora* (1997), both dealing with the subjects of sex tourism and teen porn. These films clearly indicated that the entry of many young Czechs into prostitution is closely linked to their discovery that this is a short cut to their dream life of consumerism. These films are, of course, part of the budding body of works of gay film-makers in the region.

15 These films are also being made in post-reunification Germany, often by directors who focus on the social and existential problems of the former East German lands.

16 Zanussi made films in praise of the Polish-born Pope, John Paul II, and in 1996 adapted one of his plays for the screen (published under the Pope's real name, Karol Wojtyla), *Our God's Brother* (1997).

17 Reputed Hungarian cinematographer Lajos Koltai is preparing to make a directorial debut with an adaptation of Kertesz's Holocaust novel *Fateless*

18 Some argued that *Dollybirds* undercuts its own nostalgia because the portrayal of the communists here was clearly parodic (Horton 1999b). According to Horton, the film's humorous references to repressive politics – as, for example, in the character who secretly writes reports on the others, presumably to be handed over to the secret police, and in its bitter ending, in which the safe, happy world of Communism was revealed to be based on deception – were making the choice of this film as an illustration of the 'nostalgia' business look 'slightly strange' (personal correspondence, 2003). More films of this specific 'nostalgia' genre are made across the region, specifically in Germany, where they even speak of 'Ostalgie' ('nostalgia for the East'). These include, for example, films such as Leander Haußmann's *Sonnenallee/Sun Alley* (1999) and Sebastian Peterson's *Helden wie wir/Heroes Like Us* (1999), both of which have have done extremely well at the box office. Most recently, the genre received a significant boost with the very successful *Good bye, Lenin!* (Wolfgang Becker, 2003). Set in Berlin of 1989, the plot of the film revolves around hiding the fact of the Berlin Wall's fall from the protagonist's mother. She is a devoted Communist who is in hospital with a weak heart; it would be too much of a shock for her to hear about the collapse of Communism, so the son undertakes to 'fake it' for her.

19 A special issue of the journal *Framework* (Iordanova 2003) is devoted to the cinematic

representations of Gypsies (Roma). It includes a study on the representation of Romanies in post-Communist Hungarian media and film, as well as essays on important Romani-themed films from East Central Europe such as *Pink-Tainted Dreams* and *Devils, Devils*

20   In a perceptive and illuminating study of the representation of Romanies in post-communist Hungarian media and cinema, Anikó Imre (2003) explores these trends and identifies the source of the problem which she sees in the inherent contradictions characterising the 'use' of the image of the Gypsy within the nationalist discourse of the post-Communist countries themselves. While Romanies are inherently transnational subjects, within the nationalist discourse of countries like Hungary, Poland, the Czech and Slovak republics they are still treated as 'belonging' to a nation which simultaneously rejects them.

21   Kolski also made a Holocaust themed film, *Daleko od okna/Keep Away from the Window* (2000).

22   Yet another film that deserves mention here is the German-made *Gorilla Bathes at Noon* by Yugoslav veteran exile Dušan Makavejev. The film, rich in controversial historical cross-referencing, ironically juxtaposes the images of the triumphal arrival of the Russians with the present-day story of a Soviet Army major who deserts the Soviet forces at the time of their withdrawal from Berlin and attempts to stay in the West. It also features documentary footage of the 1992 demise of the gigantic sixty-foot statue of Lenin in Berlin. For an extended discussion of *Kolya*, *Bolshe Vita* and a range of other films dealing with the changing image of the Russians, see Iordanova 2000.

Appendix

1   This collection, part of Wallflower Press' *24 Frames* series, will contain essays on a selection of some of the most important films made in the region. As with all the volumes in this series focusing on national and regional cinemas, the selection comprises texts that focus on specific films (rather than on trends or directors), and aims to cover titles representative of a variety of genres and styles.

2   A useful, though slightly outdated, site is the *East European Media and Cinema Studies* web page that I maintained between 1994 and 1997 at the University of Texas <http://www utexas edu/ftp/depts/eems/main html>.

FILMOGRAPHY

25 Firemen Street/Tüzoltó utca 25, István Szabó, Hungary, 1973
Absolute Beginners, Julien Temple, UK, 1986
Adoption/Örökbefogadás, Márta Mészáros, Hungary, 1975
Aesop/Ezop, Rangel Vulchanov, Czechoslovakia/Bulgaria, 1970
All My Good Countrymen/Všichni dobří rodáci, Vojtěch Jasný, Czechoslovakia, 1968
Amadeus, Miloš Forman, USA, 1984
Ambiguous Report About the End of the World, An/Nejasná zpráva o konci světa, Juraj Jakubisko, Czech Republic, 1997
Andrei Rublev, Andrei Tarkovsky, Soviet Union, 1969
Angels With Dirty Faces, Michael Curtiz, USA, 1938
Angi Vera, Pál Gábor, Hungary, 1979
Angry Harvest/Bittere Ernte, Agnieszka Holland, West Germany, 1985
Annunication/Angyali üdvözlet, András Jeles, Hungary, 1984
Another Way/Egymásra nézve, Károly Makk, Hungary, 1982
Apple Game, The/Hra o jablko, Věra Chytilová, Czechoslovakia, 1976
Arabian Nights/Il fiore delle mille e una notte, Pier Paolo Pasolini, Italy, 1974
Ashes and Diamonds/Popió i diamant, Andrzej Wajda, Poland, 1958
Asphalt Tango, Nae Caranfil, Romania/France, 1997
Avalon, Barry Levinson, USA, 1990
Bad Luck/Zęzowate szczęście, Andrzej Munk, Poland, 1960
Balint Fabian Meets God/Fábián Bálint találkozása Istennel, Zoltán Fábri, Hungary, 1979
Barber of Siberia, The/Sibirskiy tsiryulnik, Nikita Mikhalkov, Russia/France, 1998
Barrier/Bariera, Jerzy Skolimowski, Poland, 1966

Beast, The/La Bête, Walerian Borowczyk, France, 1975
Being There, Hal Ashby, USA, 1979
Bicycle Thieves/Ladri di biciclette, Vittorio de Sica, Italy, 1948
Big Animal, The/Duże zwierę, Jerzy Stuhr, Poland, 2000
Birch Wood, The/Brzezina, Andrzej Wajda, Poland, 1970
Birds, Orphans and Fools/Vtáčkovia, siroty a blázni, Juraj Jakubisko, Czechoslovakia/France, 1969
Bitches/Csajok, Ildikó Szabó, Hungary, 1995
Black Cat, White Cat/Crna mačka, beli mačor, Emir Kusturica, Yugoslavia/France, 1998
Black Hawk Down, Ridely Scott, USA, 2001
Black Peter (a.k.a. *Peter and Pavla*)/*Černý Petr*, Miloš Forman, Czechoslovakia, 1963
Black Swallow, The/Chernata Lyastovitza, Georgi Dyulgerov, Bulgaria/France, 1997
Blind Chance/Przypadek, Krzysztof Kieślowski, Poland, 1981
Blonde in Love, A/Lásky jedné plavovlásky, Miloš Forman, Czechoslovakia, 1965
Blow-Up/Blowup, Michelangelo Antonioni, UK, 1966
Bolshe Vita/Bolse vita, Ibolya Fekete, Hungary/Germany, 1996
Bonus/Premiya, Sergei Mikaelyan, USSR, 1974
Border Street/Ulica Graniczna, Aleksander Ford, Poland, 1949
Boxer and Death/Boxer a smrt, Peter Solan, Czechoslovakia, 1963
Boys of Paul Street, The/Pál utcai fiúk, Zoltán Fábri, Hungary, 1967
Bridgeman, The/A Hídember, Géza Bereményi, Hungary, 2002
Burial of a Potato/Pogrzeb kartofla, Jan Jakub Kolski, Poland, 1991
Buttoners/Knoflíkáři, Petr Zelenka, Czech Republic, 1997
By Touch/Przez dotyk, Magdalena Łazarkiewicz, Poland, 1985
Calamity/Kalamita, Věra Chytilová, Czechoslovakia, 1981
Camera Buff/Amator, Krzysztof Kieślowski, Poland, 1979
Canal/Kanał, Andrzej Wajda, Poland, 1957
Camouflage/Barwy ochronne, Krzysztof Zanussi, Poland, 1977
Cantata/Oldás és kötés, Hungary, Miklós Jancsó, 1963
The Canterbury Tales/I racconti di Canterbury, Pier Paolo Pasolini, Italy, 1971
Capricious Summer/Rozmarné léto, Jiří Menzel, Czechoslovakia, 1968
Casablanca, Michael Curtiz, USA, 1942
Cassandra Cat/Až přijde kocour, Vojtěch Jasný, Czechoslovakia, 1963
Cat's Play/Macskajáték, Károly Makk, Hungary, 1974
Chacho Rom, Ildikó Szabó, Hungary, 2001
Chico, Ibolya Fekete, Hungary, 2001
Chien andalou, Un, Luis Buñuel, France, 1929
Child Murders/Gyerekgyilkosságok, Ildikó Szabó, Hungary, 1993
Chinatown, Roman Polanski, USA, 1974
Citizen Kane, Orson Welles, USA, 1941
Clearcut, Ryszard Bugajski, Canada, 1991
Cleopatra, Joseph L. Mankiewicz, USA, 1963
Closely Observed Trains (UK)/*Closely Watched Trains* (USA)/*Ostře sledované vlaky*, Jiří Menzel, Czechoslovakia, 1966
Cold Days/Hideg napok, András Kovács, Hungary, 1966
Colonel Redl/Redl ezredes/Oberst Redl, István Szabó, Hungary/Germany, 1985
Colonel Wołodyjowski/Pan Wołodyjowski, Jerzy Hoffman, Poland, 1969
Competition/Konkurs, Miloš Forman, Czechoslovakia, 1963
Conductor, The/Dyrygent, Andrzej Wajda, Poland, 1979
Confidence/Bizalom, István Szabó, Hungary, 1979
Confrontation, The/Fényes szelek, Miklós Jancsó, Hungary, 1968

Filmography

Conquest, The/Honfoglalás, Gábor Koltay, Hungary, 1996
Constant Factor, The/Constans, Krzysztof Zanussi, Poland, 1980
Contract/Kontrakt, Krzysztof Zanussi, Poland, 1980
Crows/Wrony, Dorota Kędzierzawska, Poland, 1995
Csontváry, Zoltán Huszárik, Hungary, 1980
Cul-de-sac, Roman Polanski, UK, 1966
Current/Sodrásban, István Gaál, Hungary, 1963
Cutting It Short/Postřižiny, Jiří Menzel, Czechoslovakia, 1980
Daisy, The/Margaritkata, Todor Dinov, Bulgaria, 1963
Daisies/Sedmikrásky, Věra Chytilová, Czechoslovakia, 1966
Damnation/Kárhozat, Béla Tarr, Hungary, 1988
Daniel Takes the Train/Szerencsés Dániel, Pál Sándor, Hungary, 1983
Dante's Peak, Roger Donaldson, USA, 1997
Danton, Andrzej Wajda, France, 1982
Daughters of Luck/A Szerencse lányai/Cory szczęścia, Márta Mészáros, Hungary/Poland, 1998
Dear Emma, Sweet Böbe/Édes Emma, drága Böbe - vázlatok, aktok, István Szabó, Hungary, 1992
Death as a Slice of Bread/Śmierć jak kromka chleba, Kazimierz Kutz, Poland, 1994
Death of a President/Śmierć prezydenta, Jerzy Kawalerowicz, Poland, 1978
Death of Stalinism in Bohemia, Jan Švankmajer, Czechoslovakia, 1990
Debutante, The/Debiutantka, Barbara Sass, Poland, 1982
Decalogue, The/Dekalog, Krzysztof Kieślowski, Poland, 1988
Decameron/Il Decameron, Pier Paolo Pasolini, Italy, 1970
Deliverance, John Boorman, USA, 1972
Deluge, The/Potop, Jerzy Hoffman, Poland, 1974
Deserter and the Nomads, The/Zbehovia a pútnici, Juraj Jakubisko, Czechoslovakia/Italy, 1968
Devils, The, Ken Russell, UK, 1971
Devils, Devils/Diabły, diabły, Dorota Kędzierzawska, Poland, 1991
Diamonds of the Night/Démanty noci, Jan Němec, Czechoslovakia, 1963
Diary for My Children/Napló gyermekeimnek, Márta Mészáros, Hungary, 1982
Diary for My Father and Mother/Napló apámnak, anyámnak, Márta Mészáros, Hungary, 1990
Diary for My Loved Ones/Napló szerelmeimnek, Márta Mészáros, Hungary, 1987
Discreet Charm of the Bourgeoisie, The/Le charme discret de la bourgeoisie, Luis Buñuel, France/Italy/Spain, 1972,
Distant Journey (a.k.a. *The Long Journey)/Daleká cesta*, Alfréd Radok, Czechoslovakia, 1949
Dita Saxová, Antonín Moskalyk, Czechoslovakia, 1967
Divided Heaven, The/Der geteilte Himmel, Konrad Wolf, GDR, 1964
Divided We Fall/Musíme si pomáhat, Jan Hrebejk, Czech Republic, 2000
Do You Remember Dolly Bell?/Sjećaš li se, Dolly Bell, Emir Kusturica, Yugoslavia, 1981
Doll, The/Lalka, Wojciech Has, Poland, 1969
Dollybirds/Csinibaba, Péter Tímár, Hungary, 1997
Doña Flor and Her Two Husbands/Doña Flor e seus dois maridos, Bruno Bareto, Brazil, 1976
Double Life of Veronique, The/La double vie de Véronique, Krzysztof Kieślowski, France/Poland/Norway, 1991
Dybbuk, The/Dybuk, Michal Waszynski, Poland, 1937
Ear, The/Ucho, Karel Kachyňa, Czechoslovakia, 1970
Early Works/Rani Radovi, Želimir Žilnik, Yugoslavia, 1969
Ecstasy/Extase, Gustav Machatý, Czechoslovakia/Germany, 1932
Eighth Day of the Week, The/Ósmy dzień tygodnisa, Aleksander Ford, Poland, 1958
Eroica, Andrzej Munk, Poland, 1958
Eroticon, Gustav Machatý, Czechoslovakia, 1929

Escape from Liberty Cinema/Ucieczka z kina Wolność, Wojciech Marczewski, Poland, 1991

Europa, Europa/Hitlerjunge Salomon, Agnieszka Holland, Germany, 1990

Everyday Courage/Každý den odvahu, Evald Schorm, Czechoslovakia, 1964

Expulsion from Paradise/Vyhnání z ráje, Věra Chytilová, Czech Republic, 2001

Exterminating Angel, The/El Ángel Exterminador, Luis Buñuel, Mexico, 1962

Face Behind the Mask/Tvář pod maskou, Rangel Vulchanov, Bulgaria/Czechoslovakia, 1970

Family Life/Życie rodzinne, Krzysztof Zanussi, Poland, 1971

Fanatics, The/Megszállottak, Károly Makk, Hungary, 1961

Father/Apá, István Szabó, Hungary, 1966

Fever/Gorączka, Agnieszka Holland, Poland, 1981

Fidelity/La Fidélité, Andrzej Żuławski, France, 2000

Fifth Horseman is Fear, The/...a páty jezdec je Strach, Zbynek Brynych, Czechoslovakia, 1964

Fifth Seal, The/Az Ötödik pecsét, Zoltán Fábri, Hungary, 1976

Firemen's Ball, The/Hoří, má panenko, Miloš Forman, Czechoslovakia, 1967

Five Boys from Barska Street/Piątka z ulicy Barskiej, Aleksander Ford, Poland, 1954

Flowers of Reverie/Szirmok, virágok, koszorúk, László Lugossy, Hungary, 1984

Forbidden Games/Jeux interdits, René Clément, France, 1952

Forrest Gump, Robert Zemeckis, USA, 1994

Four Tank Soldiers and the Dog/Czterej pancerni i pies, Andrzej Czekalski and Konrad Nalecki, Poland, 1966

Fourteen Lives/Életjel, Zoltán Fábri, Hungary, 1954

French Lieutenant's Woman, The, Karel Reisz, UK, 1981

Fruit of Paradise, The/Ovoce stromů rajských jíme, Věra Chytilová, Czechoslovakia, 1969

Full Metal Jacket, Stanley Kubrick, USA, 1987

Garden, The/Záhrada, Martin Šulík, Slovakia, 1995

Gattaca, Andrew Niccol, USA, 1997

Generation, A/Pokolenie, Andrzej Wajda, Poland, 1954

Germany Year Zero/Germania anno zero, Roberto Rossellini, Italy, 1947

Get Carter, Mike Hodges, UK, 1971

Ghost, Jerry Zucker, USA, 1990

Girl, The/Eltávozott nap, Márta Mészáros, Hungary, 1968

Girls of Nowolipki, The/Dziewczęta z Nowolipek, Barbara Sass, Poland, 1985

Good bye, Lenin!, Wolfgang Becker, Germany, 2003

Goto, Island of Love/Goto, l'île d'amour, Walerian Borowczyk, France, 1968

Great Dictator, The, Charles Chaplin, USA, 1940

Guardian Angel/Anđeo čuvar, Goran Paskaljević, Yugoslavia, 1987

Gypsies/Cigányok, Sándor Sára, Hungary, 1962

Gypsies Are Found Near Heaven/Tabor ukhodit v nebo, Emil Loteanu, USSR, 1975

Gypsy Lore/Romani kris – Cigánytörvény, Bence Gyöngyössy, Hungary, 1997

Gypsy Magic, Stole Popov, Macedonia, 1997

Gyuri/Cséplö Gyuri, Pál Schiffer, Hungary, 1978

Hair, Miloš Forman, USA/West Germany, 1979

Hand, The/Ruka, Jiří Trnka, Czechoslovakia, 1965

Hands Up!/Ręce do góry, Jerzy Skolimowski, Poland, 1966/1981/1985

Hanele, Karel Kachyňa, Czech Republic, 1999

Hanussen, István Szabó, Hungary/Germany, 1988

Heaven, Tom Tykwer, Germany, 2002

Hero of the Year/Bohater roku, Feliks Falk, Poland, 1987

Heroes like Us/Helden wie wir, Sebastian Peterson, Germany, 1999

Hi, Tereska/Cześć Tereska, Robert Gliński, Poland, 2001

Hitler: A Film from Germany/Hitler: ein Film aus Deutschland, Hans-Jürgen Syberberg,

Germany, 1977

Holy Mountain/La Montaña sagrada, Alejandro Jodorowsky, Mexico, 1973

Holy Week/Wielki tydzień, Andrzej Wajda, Poland, 1995

Hungarian Rhapsody/Magyar rapszódia, Miklós Jancsó, Hungary, 1979

Hungarian village, A 1972–73/Istenmezején 1972–73–ban, Judit Elek, Hungary, 1973

Hungarians/Magyarok, Zoltán Fábri, Hungary, 1978

I am the Rabbit (a.k.a. *The Rabbit is Me*)*/Das Kaninchen bin Ich*, Kurt Maetzig, GDR, 1965

I Even Met Happy Gypsies/Skupljači perja, Aleksandar Petrović, Yugoslavia, 1967

Identification Marks: None/Rysopis, Jerzy Skolimowski, Poland, 1964

If..., Lindsay Anderson, UK 1968

If There Were No Music/Kdyby ty muziky nebyly, Miloš Forman, Czechoslovakia, 1963

Illumination/Iluminacja, Krzysztof Zanussi, Poland, 1973

Immoral Tales/Contes immoraux, Walerian Borowczyk, France, 1974

Inn, The/Austeria, Jerzy Kawalerowicz, Poland, 1983

Interrogation, The/Przesłuchanie, Ryszard Bugajski, Poland, 1982

Intimate Lighting/Intimní osvětlení, Ivan Passer, Czechoslovakia, 1966

Invitation/Zaproszenie, Wanda Jakubowska, Poland, 1986

Ivan and Abraham/Moi Ivan, toi Abraham, Yolande Zauberman, France/Belarus, 1993

Ivan the Terrible, parts I and II/Ivan Grozniy, Sergei Eisenstein, USSR, 1944/1946

Jahrgang '45/Born in '45, Jürgen Böttcher, East Germany, 1965

Jakob the Liar/Jakob, der Lügner, Frank Beyer, East Germany/Czechoslovakia, 1974

Jakob the Liar, Peter Kassovitz, France/Hungary/USA, 1999

Jetée, La, Chris Marker, France, 1962

Johnnie the Aquarius/Jańcio Wodnik, Jan Jakub Kolski, Poland, 1993

Joke, The/Žert, Jaromil Jireš, Czechoslovakia, 1969

Junction, The/Torowisko, Urszula Urbaniak, Poland, 1999

Junk Movie/Roncsfilm, György Szomjas, Hungary, 1992

Kapò, Gilo Pontecorvo, France/Italy, 1959

Karla, Herrmann Zschoche, GDR, 1965

Keep Away from the Window/Daleko od okna, Jan Jakub Kolski, Poland, 2000

Kiler, Juliusz Machulski, Poland, 1997

King Istvan/István, a király, Gábor Koltay, Hungary, 1984

Knife in the Water/Nóż w wodzie, Roman Polanski, Poland, 1962

Knight's Tale, A, Brian Helgeland, USA, 2000

Knights of the Teutonic Order/Krzyżacy, Aleksander Ford, Poland, 1960

Kolya/Kolja, Jan Svěrák, Czech Republic, 1996

Koportos, Lívia Gyarmathy, Hungary, 1979

Korczak, Andrzej Wajda, Poland, 1990

Kung-Fu, Janusz Kijowski, Poland, 1980

Kühle Wampe oder: Wem gehört die Welt/To Whom Does the World Belong?, Zlatan Dudow, Germany, 1932

Lady from Constantinople, The/Sziget a szárazföldön, Judit Elek, Hungary, 1969

Landscape After the Battle/Krajobraz po bitwie, Andrzej Wajda, Poland, 1970

Last Bohemian, The/Az Utolsó bohém, Michael Curtiz, Hungary, 1912

Last Butterfly, The/Poslední motýl, Karel Kachyňa, Czechoslovakia, 1990

Last Picture, The/Ostatnie zdjęcia, Andrzej Brzozowski, Poland, 2001

Last Resort, Pawel Pawlikowski, UK, 2000

Last School Bell, The/Ostatni dzwonek, Magdalena Łazarkiewicz, Poland, 1989

Last Stage, The/Ostatni etap, Wanda Jakubowska, Poland, 1948

Late Night Talks with Mother/Noční hovory s matkou, Jan Němec, Czech Republic, 2000

Legend of Paul and Paula, The/Die Legende von Paul und Paula, Heiner Carow, East Germany,

1974
Legend about the Death and Resurrection of Two Young Men/Meztelen vagy, Imre Gyöngyössy,
 Hungary, 1971
Lethal Weapon 4, Richard Donner, USA, 1998
*Life as a Fatal Sexually Transmitted Disease/Życie jako śmiertelna choroba przenoszona drogą
 plciową*, Krzysztof Zanussi, Poland, 2000
Life is Beautiful/La vita è bella, Roberto Begnini, Italy, 1997
Lightship, The, Jerzy Skolimowski, USA, 1985
Lilja 4-Ever, Lukas Moodysson, Denmark/Sweden, 2002
Little Valentino/Kis Valentinó, András Jeles, Hungary, 1979
Lord of the Flies, Peter Brook, UK, 1963
Lost Souls, Janusz Kaminski, USA, 2000
Love in Germany, A/Eine Liebe in Deutschland, Andrzej Wajda, Germany, 1983
Love Film/Szerelmesfilm, István Szabó, Hungary, 1970
Love/Szerelem, Károly Makk, Hungary, 1971
Man and a Woman, A/Un homme et une femme, Claude Lelouch, France, 1966
Man of Iron/Człowiek z żelaza, Andrzej Wajda, Poland, 1981
Man of Marble/Człowiek z marmuru, Andrzej Wajda, Poland, 1976
Man on the Moon, Miloš Forman, UK/Germany/Japan/USA, 1999
Man on the Track/Człowiek na torze, Andrzej Munk, Poland, 1957
Mandragora, Wiktor Grodecki, Czech Republic, 1997
Maria's Day/Mária-nap, Judit Elek, Hungary, 1983
Marian, Petr Vaclav, Czech Republic/France
Marketa Lazarová, František Vláčil, Czechoslovakia, 1967
Martyrs of Love/Mučedníci lásky, Jan Němec, Czechoslovakia, 1966
McCabe and Mrs Miller, Robert Altman, USA, 1971
Men of the Blue Cross/Błękitny krzyż, Andrzej Munk, Poland, 1955
Men with Guns, John Sayles, USA, 1997
Mephisto, István Szabó, Germany/Hungary, 1981
Merry-Go-Round/Körhinta, Zoltán Fábri, Hungary, 1955
Mildred Pierce, Michael Curtiz, USA, 1945
Millenial Bee, The/Tisícroná vná vela, Juraj Jakubisko, Czechoslovakia, 1983
Miracle in Milan/Miracolo a Milano, Vittorio de Sica, Italy, 1951
Mirror, The/Zerkalo, Andrei Tarkovsky, Soviet Union, 1975
Mission Impossible, Brian De Palma, USA, 1996
Monsieur Hire, Patrice Leconte, France, 1989
Moonlighting, Jerzy Skolimowski, UK/West Germany, 1982
More Than Life at Stake/Stawka większa niż życie, Andrzej Konic and Janusz Morgenstern,
 Poland, 1969
Moscow Does Not Believe in Tears/Moskva slezam ne verit, Vladimir Menshov, USSR, 1979
Mother/Mat, Vsevolod Pudovkin, USSR, 1926
Mother and Son/Mat' i syn, Aleksandr Sokurov, Russia/Germany, 1997
Mother Joan of the Angels/Matka Joanna od aniołów, Jerzy Kawalerowicz, Poland, 1961
Mother of Kings/Matka Królów, Janusz Zaorski, Poland, 1983
Murderers Are Among Us, The/Die Mörder sind unter uns, Wolfgang Staudte, 1946
Music Box, Costa-Gavras, USA, 1989
My Sweet Little Village/Vesničko má středisková, Jiří Menzel, 1985
My Twentieth Century/Az én XX. Századom, Ildikó Enyédi, Hungary, 1989
Naked Among Wolves/Nackt unter Wölfen, Frank Beyer, East Germany, 1962
Nice Neighbour, The/A kedves szomszéd, Zsolt Kézdi-Kovács, Hungary, 1979
Night and Fog/Nuit et brouillard, Alain Resnais, France, 1955

Filmography

Night on Earth, Jim Jarmusch, France/USA, 1991
Night Porter, The/Il Portiere di notte, Liliana Cavani, Italy, 1974
Night Train/Pociąg, Jerzy Kawalerowicz, Poland, 1959
Nine Months/Kilenc hónap, Márta Mészáros, Hungary, 1976
No End/Bez konca, Krzysztof Kieślowski, Poland, 1985
Nobody's Daughter/Árvácska, Gyula Mészáros and László Ranódy, Hungary, 1976
Not Angels But Angels, Wiktor Grodecki, Czech Republic, 1994
Nothing/Nic, Dorota Kędzierzawska, Poland, 1998
Oh, Lucky Man!, Lindsay Anderson, UK/USA, 1973
Oh, Bloody Life/Te rongyos élet, Péter Bacsó, Hungary, 1983
October/Oktiabr, Sergei M. Eisenstein, USSR, 1927
Old Czech Legends/Staré povesti ceské, Jirí Trnka, Czechoslovakia, 1953
Olivier, Olivier, Agnieszka Holland, France, 1992
One Day More, One Day Less/Plusz-mínusz egy nap, Zoltán Fábri, Hungary, 1973
One Flew Over the Cuckoo's Nest, Miloš Forman, USA, 1975
Open Doors/Porte aperte, Gianni Amelio, Italy, 1990
Osceola, Konrad Petzold, East Germany, 1971
Our God's Brother/Brat naszego boga, Krzysztof Zanussi, Poland, 1997
Padre Padrone, Paolo and Vittorio Taviani, Italy, 1977
Pan Tadeusz, Andrzej Wajda, Poland, 1999
Paper Heads/Papierové hlavy, Dušan Hanák, Slovakia, 1995
Party and the Guests, The/O slavnosti a hostech, Jan Němec, Czechoslovakia, 1966
Passenger/Pasażerka, Andrzej Munk, Poland, 1960/1963
Passion/Szenvedély, György Fehér, Hungary, 1998
Pawnbroker, The, Sidney Lumet, USA, 1964
Pearl in the Crown/Perła w koronie, Kazimierz Kutz, Poland, 1972
Pearls of the Deep/Perličky na dně, Věra Chytilová, Jaromil Jireš, Jiří Menzel, Jan Němec, Evald
    Schorm, Czechoslovakia, 1965
Peasants, The/Chłopi, Jan Rybkowski, Poland, 1973
People vs. Larry Flynt, The, Miloš Forman, Canada/USA, 1996
Peeping Tom, Michael Powell, UK, 1960
Persona, Ingmar Bergman, Sweden, 1966
Pharaoh/Faraon, Jerzy Kawalerowicz, Poland, 1966
Pianist, The/Le Pianiste, Roman Polanski, France/Germany/Poland, 2002
Pictures from the Old World/Obrazy starého sveta, Dušan Hanák, Czechoslovakia, 1972
Pigs/Psy, Władysław Pasikowski, Poland, 1992
Pip, The/Pestka, Krystyna Janda, Poland, 1995
Players/Gracze, Ryszard Bugajski, Poland, 1995
Ponette, Jacques Doillon, France, 1996
Possession, Andrzej Żuławski, France/West Germany, 1981
Prayer for Katherina Horovitzova, A /Modlitba pro Katerinu Horovitzovou, Antonín Moskalyk,
    Czechoslovakia, 1969
Prefab Story/Panelstory, Věra Chytilová, Czechoslovakia, 1979
Priceless Day, A/Ajándék ez a nap, Péter Gothár, Hungary, 1979
Professor Hannibal/Hannibál tanár úr, Zoltán Fábri, Hungary, 1957
Prometheus/Prometei, Todor Dinov, Bulgaria, 1969
Promised Land/Ziemia obiecana, Andrzej Wajda, Poland, 1974
Provincial Actors/Aktorzy prowincjonalni, Agnieszka Holland, Poland, 1980
Public Woman, The/La Femme publique, Andrzej Żuławski, France, 1984
Quarterly Balance/Bilans kwartalny, Krzysztof Zanussi, Poland, 1975
Quo vadis, Jerzy Kawalerowicz, Poland, 2001

Raftsmen/Tutajosok, Judit Elek, Hungary, 1989
Ragtime, Miloš Forman, USA, 1981
Rear Window, Alfred Hitchcock, USA, 1954
Red and the White, The/Csillagosok, katonák, Miklós Jancsó, Hungary, 1967
Red Earth/Vörös föld, László Vitézy, Hungary, 1982
Red Psalm/Még kér a nép, Miklós Jancsó, Hungary, 1971
Repentance/Monanieba, Tengiz Abuladze, USSR, 1986
Repulsion, Roman Polanski, UK, 1965
Requiem, Zoltán Fábri, Hungary, 1981
Requiem for a Maiden/Requiem pro panenku, Filip Renč, Czechoslovakia, 1991
Return of the Idiot/Návrat idiota, Sasa Gedeon, Czech Republic, 1999
Return of the Prodigal Son, The/Návrat ztraceného syna, Evald Schorm, Czechoslovakia, 1966
Return to Paradise Lost/Návrat ztraceného ráje, Vojtěch Jasný, USA/Czech Republic, 1999
Revenge, The/Zemsta, Andrzej Wajda, Poland, 2002
Revolt of Job, The/Jób lázadása, Imre Gyöngyössy and Barna Kabay, Hungary, 1983
Riddance/Szabad lelegzet, Márta Mészáros, Hungary, 1973
Romeo Must Die, Andrzej Bartkowiak, USA, 2000
Rose-Tinted Dreams/Ružové sny, Dušan Hanák, Czechoslovakia, 1976
Rosemary's Baby, Roman Polanski, USA, 1968
Rough Treatment (aka *Without Anesthesia*)/*Bez znieczulenia*, Andrzej Wajda, Poland, 1979
Round-Up, The/Szegénylegények, Miklós Jancsó, Hungary, 1965
Run Lola Run/Lola rennt, Tom Tykwer, Germany, 1998
Sacred Crown/Sacra Corona, Gábor Koltay, Hungary, 2001
Salo, or The 120 Days of Sodom/Salò o le 120 giornate di Sodoma, Pier Paolo Pasolini, Italy, 1975
Salt of the Black Earth/Sól ziemi czarnej, Kazimierz Kutz, Poland, 1970
Samson, Andrzej Wajda, Poland, 1961
Sanatorium under the Sign of the Hourglass/Sanatorium pod klepsydra, Wojciech Has, Poland, 1973
Saragossa Manuscript, The/Rękopis znaleziony w Saragossie, Wojciech Has, Poland, 1965
Satan's Tango/Sátántangó, Béla Tarr, Hungary, 1994
Scar/Blizna, Krzysztof Kieślowski, Poland, 1976
Schindler's List, Steven Spielberg, USA, 1993
School of Sensitivity/Érzékek iskolája, András Solyom, Hungary, 1996
Scum, Alan Clarke, UK, 1979
Second Circle/Krug vtoroy, Aleksandr Sokurov, USSR, 1990
Secret Garden, The, Agnieszka Holland, USA/UK, 1993
See You in Hell, My Friends!/Dovidenia v pekle priatelia, Juraj Jakubisko, Italy/Czechoslovakia, 1970
Sequence of Feelings/Kolejność uczuć, Radoslaw Piwowarski, Poland, 1992
Seven Beauties/Pasqualino Settebellezze, Lina Wertmüller, Italy, 1976
Seventeen Moments of Spring/Semnadtsat mgnovenij vesny, Tatyana Lioznova, USSR, 1973
Sexmission/Seksmisja, Juliusz Machulski, Poland, 1984
Shaman/Szamanka, Andrzej Żuławski, Poland/France/Switzerland, 1996
Shanghai Knights, David Dobkin, USA, 2003
Shine, Scott Hicks, Australia, 1996
Shivers/Dreszcze, Wojciech Marczewski, Poland, 1981
Shoah, Claude Lanzmann, France, 1985
Shop on the High Street, A (UK)/*Shop on Main Street* (USA)/*Obchod na korze*, Jan Kadár and Elmar Klos, Czechoslovakia, 1965
Short Film About Killing, A/Krótki film o zabijaniu, Krzysztof Kieślowski, Poland, 1988

Filmography

Short Film About Love, A/Krótki film o miłości, Krzysztof Kieślowski, Poland, 1988
Shout, The, Jerzy Skolimowski, UK, 1978
Siberian Lady Macbeth, A/Sibirska Ledi Magbet, Andrzej Wajda, Poland/Yugoslavia, 1961
Silence and Cry/Csend és kiáltás, Miklós Jancsó, Hungary, 1968
Sinbad/Szindbád, Zoltán Huszárik, Hungary, 1971
Skylarks on a String (a.k.a. *Larks on a String*)/*Skřivánci na niti*, Jiří Menzel, Czechoslovakia, 1969
Sliding Doors, Peter Howitt, UK/USA, 1998
Snowdrop Festival, The/Slavnosti sněženek, Jiří Menzel, Czechoslovakia, 1983
Solo Sunny, Wolfgang Kohlhaase and Konrad Wolf, East Germany, 1979
Somewhere in Europe/Valahol Európában, Géza von Radványi, Hungary, 1947
Sons of the Big Bear, The/Die Söhne der großen Bärin, Josef Mach, East Germany, 1966
Speed, Jan de Bont, USA, 1994
Spring to Come, The/Przedwiośnie, Filip Bajon, Poland, 2001
Stalker, Andrei Tarkovsky, Soviet Union, 1982
Stars/Sterne/Zvezdi, Konrad Wolf, East Germany/Bulgaria, 1959
Story of a Sin/Dzieje grzechu, Walerian Borowczyk, Poland, 1975
Story of Pekosiński, The/Przypadek Pekosińskiego, Grzegorz Królikiewicz, Poland, 1993
Structure of Crystals, The/Struktura kryształu, Krzysztof Zanussi, Poland, 1969
Success is the Best Revenge, Jerzy Skolimowski, France/UK, 1984
Sun Alley/Sonnenallee, Leander Haußmann, Germany, 1999
Sunday Daughters/Vasárnapi szülők, János Rózsa, Hungary, 1979
Sunshine, István Szabó, Hungary/Germany/Canada/Austria, 1999
Surveillance/Nadzór, Wiesław Saniewski, Poland, 1985
Suspended/W zawieszeniu, Waldemar Krzystek, Poland, 1987
Sweet Light in a Dark Room/Romeo, Julia a tma, Jiří Weiss, Czechoslovakia, 1960
Taking Off, Miloš Forman, USA, 1971
Taking Sides, István Szabó, UK/France/Germany/Austria, 2001
Ten Thousand Suns/Tízezer nap, Ferenc Kósa, Hungary, 1965
Tenant, The/Le Locataire, Roman Polanski, France/USA, 1976
Temptations/Kísértések, Zoltán Kamondi, Hungary, 2002
Thief/Vor, Pavel Chukhrai, Russia, 1997
Third Part of the Night, The/Trzecia część nocy, Andrzej Żuławski, Poland, 1971
Thirty Cases of Major Zeman/30 případů majora Zemana, Jiří Sequens, Czechoslovakia, 1975
Thirty Door Key/Ferdydurke, Jerzy Skolimowski, Poland, 1992
This Boy's Life, Michael Caton-Jones, USA, 1993
This Sporting Life, Lindsay Anderson, UK, 1963
Three/Tri, Aleksandar Petrović, Yugoslavia, 1965
Three Colours: Blue/Trois couleurs: Bleu, Krzysztof Kieślowski, France/Poland/Switzerland, 1993
Three Colours: White/Trois couleurs: Blanc, Krzysztof Kieślowski, France/Poland/Switzerland, 1994
Three Colours: Red/Trois couleurs: Rouge, Krzysztof Kieślowski, France/Poland/Switzerland, 1994
Three Fools, The/Trimata glupaci, Donyo Donev, Bulgaria, 1970–1985
Time of the Gypsies, The/Dom za vešanje, Emir Kusturica, Yugoslavia, 1989
To Kill a Priest, Agnieszka Holland, France/USA, 1988
To Speak the Unspeakable: The Message of Elie Wiesel/Mondani a mondhatatlant: Elie Wiesel üzenete, Judit Elek, Hungary, 1996
Top Dog/Wodzirej, Feliks Falk, Poland, 1978
Topo, El, Alejandro Jodorowsky, Mexico/USA, 1970
Total Eclipse, Agnieszka Holland, UK/France/Belgium, 1995
Train of Life/Train de vie, Radu Mihaileanu, France/Belgium/Netherlands/Israel, 1998

Transport From Paradise/Transport z raje, Zbynek Brynych, Czechoslovakia, 1962
Traps/Pasti, pasti, pastičky, Czech Republic, Věra Chytilová, 1998
Tree of Wooden Clogs, The/L'albero degli zoccoli, Ermanno Olmi, Italy/France,1978
Truce, The/La Tregua, Francesco Rosi, Italy, 1996
Truly, Madly, Deeply, Anthony Minghella, UK, 1991
Turning Point, The/Der Aufenthalt, Frank Beyer, East Germany, 1983
Twenty Hours/Húsz óra, Zoltán Fábri, Hungary, 1964
Ugetsu/Ugetsu monogatari, Kenji Mizoguchi, Japan, 1953
Under the Sand/Sous le sable, François Ozon, France, 2000
Underground, Emir Kusturica, France/Germany/Hungary, 1995
Va Banque/Vabank, Juliusz Machulski, Poland, 1981
Va Banque II/Vabank II, czyli riposta, Juliusz Machulski, Poland, 1985
Valerie and Her Week of Wonders/Valerie a týden div, Jaromil Jireš, Czechoslovakia, 1970
Velvet Hangover, The/Sametová kocovina, Robert Buchar and David Lawrence, USA, 2000
Very Late Afternoon of a Faun, The/Faunovo příliš pozdní odpoledne, Věra Chytilová, Czechoslovakia, 1983
Walkover, Jerzy Skolimowski, Poland, 1965
Ward Six/Paviljon broj VI, Lucian Pintilie, Yugoslavia, 1978
Washington Square, Agnieszka Holland, USA, 1997
Wasted Lives/Kettévált mennyezet, Pál Gábor, Hungary, 1982
We Never Die/Sose halunk meg, Róbert Koltai, Hungary, 1993
Wedding/Wesele, Andrzej Wajda, Poland, 1973
Werckmeister Harmonies/Werckmeister harmóniák, Béla Tarr, Hungary, 2000
When Father Was Away on Business/Otac na službenom putu, Emir Kusturica, Yugoslavia, 1985
When Joseph Returns/Ha megjön József, Zsolt Kézdi-Kovács, Hungary, 1975
Whooping Cough/Szamárköhögés, Péter Gárdos, Hungary, 1986
With Fire and Sword/Ogniem i mieczem, Jerzy Hoffman, Poland, 1999
Without Love/Bez miłości, Barbara Sass, Poland, 1980
Witness, The/A tanú, Péter Bacsó, Hungary, 1969
Witness Again, The/Megint tanú, Péter Bacsó, Hungary, 1994
Woman Alone, A/Kobieta samotna, Agnieszka Holland, Poland, 1981
Woman and a Woman, A/Kobieta i kobieta, Ryszard Bugajski, Poland, 1980
Woman at Thirty-Three, A/Edna zhena na trideset i tri, Hristo Hristov, Bulgaria, 1981
Woman Under the Influence, A, John Cassavetes, USA, 1974
Woyzeck, János Sázsz, Hungary, 1994
Yanoshik/Jánosik, Jerzy Passendorfer, Poland, 1974
Year of the Quiet Sun/Rok spokojnego słońca, Krzysztof Zanussi, Poland/Germany, 1984
Yentl, Barbra Streisand, USA/UK, 1983
Yesterday, Today and Tomorrow/Ieri, oggi, domani, Vittorio de Sica, Italy, 1963
Yidl with a Fiddle/Yidl mitn Fidl, Joseph Green and Jan Nowina-Przybylski, Poland, 1935

BIBLIOGRAPHY

Aitken, I. (2001) *European Film Theory and Cinema: A Critical Introduction.* Edinburgh: Edinburgh University Press.

Allan, S. & J. Sandford (eds) (1999) *DEFA: East German Cinema, 1946–1992.* New York & Oxford: Berghahn Books.

Anderson, B. (1983) *Imagined Communities: Reflections on the Origin and Spread of Nationalism.* London: Verso.

Andrew, G. (1998) *The 'Three Colours' Trilogy.* London: BFI.

Avisar, I. (1988) *Screening the Holocaust: Cinema's Images of the Unimaginable.* Bloomington: Indiana University Press.

Balio, T. (ed.) (1985) *The American Film Industry.* Madison: University of Wisconsin Press.

Balski, G. (1991) *Directory of Eastern European Film-Makers and Films 1945–1991.* Trowbridge: Flicks Books.

Becker, F. (2002) 'The ad that failed: The making and uses of Géza Bereményi's *A Hídember* (*The Bridgeman, 2002*)', Kinoeye, 2, 10. Available: http://www.kinoeye.org/02/10/becker 10.html [Accessed: 18 March 2003].

Berghahn, D. (1999) 'Censorship in East German Cinema: The Case of Spur der Steine', in S. Giles, P. Graves & P. Lang (eds) *From Classical Shades to Vickers Victorious: Shifting Perspectives in British German Studies.* Oxford: Bern, 183–97.

_____ (2000) 'The Forbidden Films: Film Censorship in East German Cinema in the Wake of the Eleventh Plenum', in D. Holmes & A. Smith (eds) *100 Years of European Cinema: Entertainment or Ideology?* Manchester: Manchester University Press, 40–50.

_____ (2002) 'Trace of Stones and Other Forbidden Films', *Icestorm web-site*, Available: http://www.icestorm-video.com/berghahn_essay.cfm [Accessed: 5 April 2002].

Berry, E. (ed.) (1995) *Postcommunism and the Body Politic*. New York: New York University Press.

Beumers, B. (ed.) (1999) *Russia on Reels: The Russian Idea in Post-Soviet Cinema*. London and New York: I.B. Tauris Publishers.

Bird, D. (2001) 'Can We Live with the Truth? Věra Chytilová's *Ovoce stromů rajských jíme*', *Central Europe Review*, 3, 17. Available: http://www.ce-review.org/01/17/kinoeye17_bird.html [Accessed 2 May 2002].

Biró, Y. (1977) *Miklós Jancsó*. Paris Editions: Albatros.

Bordwell, D., J. Staiger & K. Thompson (1985) *The Classical Hollywood Cinema: Film Style and Mode of Production to 1960*. London: Routledge & Kegan Paul.

Bordwell, D. (1993) *The Cinema of Eisenstein*. Cambridge: Harvard University Press.

Bren, F. (1986) *World Cinema 1: Poland*. Trowbridge: Flicks Books.

Burns, B. (1996) *World Cinema 5: Hungary*. Trowbridge: Flicks Books.

Clark, G. & L. Federlein (2002) 'The Smell of Things: Ibolya Fekete interviewed', *Kinoeye*, 2, 4. Available: http://www.kinoeye.org/02/04/clarkfederlein04.html [Accessed: 18 February 2002].

Coates, P. (1985) *The Story of the Lost Reflection: The Alienation of The Image in Western and Polish Cinema*. London: Verso.

_____ (1996) 'The Sense of an Ending: Reflections on Kieślowski's Trilogy', *Film Quarterly*, 50, 2, 19–26.

_____ (ed.) (1999) *Lucid Dreams: The Films of Krzysztof Kieślowski*. Trowbridge: Flicks Books.

Condee, N. (ed.) (1995) *Soviet Hieroglyphics: Visual Culture in Late Twentieth Century Russia*. London: BFI.

Connolly, K. (2000) 'Bohemian Rhapsodist: Interview with Věra Chytilová', *The Guardian*, *Friday Review*, 11 August, 3.

_____ (2002) 'Bridge for Hire: $7,000 a Morning', *The Guardian*, *Friday Review*, 12 April, 8–9.

Craig, C. (2001) 'Rooms without a View', in G. Vincendeau (ed.) *Film/Literature/Heritage*. London: BFI, 3–6.

Cunningham, John (2004) *Hungarian Cinema: From Coffee House to Multiplex*. London: Wallflower Press.

Dale, M. (1997) *The Movie Game: The Film Business in Britain, Europe, and America*, London: Cassell.

Davies, N. (1981) *God's Playground: A History of Poland, volume II – 1795 to the Present*. Oxford: Clarendon Press.

Downing, J. D. H. (1996) *Internationalizing Media Theory: Transition, Power, Culture: Reflections on Media in Russia, Poland and Hungary, 1980–95*. London: Sage.

Drakulić, S. (1991) *How We Survived Communism and Even Laughed*, New York: Harper Perennial.

Dyer R. & G. Vincendeau (eds) (1992) *Popular European Cinema*. London and New York: Routledge.

Eagle, H. (1981) *Russian Formalist Film Theory*. Ann Arbor: Michigan Slavic Publications.

_____ (1982) 'Andrzej Wajda: Film Language and the Artist's Truth', in *Cross Currents: A Yearbook of Central European Culture*. Ann Arbor: University of Michigan, 339–53.

_____ (1991) 'Dada and Structuralism in Chytilova's *Daisies*', in *Cross Currents 10: A Yearbook of Central European Culture*. Ann Arbor: University of Michigan, 223–34.

Einhorn, B. (1993) *Cinderella Goes to Market: Citizenship, Gender and Women's Movements in East Central Europe*. London and New York: Verso.

Elsaesser, T. (1999) 'Ethnicity, Authenticity, and Exile: A Counterfeit Trade? German Film-makers and Hollywood', in H. Naficy (ed.) *Home, Exile, Homeland: Film, Media and the*

Politics of Place. New York and London: Routledge, 97–125.

Elsaesser, T. & M. Wedel (eds) (2000) *The BFI Companion to German Cinema.* London: BFI.

Esteve, M. & Y. Biró (1994) *Krzysztof Kieślowski.* Paris: Lettres Modernes.

Falkowska, J. (1996) *The Political Films of Andrzej Wajda: Dialogism in Man of Marble, Man of Iron, and Danton.* Providence and Oxford: Berghahn Books.

_____ (ed.) (2000) 'National Cinemas in Postwar East-Central Europe', Special issue of *Canadian Slavonic Papers,* XLII, 1–2.

Faraday, G. (2000) *Revolt of the Film-makers: The Struggle for Artistic Autonomy and the Fall of the Soviet Film Industry.* University Park: Penn State University Press.

Finney, A. (1996) *The State of European Cinema: A New Dose of Reality.* London: Cassell.

Forbes, J. & S. Street (2000) *European Cinema.* Basingstoke: Palgrave.

Forman, M. & J. Novák (1994) *Turnaround: A Memoir.* London: Faber & Faber.

Frucht, R. (ed.) (2000) *Encyclopedia of Eastern Europe: From the Congress of Vienna to the Fall of Communism.* New York: Garland Publishing.

Funk, N. (1993) *Gender Politics and Post-Communism: Reflections from Eastern Europe and the Former Soviet Union.* New York and London: Routledge.

Gal, S. (1991) 'Bartók's Funeral: Representations of Europe in Hungarian Political Rhetoric', *American Ethnologist,* 18, 3, 440–58.

Gal, S. & G. Kligman (eds) (2000) *Reproducing Gender: Politics, Publics, and Everyday Life after Socialism.* Princeton, NJ: Princeton University Press.

Gálik, M. (1998) 'Who Laughs Last: Film and Broadcasting in Hungary', in P. Boorsma, A. van Hemel & N. van der Wielen (eds) *Privatization and Culture.* Boston-Dordrecht and London: Kluwer Academic Publishers, 131–41.

Gallagher, M. (1980) 'Angi Vera: A Conversation with Pál Gábor', *Cineaste,* 10, 2, 32–3.

Garbowski, C. (1996) *Krzysztof Kieślowski's Decalogue Series: The Problem of The Protagonists and Their Self-Transcendance.* Boulder CO: East European Monographs.

Garton Ash, T. (1983) *The Uses of Adversity: Essays on the Fate of Central Europe.* London: Jonathan Cape.

Gehler, F (ed.) (1987) *Regiestühle International.* Berlin: Henschelverlag.

Gomery, D. (1986) *The Hollywood Studio System.* New York: St. Martin's Press.

_____ (1992) *Shared Pleasures: A History of Movie Presentation in the United States.* Madison: University of Wisconsin Press.

Goulding, D. (ed.) (1989) *Post New-Wave Cinema in the Soviet Union and Eastern Europe.* Bloomington: I ndiana University Press.

_____ (ed.) (1995) *Five Filmmakers: Tarkovsky, Forman, Polanski, Szabó, Makavejev.* Bloomington: Indiana University Press.

Hadjimichalis, C. & D. Sadler (eds) (1995) *Europe at the Margins: New Mosaics of Inequality.* New York: John Wiley and Sons.

Hall, S. & B. Gieben (eds) (1992) *Formations of Modernity.* Milton Keynes: Open University Press.

Haltof, M. (1995) 'A Fistful of Dollars: Polish Cinema after 1989', *Film Quarterly,* 48, 3, 15–25.

_____ (2001) Review of BFI's Companion to Eastern European and Russian Cinema, *Canadian Slavonic Papers,* XLIII, 2–3, 381–2.

_____ (2002) *Polish National Cinema.* New York and Oxford: Berghahn Books.

Hames, P. (1985) *The Czechoslovak New Wave.* Berkeley: University of California Press.

_____ (ed.) (1995) *Dark Alchemy: The Films of Jan Svankmajer.* Trowbridge: Flicks Books.

_____ (2000a) 'Czech Cinema: From State Industry to Competition', *Canadian Slavonic Papers,* 42, 1, 63–85.

_____ (2000b) 'In the Shadow of the Werewolf: František Vláčil's Markéta Lazarová revived in the UK', *Central Europe Review,* 2, 35. Available: http://www.ce-review.org/00/35/

kinoeye35_hames.html [Accessed: 19 September 2002].

_____ (2001) 'Enfant Terrible of the Czech New Wave: Jan Němec's 1960s films', *Central Europe Review*, 3, 17. Available: http://www.ce-review.org/01/17/kinoeye17_hames.html [Accessed: 19 September 2002].

Haraszty, M. (1987) *The Velvet Prison: Artists Under State Socialism*. Basic Books: New York.

Havel, V. (1990) 'The Power of the Powerless', in W. M. Brinton & A. Rinzler (eds) *Without Force or Lies: Voices from The Revolution of Central Europe in 1989-90*, San Francisco: Mecrury House, 43–128.

Hayward, S. (2000) 'Framing National Cinemas', in M. Hjort & S. MacKenzie (eds) *Cinema and Nation*. London and New York: Routledge, 88–103.

Hegyi, L. (1992) 'Eastern Art – State Art – Official Art in The Former Eastern Bloc Countries', in *Reductivism – Abstract Art in Poland, Czechoslovakia and Hungary 1950-1980*, published by the Museum of Modern Art Foundation Ludwig Vienna, 11–43. Available: http://www.aspectspositions.org/essays/hegyi2.html [Accessed: 19 September 2002].

_____ (2001) 'Central Europe as a Hypothesis and a Way of Life', in *Catalogue to Aspects/ Positions: 50 Years of Art in Central Europe 1949–1999*. Published by The Museum of Modern Art Foundation Ludwig Vienna. Available: http://www.aspectspositions.org/essays/hegyi1.html_ [Accessed: 19 September 2002].

Helman, A. (2000) 'The Masters Are Tired', *Canadian Slavonic Papers*, XLII, 1-2, 99–113.

Hoberman, J. (1998) *The Red Atlantis: Communist Culture in the Absence of Communism*. Philadelphia Temple: University Press.

Holloway, R. (1972) *Z is for Zagreb*. London: Tantivy Press.

Horton, A. J. (1999a) 'Hitchhiking: The Perils and The Romance: Věra Chytilova's *Pasti, pasti, pasticky*', *Central Europe Review*, 0, 17. Available: http://www.ce-review.org/kinoeye/kinoeye17old1.html [Accessed 2 May 2002].

_____ (1999b) 'Unsentimental Reveries: Peter Timar's *Csinibaba*', 0, 18. Available: http://www.ce-review.org/kinoeye/kinoeye18old2.html [Accessed: 19 March 2003].

Huntington, S. (1993) 'The Clash of Civilisations?' *Foreign Affairs*, 72, 3, 22–50.

Hughes, H. M. (1999) 'Were We Looking Away? – The Reception in the West of Art from Central and East Central Europe at the Time of the Cold War'. Available: http://www.aspectspositions.org/essays/hughes.html [Accessed: 19 September 2002].

Imre, A. (1999) 'White Man, White Mask: Mephisto Meets Venus', *Screen*, 40, 4, 405–23.

_____ (2003) 'Screen Gypsies', in Special issue of *Framework: The Journal of Film and Media*, 44, 2, 13–33.

Insdorf, A. (1989) *Indelible Shadows: Film and The Holocaust*. Cambridge and New York: Cambridge University Press. [Third Edition, 2003].

_____ (1999) *Double Lives, Second Chances: The Cinema of Krzysztof Kieślowski*. New York: Miramax Books.

Iordanova, D. (1999a) 'East Europe's Cinema Industries since 1989: Financing Structure and Studios', *Javnost/The Public*, VI, 2, 45–60.

_____ (1999b) 'College Course File: Eastern European Cinema', *Journal of Film and Video*, 51, 1, 56–77.

_____ (2000) 'The New Russians in Film: Nostalgia for the Occupier, Commiseration for the Immigrant', *Canadian Slavonic Papers*, XVII, 1–2, 113–31.

_____ (2001) *Cinema of Flames: Balkan Film, Culture and the Media*. London: BFI.

_____ (2002a) 'Feature Film-making Within the New Europe: Moving Funds and Images Across the East-West Divide', *Media, Culture and Society*, 24, 4, 517–37.

_____ (2002b) *Emir Kusturica*. London: BFI.

_____ (ed.) (2003) 'Images of Romanies (Gypsies) in International Cinema', Special issue of *Framework: The Journal of Film and Media*, 44, 2.

Jäckel, A. (1996) 'European Co-Production Strategies: The Case of France and Britain', in

A. Moran (ed.) *Film Policy: International, National, and Regional Perspectives*, London and New York: Routledge, 85–98.

Jameson, F. (1992) *The Geopolitical Aesthetic: Cinema and Space in the World System*. London: BFI.

Jones, D. (ed.) (2001) *Censorship: A World Encyclopedia*. 4 volumes. London and Chicago: Fitzroy Dearborn.

Kaes, A. (1992) 'Holocaust and the End of History: Postmodern Historiography in Cinema', in S. Friedlander (ed.) *Probing the Limits of Representation: Nazism and the 'Final Solution'*. Cambridge and London: Harvard University Press, 216–23.

Kieślowski, K. & K. Piesiewicz (1991) *Decalogue: The Ten Commandments*. translated by P. Cavendish & S. Bluh, foreword by S. Kubrick. London: Faber.

Kindem, G. (ed.) (2000) *The International Movie Industry*. Carbondale: Southern Illinois University Press.

Koch, G. (1993) 'On The Disappearance of The Dead Among The Living: Holocaust and The Confusion of Identities in The Films of Konrad Wolf', *New German Critique*, 60, 57–75.

Kuhn, A. & S. Radstone (ed.) (1990) *The Women's Companion to International Film*. Berkeley: University of California Press.

Lev, P. (1993) *The Euro-American Cinema*. Austin: University of Texas Press.

Liehm, A. J. (1974) *Closely Watched Films: The Czechoslovak Experience*. New York International Arts and Sciences Press.

_____ (1975) *The Miloš Forman Stories*. New York: International Arts and Sciences Press.

Liehm, M. & A. Liehm (1977) *The Most Important Art: Soviet and East European Film After 1945*. Berkeley: University of California Press.

Macnab, G. (2002) 'Heaven Can't Wait (An interview with Andrzej Wajda)', *Guardian, Friday Review*, 24 May, 6.

Malcolm, D. (2002) 'Tom Tykwer's Heaven', *Guardian*, 8 February, 18.

Mattelart, A, X. Delacourt & M. Mattelart (1984) *International Image Markets*. London: Comedia.

Mazierska, E. (1999) 'Any Town? Postcommunist Warsaw in *Girl Guide* and *Kiler* by Juliusz Machulski', *Historical Journal of Film, Radio and Television*, 19, 4, 515–30.

_____ (2000a) 'Between The Sacred and The Profane, The Sublime and The Trivial: The Magic Realism of Jan Jakub Kolski', *Scope*, 1. Available: http://www.nottingham.ac.uk/film/journal/articles/jan_jakub_kolski.htm. [Accessed: 19 September 2002].

_____ (2000b) 'Life and Work in Silesia According to Kazimierz Kutz', in V. Mainz & G. Pollock (eds) *Work and its Representation: From Painting to Cinema*. Aldershot: Ashgate, 177–92.

_____ (2000c) 'Non-Jewish Jews, Good Poles and Historical Truth in Films of Andrzej Wajda', *Historical Journal of Film, Radio and Television*, 20, 2, 213–26.

_____ (2001a) 'In the Land of Noble Knights and Mute Princesses: Polish Heritage Cinema', *Historical Journal of Film, Radio and Television*, 21, 2, 167–82.

_____ (2001b) 'Wanda Jakubowska's Cinema of Commitment', *European Journal of Women Studies*, 2, 221–38.

_____ (2002) 'Witches, Shamans, Pandoras – Representation of Women in the Polish Postcommunist Cinema', *Scope*, 3, 2, Available: http://www.nottingham.ac.uk/film/journal/articles/witches-shamans-pandoras.htm [Accessed: 25 September 2002].

Mazierska, E. & L. Rascaroli (2003) *From Moscow to Madrid: Postmodern Cities, European Cinema*. London: I.B. Tauris.

Medhurst, A. (2001) 'Sexuality and Heritage', in G. Vincendeau (ed.) *Film/Literature/Heritage*. London: BFI, 11–14.

Menashe, L. (2001) 'Moscow Believes in Tears: The Problems (and Promise?) of Russian Cinema in The Transition Period', *Cineaste*, 26, 3, 10–17.

Michałek, B. (1973) *The Cinema of Andrzej Wajda*. London: The Tantivy Press.

_____ (1992) *Le Cinema Polonais*. Paris: Centre Pompidou.

Michałek, B. & Turaj F. (1988) *Modern Cinema of Poland*. Bloomington and Indianapolis: Indiana University Press.

Miljacki, A. (2002) 'Closely Watched Films: On the Transformations of Eastern European Urbanism', *Blok*, 1, 98–120.

Miller, T., N. Govil, J. McMuria & R. Maxwell (2001) *Global Hollywood*. London: BFI.

Murri, S. (1997) *Krzysztof Kieślowski*. Il Castoro: Milano.

Némes, K. (1985) *Fims of Commitment: Socialist Cinema in Eastern Europe*. Budapest: Corvina.

Nemeskűrty, I. (1968) *Word and Image: History of the Hungarian Cinema*. Budapest: Corvina.

Naficy, H. (2001) *Accented Cinema: Exilic and Diasporic Film-making*. Princeton: Princeton University Press.

Oleksy, E. H., E. Ostrowska & M. Stevenson (eds) (2000) *Gender in Film and the Media: East-West Dialogues*. Frankfurt Main: Peter Lang.

Orr, J. (2000) *The Art and Politics of Film*. Edinburgh: Edinburgh University Press.

Ostrowska, E. (1998) 'Filmic Representations of the 'Polish Mother' in Post-Second World War Polish Cinema', *The European Journal of Women's Studies*, 5, 419–35.

Paskin, S. (ed.) (1999) *When Joseph Met Molly: A Reader on Yiddish Film*. Nottingham: Five Leaves Press.

Paul, D. (ed.) (1983) *Politics, Art and Commitment in the East European Cinema*. New York: St. Martin's Press.

Petrie, G. (1978) *History Must Answer to Man: The Contemporary Hungarian Cinema*. Budapest: Corvina Kiadó.

_____ (1998) *Red Psalm*. Trowbridge: Flicks Books.

Petrie, G. & R. Dwyer (1990) *Before The Wall Came Down: Soviet and East European Film-makers Working in The West*. Lanham: University Press of America.

Pines, J. & P. Willemen (eds) (1989) *Questions of Third Cinema*. London: BFI.

Portuges, C. (1992) 'Border Crossings: Recent Trends in East and Central European Cinema', *Slavic Review*, 51, 3, 531–35.

_____ (1993) *Screen Memories: The Hungarian Cinema of Márta Mészáros*. Bloomington: University of Indiana Press.

_____ (1995) 'Post-Transition Hungarian Cinema and its National Imaginary', *Slavic Review*, 54, 4, l004–9.

_____ (1997) 'Hidden Subjects, Secret Identities. Figuring Jews, Gypsies, and Gender in 1990s Cinema of Eastern Europe', in G. Brinkler-Gabler & S. Smith (eds) *Writing New Identities: Gender, Nation, and Immigration in Contemporary Europe*. Minneapolis: University of Minnesota Press, 196–215.

Portuges, C. (2001) 'Home Movies, Found Images and "Amateur Film" as a Witness to History: Péter Forgács's *Private Hungary*', *The Moving Image*, Fall, 107-125.

Quart, B. (1988) 'Eastern European Women Directors' in *Women Directors*. New York: Praeger, 191–239.

Quart, L. (1980) 'Angi Vera', *Film Quarterly*, 34, 1, 45–47.

Radkiewicz, M. (2002) 'Angry young girls: Gender representations in Věra Chytilová's *Sedmikrásky* and *Pasti, pasti, pastičky*', *Kinoeye*, 2, 8. Available: http://www.kinoeye.org/02/08/radkiewicz08.html [Accessed: 2 May 2002].

Roberts, G. (2000) 'Double Lives: Europe and Identity in the Later Films of Krzysztof Kieślowski', in J. Andrew, M. Cook, D. Holmes & E. Kolinsky (eds), *Why Europe? Problems of Culture and Identity, Vol. 2: Media, Film, Gender, Youth and Education*. Basingstoke:

Macmillan Press, 37–51.

Rosenstone, R. (1995) 'The Historical Film as Real History', *Film-Historia*, V, 1, 5–23.

Rupnik, J. (1988) *The Other Europe: The Rise and Fall of Communism in East Central Europe*. London: Weidenfeld and Nicholson.

Shohat, E. & R. Stam (1994) *Unthinking Eurocentrism: Multiculturalism and the Media*. London and New York: Routledge.

Škvorecký, J. (1971) *All the Bright Young Men and Women: A Personal History of the Czech Cinema*. Toronto: Peter Martin Associates.

Skwara, A. (1992) 'Film Stars do not Shine in the Sky over Poland: The Absence of Popular Cinema in Poland', in R. Dyer & G. Vincendeau (eds) *Popular European Cinema*. London and New York: Routledge, 220–32.

Slater, T. J. (1987) *Miloš Forman: A Bio-Bibliography*. New York and London: Greenwood.

_____ (ed.) (1992) *Handbook of Soviet and East European Films and Film-makers*, New York: Greenwood Press.

Sneé, P. (1998) 'The Award of Success', *Filmkultura*, Available: http://www.filmkultura.iif.hu:8080/articles/films/csinibaba.en.html [Accessed: 19 March 2003].

Sparks, C. (1997) 'Post-Communist Media in Transition', in J. Corner, P. Schlesinger & R. Silverstone (eds) *International Media Research: A Critical Survey*. London and New York: Routledge, 96–122.

Sparks, C. & A. Reading (1998) *Communism, Capitalism and the Mass Media*. London: Sage Publications.

Stöhr, L. (1998) 'Feature film potentials in Hungary', *Filmkultura*, Available: http://www.filmkultura.iif.hu:8080/articles/films/csini.en.html [Accessed: 19 March 2003].

Stok, D. (ed.) (1993) *Kieślowski on Kieślowski*. London: Faber.

Stolarska, B. (1995) 'In Search for Hope: On the Films of Andrzej Munk', *Bulletin de la Societé des sciences et de letters de Łódź*, XLV, Recherches sur les Arts, VI, 21–39.

Stringer, J. (2001) 'Global Cities and the International Film Festival Economy', in M. Shiel & T. Fitzmaurice (eds) *Cinema and the City: Film and Urban Societies in a Global Context*. Oxford: Blackwell, 134–44.

Švankmajer, J. (1996) *Faust: The Script*. Trowbridge: Flicks Books.

Taylor, R., J. Graffy, N. Wood & D. Iordanova (eds) (2000) *The BFI Companion to Eastern European and Russian Cinema*. London: BFI.

Todorova, M. (1997) *Imagining the Balkans*. New York: Oxford University Press.

Turan, K. (2002) *Sundance to Sarajevo: Film Festivals and the World They Made*. Berkeley: University of California Press.

Usai, P. C. (1994) *Burning Passions: An Introduction to the Study of Silent Cinema*. London: BFI.

Vaculik, L. (1987) *A Cup of Coffee with My Interrogator*. London: Readers International.

Vincendeau, G. (ed.) (1995) *Encyclopedia of European Cinema*. London: Cassell and BFI.

_____ (2001) 'Introduction', in G. Vincendeau (ed) *Film/Literature/Heritage*. London: BFI, xi–xxv.

Wajda, A. (1986) *Double Vision: My Life in Film*. New York: Henry Holt.

Wayne, M. (2001) *Political Film: The Dialectics of Third Cinema*. London: Pluto Press.

Wexman, V. W. (1985) *Roman Polanski*. Boston: Twayne.

Willemen, P. (1995) 'The National', in L. Devereaux & R. Hillman (eds) *Fields of Vision: Essays in Film Studies, Visual Anthropology, and Photography*. Berkeley: University of California Press, 21–34.

Wolff, L. (1994) *Inventing Eastern Europe*. Stanford: Stanford University Press.

Žižek, S. (2001) *The Fright of Real Tears: Krzysztof Kieślowski between Theory and Post-theory*. London: BFI.

INDEX

East European Cinema From Wallflower Press

Hungarian Cinema
From Coffee House to Multiplex

John Cunningham

In the 1960s Hungary entered a period of relative stability and increasing cultural relaxation, resulting in an astonishing growth of film-making. Innovative and groundbreaking directors such as Miklós Jancsó (*Hungarian Rhapsody, The Red and the White*), István Szabó (*Mephisto, Sunshine*) and Márta Mészaros (*Little Vilma*) emerged and established the reputation of Hungarian films on a global scale. This is the first book to discuss all major aspects of the history of Hungarian cinema and its place in the development of Hungarian society. It focuses on film-makers as diverse and significant as Zoltán Fábri (*The Storm*) and Béla Tarr (*Satantango*), and includes coverage of under-explored areas including avant-garde film-making, animation, and representations of the Gypsy and Jewish minorities.

"An accessible and enjoyable introduction to Hungarian cinema. I would not hesitate to recommend it to students of Central and East European Cinema and to others in search of approachable materials for undergraduates."
– Catherine Portuges, University of Massachusetts Amherst

John Cunningham teaches Film Studies at Sheffield Hallam University and at the London Centre, University of Notre Dame, Indiana.

2004   1-903364-79-5   224pp   £15.99

East European Cinema From Wallflower Press

The Cinema of Andrzej Wajda
The Art of Irony and Defiance

Edited by John Orr & Elzbieta Ostrowska

This book is a major re-assessment of the great Polish director Andrzej Wajda, who received a Lifetime Achievement Academy Award in 2000. It covers all aspects of his work from his early trilogy of the 1950s – *A Generation, Kanal, Ashes and Diamonds* – to his 1999 epic *Pan Tadeusz*, and looks at his daring innovations in style, his concern with Polish history and nationhood, and his artistic defiance of authoritarian rule during the Cold War. A timely look at a prolific film-maker whose work over four decades reflects the changing nature of cinema itself.

"The most comprehensive and multifaceted compilation on Wajda's film-making published in English ... A desideratum for anyone drawn to Wajda's films or Polish cinema in general."
    – Renata Murawska, Macquarie University

John Orr is Professor Emeritus at Edinburgh University and the author of *Contemporary Cinema* (1998) and *The Art and Politics of Film* (2001). Elzbieta Ostrowska teaches film at the University of Lódz. She is co-editor of *Gender in Film and the Media* (2000).

2003   1-903364-89-2   208pp   £14.99

Other titles in the *Directors' Cuts* series include volumes on Wim Wenders, Ken Loach, Kathryn Bigelow, Robert Lepage, Terrence Malick, David Lynch and Nanni Moretti. Forthcoming are volumes on Krzystof Kieslowski, Mike Leigh, Ang Lee, Theo Angelopouls and Lars von Trier.

East European Cinema From Wallflower Press

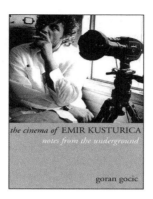

The Cinema of Emir Kusturica
Notes from the Underground

Goran Gocic

The Cinema of Emir Kusturica is the first book on the Sarajevan film-maker to be published in English. With each of his films winning prizes at major festivals around the world, Kusturica is already established as one of the most important of contemporary film-makers. In covering films such as *Underground*, *Arizona Dream* and *Black Cat, White Cat*, this timely study delves into diverse facets of Kusturica's work, much of which is passionately dedicated to the marginal and the outcast, as well as discourses of national and cultural identity.

Goran Gocic is a film critic and print and broadcast journalist, and has published widely on cinema and media.

"This is a comprehensive and fascinating study of one of Europe's most important film directors. A sharp and perceptive monograph and long overdue as far as English-language film criticism is concerned. This is a must read."
— John Orr, Edinburgh University

"An intruiging book that combines original and up-to-date research on the artistic, cultural and political circumstances of Kusturica's cinematography. It offers sources and stimuli for students of film, Balkan history and politics, cultural and social studies."
— Aleksandar Dundjerovic, Brunel University

2001   1-903364-14-0   208pp   £14.99